NO SIGN OF LIF

Officer Eloy Escareno was the first t
house. He was followed by Officer Tell
kids!" Tello called out. "You can come

Escareno made his way down the d
and slowly approached the door of th
bedroom with his shotgun drawn. The door was
slightly ajar and with his free hand he pushed it
open. The room was pitch dark and silent. Escareno went in. He panned his flashlight across
the room but his eyes hadn't adjusted to the darkness of the room and all he could see were the
outlines of shapes beginning to form. Three large
coffins were leaning up against the wall. Officer
Tello entered the room and found a light switch
along the wall. He flipped it on.

Escareno gasped and dropped his shotgun.

The bodies were stacked on the other side of the
coffins in the northeast corner of the room, where
a large pool of blood had formed on the floor.

The oldest victims were the most visible: they
were covering the bodies of the children . . .

BY THEIR FATHER'S HAND

THE TRUE STORY OF THE
WESSON FAMILY MASSACRE

MONTE FRANCIS

HARPER

An Imprint of HarperCollins*Publishers*

By Their Father's Hand is a journalistic account of the 2004 deaths of nine members of the Wesson family in Fresno, California. The events recounted in this book are true. The actions and conversations portrayed in this book have been constructed using extensive interviews, court documents, trial transcripts, letters, personal papers, and press accounts.

HARPER

An Imprint of HarperCollins*Publishers*
10 East 53rd Street
New York, New York 10022-5299

ISBN: 978-0-06-087824-5
ISBN-10: 0-06-087824-X

First Harper paperback printing: June 2007

10   9   8   7   6

INTRODUCTION

When I began covering the Wesson murders for Fresno television station KSEE, I had just finished reporting on what turned out to be the most closely followed trial in the country since O. J. Simpson's: the murder trial of Scott Peterson. Peterson was convicted of killing his pregnant wife and dumping her body in the waters of San Francisco Bay, and the case had captivated much of the country. As horrific and disturbing as the Wesson murders were, after a few days the national spotlight dimmed. I had stood in front of the Wesson house as the bodies of seven children, a teenager, and an adult were carried out one by one in body bags, so it perplexed me when no one in the national media arrived to cover the trial on the day of opening statements. Following the media circus that was the Scott Peterson trial, I wondered why no one seemed to care about nine dead family members in Fresno, California, only ninety miles away.

Granted, the story was unsettling. The details of incest alone made you want to look the other way. Surprisingly, the Wesson family was met with similar disregard long before the murders; for years, people who knew them realized a potential disaster was just around the corner and looked the other way. Just months before the killings, Wesson's own father wrote to his daughter-in-law to plead with her to bring the children to Washington and enroll them in a private school, fearing the authorities would discover the children Marcus Wesson had fathered with his daughters and nieces. I was constantly surprised while writing this book by the number of neighbors and family acquaintances who told me they, too, feared something awful was about to happen and said nothing, or by those who were not surprised to learn of the mass murder.

Just after Scott Peterson was sentenced to death, the West Coast contingent of reporters packed up and left Redwood City, passed by Fresno, and promptly descended on Santa Maria, where its most famous resident, Michael Jackson, was about to face charges of child molestation. The national media's preoccupation with that case, coupled with what one reporter described to me as the "gross-out factor," became the clear reasons in my mind why the Wesson murders went unnoticed by most of the country. It had more to do with audience demographics and what network executives thought would "sell" to their target audiences than with the gravity of what had happened. The more pressing question that still lingers in my mind is whether something could have been done to save the Wesson children from their deaths.

After covering Wesson's three-month trial, my biggest disappointment was that I hadn't heard his side of the story. So many questions remained: Did he shoot some or all of the children? Did he admit to ordering the killings, or did he claim to be innocent of the crimes? All the eyewitnesses were dead except for Wesson himself, and he was the only one left who really knew what had happened. During the trial the public defender opted not to call Wesson to testify, and the prosecutor decided not to enter Wesson's tape-recorded statements to the police into evidence. I wrote to Wesson on Death Row and he answered many of my questions. His responses appear within these pages.

The following is my attempt to construct a truthful and coherent narrative of what led to the murders of nine people in a Fresno home on March 12, 2004. It is based on my research, testimony, interviews, and court transcripts. Nearly all of the dialogue that appears in the initial chapters was transcribed verbatim from an audio recording made on the day of the murders. The dialogue between Marcus and Elizabeth Wesson during a jail visit is also taken verbatim from a transcript of a recording made by the Fresno County Sheriff's Department. At times, family members provided conflicting accounts of what occurred on the day of the killings. The events of March 12, 2004, as depicted in this book have been corroborated by at least two witnesses, unless otherwise noted. Marcus Wesson's unpublished book, "In the Night of the Light for the Dark," and the dairies of the young women in the family, were all entered into evidence by the district attorney and are part of the public record.

It is an accepted ethical practice to not reveal the names of minors who are the victims of sexual abuse. In this case those victims are now dead or their names became public after the murders. The incestuous relationships between Marcus Wesson and his daughters and nieces created the complicated family tree, and resulted in the births of seven of the nine murder victims.

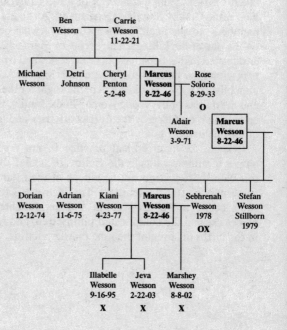

THE WESSON FAMILY

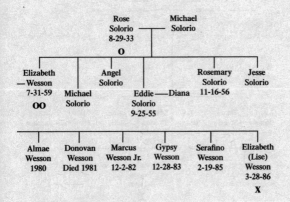

Rose Solorio 8-29-33 — Michael Solorio
O

Elizabeth —Wesson 7-31-59 **OO** — Michael Solorio

Angel Solorio

Eddie Solorio 9-25-55 — Diana

Rosemary Solorio 11-16-56

Jesse Solorio

Almae Wesson 1980

Donovan Wesson Died 1981

Marcus Wesson Jr. 12-2-82

Gypsy Wesson 12-28-83

Serafino Wesson 2-19-85

Elizabeth (Lise) Wesson 3-28-86 **X**

KEY	
Murder Victim:	X
Married to Wesson:	OO
Had Children with Wesson:	O

THE SOLORIO FAMILY

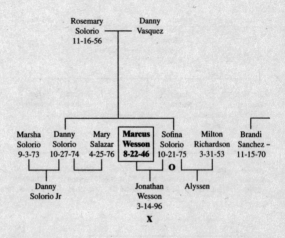

Rosemary Solorio 11-16-56 — Danny Vasquez

Marsha Solorio 9-3-73

Danny Solorio 10-27-74

Mary Salazar 4-25-76

Marcus Wesson 8-22-46

Sofina Solorio 10-21-75 **O**

Milton Richardson 3-31-53

Brandi Sanchez – 11-15-70

Danny Solorio Jr

Jonathan Wesson 3-14-96 **X**

Alyssen

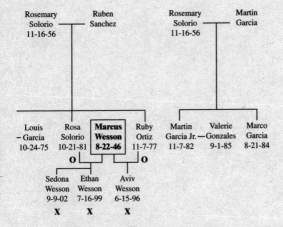

Rosemary Solorio 11-16-56	—	Ruben Sanchez		Rosemary Solorio 11-16-56	—	Martin Garcia

Louis – Garcia 10-24-75	Rosa Solorio 10-21-81	**Marcus Wesson 8-22-46**	Ruby Ortiz 11-7-77		Martin Garcia Jr. 11-7-82	Valerie — Gonzales 9-1-85	Marco Garcia 8-21-84

O

Sedona Wesson 9-9-02	Ethan Wesson 7-16-99	Aviv Wesson 6-15-96
X	**X**	**X**

KEY	
Murder Victim:	X
Married to Wesson:	OO
Had Children with Wesson:	O

PROLOGUE

Off the coast of Marshall, California, 1998

Sofina loaded the gun. She shook nervously, sliding the magazine into her uncle's .22 caliber pistol. The sound of metal against metal and the weight of the gun in her hands made her feel a sense of urgency. It was something she hadn't experienced when rehearsing it so many times in her mind. She was not the one Marcus Wesson called his "strong soldier," but she would prove that she could be one. She gathered the children together and instructed those who could write to compose suicide notes. The children were scared but they knew what they were supposed to do. Sixteen-year-old Gypsy scribbled on a piece of paper: "We did this ourselves. It's nobody's fault. We don't want to be separated."

The family lived aboard a tugboat called the *Sudan*, moored just one hundred feet off the Northern California shore. Just minutes before, one of the boys had arrived belowdeck with some disturbing news: While on deck he had spotted a conspicuous white vehicle. Sofina led two of the older girls upstairs to the deck of the *Sudan* to investigate. As they watched, a white truck with the word "Progressive" written on the side drove by slowly and then disappeared. Five minutes later it passed by again. This time there were two white trucks with the word "Progressive" written on them. Then three. Sofina panicked. Not realizing that Progressive was the name of an insurance company, she and the others were convinced that the government had arrived to take them away. Their father, Marcus Wesson, was in Fresno looking for his niece Ruby, who had run away from home. But in his absence the children knew what he had taught them: that it was better to be with the Lord than to let the government separate the family.

Even with that notion in the minds of the Wesson children, Sofina knew things her siblings and cousins did not. Marcus had told her that when the time came he would need "strong soldiers" to seek out and kill other family members who had already grown up and left the family home. He reasoned that he didn't want them to "lose the Lord" and wanted to see them in Heaven. Once the whole family was dead, Marcus said he would be the only one left alive. He reasoned that someone had to stay behind to explain to the world what had happened. Because of this, Sofina was always ready. She had even rehearsed the method of the murder-suicide; the older children would kill the younger ones by putting the gun in their mouths and pulling the trigger. Then the older children would kill themselves. It would be over before the police or CPS—Child Protective Services—ever arrived.

Belowdeck, Sofina arranged the children in a circle. One of the older girls went to the front of the boat, where Marcus kept a brown leather bag. She removed a pistol and ammunition and carried the gun to Sofina. They held hands and prayed. Sofina had loaded the gun but something didn't feel right. She couldn't shake the feeling that they needed affirmation from the family's patriarch, some final approval. How would they explain it to Marcus, she reasoned, if he came home to find them all dead?

"Who wants to go call him and let him know we're going to do this?" Sofina asked the others. Two of the older girls volunteered to carry word to their father. They untied the small rowboat from the *Sudan* and waited for the white vehicles to pass. Then they frantically rowed ashore. They secured the boat on the pier and ran to the town store. The woman who ran the store was generous and had said she would let them use the phone if it was an emergency, and this most certainly qualified.

Once on the line, Marcus Wesson told them to stop. In a calm voice he ordered them to carry the word to the others: "Put that stuff away," he said. "It's not time yet."

PART ONE:

THE MURDERS

ONE

In the Wesson home, the youngest children lived like vampires. Some of the older children thought of it as an elaborate game invented by their father, but the facts were undeniable: The young ones slept on oversized mahogany coffins and seldom saw the light of day. Marcus Wesson had even given many of the children names associated with vampires. One of the babies was named Jeva, a combination of the words "Jesus" and "vampire." Sedona and Marshey, both one and a half years old, were named after characters in their father's magnum opus, a one thousand page work he referred to as a bible for vampires. The babies along with the other children—8-year-old Illabelle, 7-year-old Jonathan, 7-year-old Aviv, and 4-year-old Ethan—were under their father's strict control. At his orders, they could not go outside to play. Neighbors would later say they had no idea so many children were living inside the small home.

In truth, no one was supposed to live at 761 West Hammond Avenue. The small, flat-roofed building was zoned as a business and sat on the corner of a busy intersection of the Golden State Freeway, which runs parallel to the Union Pacific railroad tracks. The frequent and thunderous sound of passing trains was a constant reminder of the home's precarious location, situated between a residential neighborhood and what was once one of Fresno's thriving business districts. All that remained to the west of the railroad tracks was a strip of liquor stores and a run-down motel. A sprawling park, home to many of the city's homeless and to the city zoo, sat between the Union Pacific line and Highway 99, the thoroughfare that vertically divides California in half.

The Wesson family had lived in a shed, a tugboat, and a campsite in the mountains. As far as domiciles went, this was perhaps the most conventional. However, the city had just discovered the family's violation of the zoning laws, and since the building was clearly not being used as a place of business, the city had served notice that the Wessons were to evacuate the home immediately. But such warnings didn't faze the family's leader.

On March 12, 2004, Elizabeth Wesson woke up before everyone else. It was the only time the house was completely silent. Her husband and the children were not yet stirring, and she felt that short time in the early morning belonged just to her. She showered and dressed. When she left the house to make her usual trip to Circle K to get a cup of coffee, the younger children were still asleep on their coffins. She knew that if people were aware of her husband's obsession with vampires, the sleeping arrangements might have seemed strange, but she reminded herself that Marcus was using the antique caskets to build furniture, and at any rate it was more comfortable than sleeping on the floor.

When Elizabeth returned to the house with her coffee around 7:30 A.M., the rest of the family was just waking up. She turned on the TV to watch the news. Marcus came out of the bathroom and sat next to his wife and they watched television. Their daughter Kiani was bathing her baby. The other women in the house were caring for the children and cooking breakfast. Seventeen-year-old Lise was preparing the children's schoolwork for the day.

After lunch, Elizabeth left to visit her nephew's girl-friend. Marcus and their 25-year-old daughter Sebhrenah were working on the school bus parked in front of the house. The city had served notice that the strange-looking yellow bus decorated with shiny chrome was violating city code by sitting in the driveway, but Marcus didn't care. It was his latest project, in which he had the whole family involved. He told his children they had to finish transforming the bus into a motor home since the city seemed anxious to evict them from the house. He told them they would drive the bus to Washington to visit his ailing father and then embark on a cross-country journey. As Marcus saw it, the transformation would render the yellow school bus like none other; the rear upper portion of the bus had already been cut off and a hot tub was installed. He planned to gut the inside of the bus, and for seats, use the lids from the ten antique coffins the children had been using as beds. Neighbors described seeing the women in the family dressed in long black dresses, working on the bus at all hours of the day and night under Marcus Wesson's careful supervision. They did labor both of a mechanical and cosmetic nature, making frequent trips between the house and a storage facility where Wesson kept another bus he was using for spare parts.

In truth, Wesson was more than a father to the girls and the women who lived in the house, and notwithstanding his obsession with vampires, that fact would be the one thing he knew the outside world would not understand: He believed in polygamy and incest. He told his young daughters and nieces that it was his job to instruct them on how to please a man, and he felt it was his duty to adequately prepare them for marriage. The girls wore rings he had given them. At his whim, they cleaned his ropelike dreadlocks and scratched his armpits. He shared unofficial marriage vows with several of his own daughters and three of his nieces. The young children in the Wesson family were the result of those incestuous relationships; some were both his children and his grand-children.

Providing for a family of fourteen was not easy, consid-ering that neither Marcus nor his wife Elizabeth worked. Despite Wesson's conviction for welfare fraud in 1990, for which he served jail time, the family continued to collect government benefits, as well as depending on the income of the women in the household. Many of the older girls had worked catering jobs or at fast food restaurants and turned over their paychecks directly to Wesson, who managed the family's finances. While the family struggled to provide food for the children, he ate heartily and used the family's money to purchase a number of salvaged boats that he kept docked in Tomales Bay, off the Northern California coast. He talked about buying a "world cruiser" and sailing it around the world.

Wesson maintained control over almost all the women in his life. It was therefore noteworthy that his nieces Sofina Solorio and Ruby Ortiz had managed to escape their uncle's control and attempted to start their lives over on their own terms. But both women were left with an insurmountable regret. On March 12 they decided that would finally change. Having received word of the fami-ly's impending eviction and Marcus's plan to move the family elsewhere, Ruby and Sofina decided they had to act fast to retrieve their children from the Wesson home.

Knowing that Marcus would not easily surrender their children, Sofina and Ruby decided they would arrive at the Wesson home accompanied by an entourage of broth-ers, uncles, and cousins from their mother's side of the family. They gathered at Ruby's house in Fresno to dis-cuss the plan and to assign roles to all those involved. Their strategy was simple: Sofina and Ruby would de-mand that Marcus turn over their children. If he refused, they would grab the children and run. The male family members would handle Marcus while the women made a quick getaway.

Sofina and Ruby were careful not to talk to family members who might warn Marcus of their plan, which is why they both became concerned when Marcus's wife, Elizabeth, unexpectedly showed up at Ruby's house that afternoon. Fortunately, their aunt Elizabeth didn't immediately figure out why so many uncles and cousins were gathered at Ruby's house. They told Elizabeth they were having a barbecue and needed to get some things from the store. Ruby told Elizabeth to wait until they returned. The group loaded up in their cars and made their way to the Wesson home. Elizabeth stayed at Ruby's house for about an hour before she got a call from her nephew's girlfriend.

"Elizabeth, this can all end," she said. "You can get out of the situation. You can all leave."

Elizabeth paused. She seemed to be struggling to make sense of what she was hearing. After a long silence she shook her head, realizing Sofina and Ruby were already at the house on Hammond Avenue trying to take their children.

"I've got to go," Elizabeth replied frantically. "I've got to go."

TWO

When Sofina and Ruby arrived at the Wesson home that afternoon, they knew their uncle would not easily give in to their demands. He manipulated those around him and could talk his way out of almost any situation. But Sofina vowed she would not leave without her 7-year-old son Jonathan, and Ruby swore the same about her 7-year-old daughter, Aviv. Wesson's name didn't appear on the birth certificates of the children he fathered with his daughters and nieces. He mistrusted the government and knew the outside world would not understand his desire to create a pure vampire race.[1] To that end, Sofina and Ruby thought themselves fortunate to have their children's birth certificates, which named them as the mothers. They reasoned that it put them at an advantage in case the police showed up and wanted to determine to whom the children truly belonged.

The group had decided that Sofina would be the one to enter the house and retrieve the children because Marcus trusted her the most. Sofina regularly delivered groceries, baby formula, and money to the family, so there was nothing odd about her arrival at the house

---

[1] Wesson felt he was the "master" of a new spirituality that mixed vampirism and Christianity. He spoke about this in a letter he wrote from Death Row that appears in the last section of this book.

that day. Marcus was outside with three of the older girls, who were working on the school bus. At five-nine and weighing more than 300 pounds, he was an imposing figure. At the age of 57, Wesson's graying dreadlocks hung almost to his knees. He had vowed to let his hair grow until Jesus returned to the earth, and while it was a practice borrowed from the Rastafarians, Wesson didn't follow any institutionalized or known spirituality. He only adopted religious concepts, using them for what benefit they offered while expelling those he considered unhelpful.

As Sofina approached the house, she made eye contact with her younger sister Rosa,[2] who was standing in the driveway. Wesson's daughter, 25-year-old Sebhrenah,[3] was holding a drill and was at work on the family's bus.

"Mom's not here right now," Rosa said nonchalantly, referring to their aunt Elizabeth.

"That's okay," Sofina replied. She brushed past Marcus and entered the house. She found her son in the front room. Jonathan was dressed in overalls and a plaid button-up shirt.

"Come on, Jonathan. You come with Mommy," Sofina told the boy, taking him by the hand.

"What are you doing?" Rosa asked her sister, having followed her into the house.

"I came here for my son," Sofina replied.

The look on Rosa's face quickly changed from skepticism to anger.

"You can't do this," Rosa said, her voice trembling.

---

[2] Rosa Solorio (nicknamed Rosie) gave birth to two of her uncle's children: 4-year-old Ethan and 1½-year-old Sedona; both were among those killed. Rosa remained faithful to her uncle, and she was the one he called "the good soldier."

[3] Sebhrenah Wesson was also found dead in the southeast bedroom. She gave birth to one of her father's children, who was also among those killed, one-year-old Marshey.

Wesson's 27-year-old daughter Kiani[4] entered the room and asked what was going on.

"I just came here to get my son," Sofina replied resolutely.

Outside, near the front door, Ruby and the others talked to Marcus. The longtime boyfriend of Brandi Solorio,[5] Louis Garcia, had just purchased a digital audio recorder. Thinking all might not go as planned, he began to secretly record the ensuing conversation.

"So what do you guys think?" Marcus asked Ruby in a calm and gentle voice. "I need your passports now."

"Our passports?" Ruby replied, confused by the request.

"Yeah. Now."

"No, I want to see Aviv," Ruby said.

"Aviv wants you to get her passport," Marcus insisted.

"Why do you guys need her passport?" Ruby asked.

"We get 'em every year," Marcus explained. "You know . . . you know how we always get 'em? We always get 'em. And . . . she's been told . . . she said she's been contacting you 'cause we want you . . ."

He paused, hearing the sound of women screaming from inside the house. The dispute between Sofina and the other women had escalated. Sofina pulled her son by the hand and began to lead him out of the house. Rosa seized the boy's other arm and the two women began to pull him back and forth. Eventually Rosa pried the boy from his mother's grasp. Rosa pulled Jonathan behind her, using her body as a barrier to keep Sofina from

---

[4] Kiani Wesson gave birth to two of her father's children: 8-year-old Illabelle and 1-year-old Jeva. Both children were killed on March 12, 2004.

[5] Brandi Solorio, Ruby and Sofina's sister, testified that she, too, had been molested by Marcus Wesson. Unlike her sisters, she did not give birth to any of his children.

reaching her son. Wesson's daughter Sebhrenah entered the room.

"Get the fuck out of my house!" Sebhrenah yelled at Sofina. "You're not taking any of these!" she said, referring to the children. Sofina pushed Sebhrenah away and picked up a chair, threatening to break a window. The other young women backed off. Sebhrenah clenched her fist.

Marcus remained at the front door and addressed Sofina in his usual calm tone.

"Sofia, what's going on in there?" he said, referring to Sofina by one of her nicknames. There was no answer.

"I just want my daughter, that's it! I want my baby, Marcus!" Ruby pleaded with her uncle.

"Not under kidnapping conditions," Marcus replied. "You can't kidnap her."

"I'm not leaving without my baby," Ruby warned.

Wesson made eye contact with some of the male family members trying to edge their way past him in the doorway. "Look, you guys can't come into my house without permission," he said.

"Marcus, she wants her daughter!" one of the brothers blurted out.

Marcus remained calm. "Come on, don't do the kidnapping. No, no, no," he said. "Please go."

"She wants her daughter, Marcus," one of the brothers repeated.

"I was gonna give her her daughter. But you guys can't come into my house without permission, please," Marcus said.

"All right. If we leave, when's Sofia coming out?" a brother asked. "Sofia has to come out."

"Sofia?" Marcus called out. More screaming could be heard coming from inside the house. "You guys . . . don't call the police," Marcus said.

With one of the babies in her arms, Sebhrenah made her way to a bedroom at the rear of the house. Sofina followed. Just behind Sofina was 17-year-old Lise,[6] holding the hands of 4-year-old Ethan and 7-year-old Aviv. Rosa had a firm grip of Jonathan's hand and led him into the bedroom with the other children. Eight-year-old Illabelle was already in the room, and Jeva was in her crib. One-year-old Marshey sat motionless on the floor. Sofina again grabbed Jonathan by the hand.

"Sofia, you can't take him," Rosa pleaded. "You know he's mine!"

"No, Rosa! He's my son, and I want to take him now," Sofina shouted back.

"Please, Sofia. Don't do this to me," Rosa cried. "Don't do this to me, please!"

"Shut up! Shut up! Get in here!" Lise told the children, pushing them into the room.

"You know, you don't need to talk like that," Sofina told Lise. "You don't need to be mean to them."

"You know what, shut up!" Sebhrenah interrupted. "And you get the fuck out of our house, you fat bitch!" she shouted at Sofina. Sebhrenah spoke in a voice that no one seemed to recognize. Family members would later describe it as a demon possession, saying that her voice was uncharacteristically deep and sounded like a man's.

"If you want to get nasty, I'll get nasty!" Sofina yelled. "I'm taking my son out of here no matter what happens!" Lise began to pull Sofina's hair, and Sofina screamed.

"Sofia, Jonathan doesn't want to go with you!" Rosa scoffed. "Why don't you ask him?"

"Do you want to come with Mommy?" Sofina asked the boy.

"No," the boy replied. A tear welled up in his eye.

Sofina could hear Marcus calling her from the front

---

[6] Nickname for 17-year-old Elizabeth (named after her mother), who was among the murder victims. She was also called "Little Elizabeth" by her family.

door. She left the bedroom, and Sebhrenah, Lise, and Rosa followed. The children remained in the bedroom.

"Ruby, why are you doing this?" Kiani yelled. "Why do you have to do this?"

"The cops are coming," Ruby repeated. "We already called the cops."

"You're a whore and an adulterer!" Sebhrenah shouted at Ruby. "Bow down to your master!"

"Yeah, bow down to your master!" Kiani joined in, pointing at her father's feet.

Still inside the house, Sofina turned toward Marcus, who had his back to her, and she struck him near his shoulder. "Marcus, what are they talking about . . . bow down to your master?" she asked. He did not respond.

Sebhrenah repeated the same command to Sofina. "Bow down to your master!" she cried in the same low, husky voice.

"Jesus Christ is my master!" Sofina replied, holding her hands skyward.

"You don't know who God is!" Sebhrenah retorted.

"Jesus Christ is not in this house and I am taking my son!" Sofina said.

Sebhrenah and Lise began to taunt Sofina. They chanted, *"Judas, Judas, Judas . . ."* and marched toward the back bedroom where the children were gathered. They entered the room and closed the door behind them. Desperate, Sofina followed.

"You don't know Jesus Christ," Kiani mocked. "If you did, you wouldn't be betraying us. You're just a Judas," she said to Sofina, following behind her.

The door was shut and Sofina could hear shuffling sounds coming from inside the room. She opened the door, and Lise began to push it shut from the other side. Using all her strength, Sofina managed to wedge herself halfway inside the room. She saw Sebhrenah rummaging through a brown leather bag. The children were all in the room. Ethan and Aviv were standing to her left.

Marshey was sitting on the floor with a baby bottle in his hands. Jonathan was standing near a bedroom window behind the crib where one of the babies sat quietly. Illabelle also stood silently. None of the children cried. None of them spoke as much as a word. As Sofina pushed against the door with all her might, she noticed a large pile of clothes near the door. At that moment Kiani and Rosa approached and began to pull her out of the room. She could not match their strength and the bedroom door slammed shut.

As the fight escalated, two women from the Solorio side of the family placed a total of five frantic calls to 911. Mary Salazar and Valerie Gonzalez made the calls from their cell phones. The calls were answered by a California Highway Patrol dispatcher, who transferred the calls to Fresno police. Salazar placed the first 911 call at 2:13 P.M. According to the police department, the first officer was dispatched to the scene ten minutes later, at 2:23 P.M., but officers didn't arrive at the scene until 2:35 P.M., twenty-two minutes from the time of the first call. Authorities were later criticized by family members for what they felt was a slow response. Salazar placed the first three calls:

CALLER: We need a police officer on Weber and . . . I'm trying to get my daughter, and the person who has her won't let me take her. Hammond and Weber.
(Recording ends abruptly.)

A few minutes later she made a second call:

CALLER: I need officer assistance right now. A man has my daughter.
DISPATCHER: Who is the man who has your daughter?
CALLER: I don't know. I need officer assistance!
(Call is transferred.)
CALLER: It's actually not my daughter, but we need officer assistance. It's not my daughter, it's my friend's.

DISPATCHER: What's your name?
CALLER: Mary.
DISPATCHER: Mary what?
CALLER: Mary Salazar.

Several minutes passed and Salazar made a third 911 call:

CALLER: This the lady who called before. It's getting really ugly out here.
DISPATCHER: Hold on, let me give you the police.
(Dispatcher transfers call to Fresno police.)
CALLER: It's getting really physical out here. We called like ten minutes ago. We really need someone out here! It's getting really physical!

As the conflict worsened, Valerie Gonzalez made the fourth call to 911:

CALLER: I need some kind of help! It's getting physical!
DISPATCHER: I know that. Let me transfer you over there again.
CALLER: Hello? I need some police assistance. It's getting physical.
DISPATCHER: Are you Mary?
CALLER: No.
DISPATCHER: Mary just called. Police are on the way.

Salazar made one last 911 call:

CALLER: This is domestic violence, someone has a gun. We've called several times and no one's come here. When I called 911, they transferred me to . . . I don't know.
DISPATCHER: What city is this in?
CALLER: Fresno.
DISPATCHER: Okay, let me transfer you.

The CHP dispatcher chuckled and said the following to the police dispatcher:

DISPATCHER: Every time we transfer the calls, they get more embellished. Now someone has a gun. I'm not sure, I'll let you tell, but I think it's embellished.
CALLER: This is Mary. It's getting really physical. More people have shown up and it's getting physical.
DISPATCHER: Are they fighting?
CALLER: Not all of 'em.
DISPATCHER: We have officers on the way, okay?

Again Marcus summoned Sofina to the front door. He explained they needed to talk and that she couldn't take the kids with force. He advised the women to sit down and sort it out.

"Okay then, let's talk," she said. "The reason why I came to get my son is you guys are not raising them in the way that Marcus promised that he would raise them," Sofina explained. "First of all, you know, Dad is still having, you know, children by his own girls. And the agreement that we made was he was not supposed to ever do that again," she said.

Kiani and Rosa looked at each other, confused.

"That's so stupid," Kiani said.

"You know what, you're just jealous," Rosa added.

"You guys are not teaching the kids like you're supposed to. Nobody is working to support the kids," Sofina pointed out.

"I'd rather have the police here," Marcus blurted out. "I'd rather have them do it, than force."

Ruby told Marcus she was afraid the family would leave town and that she would never see her daughter again.

"Aviv is my daughter and that's the best I got," she said.

Sofina exclaimed, "No matter what happens I'm not leaving until Jonathan walks out this door!"

"I'm not either!" Ruby agreed.

"Come on guys . . . please get out of my house!" Marcus yelled.

At this point Elizabeth Wesson's sister, Rosemary Solorio, arrived. Rosemary, who spent much of her adult life struggling with a drug addiction, had given her children—including Sofina and Ruby—to her sister and Marcus Wesson to raise. Rosemary strongly objected to having her grandchildren removed from the Wesson home and she began to fight with her daughters and her sons.[7]

"Get out of here!" Rosemary said to her children. "Get out of here now!"

"No!" Sofina said defiantly. Now in the doorway, Rosemary swung at her daughter, grazing her mouth. Marco Garcia[8] blocked his mother's fist with his arm, and in retaliation Sofina tried to kick her mother, aiming for her stomach, but missed. Marco pushed Rosemary away.

"Respect your mom!" Marcus pleaded. "Come on you guys, respect your mom! Please!"

"Where are the cops at?" a male family member asked nervously. "Where the fuck are they at?"

"What I see here . . . it's not right!" Ruby yelled. "Marcus! You're not supposed to have kids with your fucking kids, okay?" Ruby began to sob. "It's wrong!"

---

[7] Marcus Wesson came into the Solorio family when Elizabeth and Rosemary were just girls. He first had a relationship with their mother, Rosemary Maytorena, and fathered one of her children before he married a teenage Elizabeth Solorio. There was no known sexual relationship between Rosemary Solorio (the daughter) and Wesson, although he seemed to have an important role in her life. In addition to giving him custody of her children, she declared at his sentencing hearing, "My brother-in-law, he's always been a blessing to me. He saved me from a lot. I know that I always will have Marcus in my heart."

[8] Marco Garcia, a son of Rosemary Solorio, lived with the Wessons for a period of time during his adolescence and at one time considered Marcus a father figure. He was one of Ruby and Sofina's brothers who came to the Hammond Avenue house to help them regain custody of their children on March 12, 2004. Marco's job was to remain at the front door; he wedged himself in the doorway to prevent Marcus from closing it.

"That's not happening," Marcus responded.

"Yes it is! Don't fuckin'—" Ruby began.

"What the hell are you talking about?" Rosemary asked her daughter.

"Okay, ask him!" Ruby said between sobs, pointing at Marcus.

The shouting grew louder between Rosemary and her children in the front yard. She attacked her son Danny, who had come to help Sofina and Ruby get their children. Danny held his mother's hands down at her side and then forced her into a headlock.

"Rosemary, please!" Marcus shouted at his sister-in-law.

"When is it gonna stop?" Ruby asked, turning to Marcus. "When is it gonna stop?"

"You guys are bullshit!" Marcus yelled.

The men who accompanied Sofina and Ruby to retrieve the children were becoming impatient. The police had been called but still had not arrived.

"What's wrong with you?" Rosemary screamed. She swung at her daughter, hitting Ruby in the stomach.

"Rosemary, no!" Marcus yelled.

"Don't touch me!" Ruby said, doubled over in pain. "Nobody touches me! Don't touch me!"

"Come on, guys! Man, I . . . I can't believe it. It's like nobody can talk intelligently around here," Marcus exclaimed.

Ruby continued to plead with Marcus to turn over her daughter Aviv.

"You know what she believes?" Sofina said to Marcus, pointing to her mother. "You know what she believes? She wants us to stay here and get married to you! And keep having kids!"

"Come on, *mija*,[9] that's—" Marcus began.

"That's what she wants!" Sofina assured.

---

[9] In Spanish, *mija* is a term of endearment meaning "my daughter."

"I don't agree with that!" Marcus said, shaking his head.

Marcus promised Sofina and Ruby they could have visitation rights if they left peacefully. They wouldn't budge and insisted they weren't leaving without their children.

Sofina was growing impatient. "The point is this: We want to take our children," she announced. "We want to raise them, and that's . . . put the period at the end of it."

"Come on! These kids are happy!" Marcus replied.

Ruby let out a sigh of frustration. "They're happy, Marcus, because that's all they know," she said.

"Well then, what does the Lord say?" Marcus asked. "What other foundation can be laid but what is laid?"

Sofina had again left the vicinity of the front door, and the sound of women arguing could be heard coming from inside the house.

"Sofia! Get out of the house!" Marco yelled at his sister, his foot still wedged into the front doorway.

A police cruiser pulled in front of the house and Fresno police officer Frank Nelson got out and approached.

"All right. Whose house is this?" Nelson asked.

"This is our house," Marcus replied.

It took Nelson several minutes to figure out the source of the dispute because everyone was trying to explain the situation at once. Having returned to the front door, Sofina explained to the officer that she and Ruby simply wanted custody of their children.

"We tried to, um . . . do this in a nice way," Sofina told the officer. "It was not working . . . that's why—"

"These guys are here to protect us from acting like idiots," Marcus interrupted, referring to the police.

"We'll just make sure nobody gets hurt," Officer Nelson assured them.

Sofina motioned to her brother Danny to retrieve Jonathan's birth certificate from her car.

"Sofia . . . you're not gonna let . . ." Marcus said, with

desperation in his voice. He turned to officer Nelson. "She has never had that baby," he said.

Danny returned from the car and handed Sofina the birth certificate. She presented it the police officer along with her ID. "Sofina R. Solorio," she announced, pointing to the paper.

"And, eh . . . uh . . . we're talking about Jonathan?" the officer asked.

"Yes, Jonathan," she replied. Sofina explained that her son would turn eight the next Sunday.

Marcus sighed. "We gotta work this out," he said. "Sofia has the power to stop all of this."

After Nelson had heard explanations from both Sofina and Ruby and examined Jonathan and Aviv's birth certificates, he told Marcus that unless he had court papers showing that he had legal custody, he would have to turn over the children.

"Yeah, see, this is what they've done," Marcus said. "They've taken half of a story within their own . . . lack of integrity, and they're presenting it to you."

"I don't think they want to hear *that*," Ruby interjected sarcastically.

"They're . . . they're presenting to you that they're the mother of the children, but they're not," Marcus explained.

"Yeah, hold on real quick," Officer Nelson said. He held up Sofina's passport. "This is Sofina Solorio. She's mom. That's what this says. So there is no question, unless somebody's got court papers here saying they're the guardian through the court . . . this lady gets her child." Nelson pointed to Ruby. "And that one gets hers," he said.

"That baby has never lived with her in her life," Marcus retorted. "Ruby, you know you're not the mother of that baby!"

"I am the mother, Marcus," Ruby said. "I have proof."

Officer Nelson explained to Marcus that he had little recourse since nothing was done through the courts.

"You can't just randomly say, 'I'm gonna give you a baby and not have any kind of papers' . . . a word of mouth . . . a handshake? That doesn't cut it. I'm telling you the courts have to be involved."

Assisting police officer Benny Martinez was trying to move the group of family members gathered near the front door farther away from the house. He told them to stand by the sidewalk. Martinez could see Nelson was getting nowhere in his attempt to talk sense to Wesson. Martinez tapped the radio microphone clipped to his lapel to get Officer Nelson's attention. Nelson looked over, and Martinez mouthed the words, *Call sergeant.* Nelson nodded his head.

"We're gonna resolve this in the next couple of minutes," Nelson said to Marcus. "Where's her child at?"

Ruby whispered something to Nelson.

Nelson asked, "Where are these kids at?"

"In back," Louis Garcia answered. "In the back room."

Marcus continued to protest, and Nelson agreed to call over his superior, Sergeant Patrick Jackson. "Let's try to get this . . . these kids are gonna go with their mom," Nelson said, looking firmly at Marcus. "That's all there is to it."

Nelson returned a minute later with Sergeant Jackson.

"This is my boss," Nelson said to Marcus.

"How are you doing?" Marcus asked.

Sergeant Jackson nodded.

Nelson attempted to explain the situation to Jackson, providing the basics: Sofina and Ruby had given their children to Marcus eight years ago and no one ever filed custody papers and now the women wanted their children back.

Sergeant Jackson pulled Louis aside and they talked quietly. Jackson returned to the front door and told Marcus, "Well, we'll call CPS and they'll get involved . . . and . . . they wanna make a decision as to . . ."

His voice was drowned out by the sound of passing cars.

Officer Nelson spoke up. "What's gonna happen is these kids are gonna go with us. All right?"

"The kids are here?" Jackson asked.

"They are," Louis affirmed.

Jackson looked at Marcus. "May I ask you to—"

At this point Rosemary again became violent, punching her daughter Sofina in the stomach. Rosemary's sons moved in to restrain her. More officers had arrived and one ran over to help.

Sergeant Jackson explained to Marcus that if he wanted custody of the children, he would have to file paperwork with the courts. Marcus said he had a verbal agreement and that should be enough.

"That child's not hers," he said, gesturing toward Sofina.

"I'm going to call CPS," Jackson announced. He stepped away and pulled out his radio. Kiani and Rosa began whispering something to Marcus, who retrieved a small black pouch from his pocket and opened it. He removed a small key and handed it to Rosa. She took the key and disappeared into the house.

"It's either me or CPS," Sofina said to Marcus.

"Mija," Marcus pleaded. "If you do this right . . . if you do this right . . . you can have the children. You know why."

At 2:50 P.M., Sergeant Jackson called the city attorney to find out if he and his officers had a legal right to enter the house without Wesson's permission. The attorney assigned to advise the police department told Jackson they did not have legal cause to enter the home. At 3:03 P.M., Jackson called Child Protective Services for a consultation. Sergeant Jackson returned to the front door and told Marcus he would be forced to arrest him if he refused to give up the children.

"I'm not gonna argue," Jackson said. "I'm telling you that when CPS gets here, we'll ask them if they wanna do something with these kids."

"Marcus, the cops, they're gonna do this now or later," Ruby said. "We tried to discuss it."

"No, I'm not arguing anything," Marcus said. "I feel constricted here. I just can't believe what you're doing."

Marcus pleaded with Sofina and Ruby to talk to him in private. Both refused.

Officer Nelson, who was writing something in a notebook, looked up. "There's no other kids here, right?" He paused. "I don't think there are . . . the only reason I say that is . . . once CPS gets here . . . they will make a decision . . ."

Marcus continued trying to convince Sofina and Ruby to come into the house, and Officer Nelson lost his patience. He told Marcus that if he continued to be uncooperative, he would end up in the Fresno County Jail, and if there were other kids in the house, CPS would probably take them.

Marcus shook his head in protest. "No . . . no . . . oh, no!"

At this point Marcus Wesson's 19-year-old son Serafino arrived at the house. The sight of police cruisers parked in front immediately sent him into a panic. He brushed past the officers, ducked under his father's arm and entered the house. In the living room, he angrily addressed Sofina and the others. "What's going on? What's happening?" he demanded.

Rosa was the first to respond. "Serafino," she said, "Sofina and Ruby are here to come and get Aviv and Jonathan."

Serafino began pacing back and forth, holding his forehead.

Marcus continued to whisper something to Kiani.

"Sofia, what are you doing?" Serafino demanded.

"I came here to get Jonathan," Sofina replied.

Serafino turned frantically to his father. "Dad, just say the word and I'll get the kids right now," he said. "I'll go through the back and I'll have a car out there and we'll take them."

"No Serafino, no," Marcus said coolly.

Seventeen-year-old Lise was standing in the living room crying. She approached her brother Serafino and said, "Fino, I'm scared. They're trying to take the kids away."

"Lise, don't worry," he said. "I won't let nothing happen to you. Everything is going to be okay." But inside, Serafino was boiling with rage. How could his cousins be so selfish as to break a promise they made to his father? he wondered.

Over Lise's shoulder Serafino could see his sister Sebhrenah blocking the doorway of the southeast bedroom. He approached her and asked, "Sebhrenah, what's going on?"

She began to cry but had an eerie smile on her face. She explained to her brother that Sofina had come for Jonathan and had started a fight. Serafino continued pacing and then exited the house, where his cousin Marco was still guarding Marcus at the front door.

"You know, I ought to snap your neck right now," Serafino told Marco.

"You know what?" Sofina interjected. "Forget it. This is getting violent. Marcus, I'm getting my son out of here."

By this time several more police officers had arrived, and one of them attempted to enter the house. Serafino grabbed the officer and pushed him back.

"You don't have a warrant," Serafino said.

"Don't disrespect the officers," Marcus advised his son.

The officer told Serafino not to touch him again, but backed away.

Officer Nelson turned to Marcus. "He's gonna call our city attorney. I don't know if we're gonna wait for CPS."

"Well, how long is that gonna take?" Marcus asked.

"Once he makes the call and we get the word from the

city attorney as far as . . . I don't think that we even . . . we don't need a warrant to go in. We can just go in," Nelson said. "What that means is that once we cross the threshold, then I know a few people that are being arrested. I hate to say that . . . okay?"

More commotion could be heard, and for the first time since the police arrived, Marcus left his post at the front door and entered the house.

"Don't let him walk around in the house," Louis advised the officers. "Keep an eye on that big guy."

Ruby was becoming increasingly nervous. She turned to one of the officers and said, "Uh . . . Marcus . . . that . . . that . . . big gentleman . . . can you just watch him? I want my daughter and I don't trust him."

"Well, okay, eight years ago you made a real bad mistake," Nelson said to Ruby.

Marcus pleaded with Ruby to come inside the house and talk, and then he paused. Elizabeth Wesson had just arrived at the house. She stumbled as she made her way to the front door. She seemed confused and disoriented.

"Aunt Lise," Sofina said to Elizabeth. "I love you with all my heart but I want you to stay out of it."

"What do you mean stay out of it?" Elizabeth replied. "I don't believe it!"

"I told you last week what we were gonna do," Sofina said to Elizabeth. "I told you last week that I want Jonathan."

"Didn't I say 'Talk to him'?" Elizabeth said, referring to Marcus.

"Ruby and I got together . . . we talked about it. We thought the only way to do it . . . is to do this. And we did it!" Sofina said.

"No!" Elizabeth exclaimed. "You guys didn't even give a shit! How can you . . . you didn't even give a damn warning!"

"Where's Marcus?" Ruby asked, with panic in her voice. "I tried to talk to him already. To be honest, I don't feel safe in there."

"What do you mean?" Elizabeth asked.

"Where's Marcus?" Ruby repeated, her voice beginning to tremble. "Marcus is back there?"

"He got in," one of the brothers said.

Ruby peered into the house and saw Kiani barricading the bedroom door with a table.

"Ruby, you know . . . that there is nothing going on inside," Kiani said.

"Who . . . *What?*" Louis exclaimed.

"Kiani, what is going on in there?" Ruby demanded.

"Nothing's going on right now," Kiani replied.

"Honestly . . . what's going on in there?" Ruby repeated frantically.

Elizabeth entered the house, followed by Kiani, Rosa, and Serafino. Elizabeth made her way to the back bedroom. A table was blocking the bedroom door, so she moved it aside. She opened the door and entered the room. She saw her husband bent down on the floor, holding their 17-year-old daughter Lise in his arms. Elizabeth fixated on her daughter's eyes.[10]

"Come here, Bee,"[11] Marcus said, motioning for his wife.

Elizabeth was overcome with terror.

Outside, Sofina walked from the front door and into the front yard, where her brothers were gathered. She glanced back over her shoulder and saw that Marcus had left his

---

[10] Elizabeth Wesson claimed not to remember seeing anyone else in the room besides her husband and daughter Lise. In her interviews with police and on the witness stand, she became hysterical when asked to recall what she observed at that moment in the southeast bedroom.

[11] A nickname used by Marcus Wesson for his wife.

post at the front door. Sofina panicked. She ran back to the front door, where Sergeant Jackson was still on his cell phone consulting the police department's legal advisor.

"He left!" she exclaimed to Jackson. "He went in the back! Back there! He's going to kill the kids!"

Jackson held up his hand, indicating that he was on the phone.

Desperate, Sofina ran to Officer Nelson, who was sitting in his police cruiser parked in front of the house.

"Officer, you need to go in there right now!" she exclaimed. "Marcus isn't at the door! He's in the back! He's going to kill the kids!"

Serafino had taken his father's place guarding the front door.

"Step aside, son," an officer told him.

"No!" Serafino replied defiantly. "You have no warrant. You're not coming in."

The officer pulled his gun out of its holster. Serafino stepped aside but did not exit the house. Several officers entered the house, their guns drawn. One officer cocked his shotgun as he passed through the doorway.

"Don't you dare shoot my father!" Serafino shouted, approaching the officer.

"Get him out of here!" the officer said.

Two more officers grabbed Serafino by the arm and pulled him out of the house. As he walked into the yard he began to cry.

Sofina ran to him. "Serafino, what did you see? What happened?" she asked.

Serafino shook his head and wept. "I think Dad shot Sebhrenah and Lise," he said.[12]

---

[12] According to Sofina, Serafino made this statement. Dorian Wesson (who was not present the day of the murders) testified that Serafino told him later, "Dad killed the kids." Oddly, when Serafino testified, he was not asked about making any statement to that effect.

Elizabeth Wesson then emerged from the back bedroom with a look of terror on her face. She ran out of the house and into the yard.

"They're all gone! They're all gone!" she cried. Elizabeth fell into Sofina's arms.

Sofina and Ruby began to scream. "No . . . *Noooo!*"

"*Nooooo!*" Ruby cried.

"*Oh my God!*" Sofina yelled.

The women all began to scream.

"*Shoot his fuckin' ass!*" Louis shouted at the police. "Kill that son of a bitch! That's what he gets! I hope he dies right now!"

"*Get in there! He's doing something to the kids!*" Louis exclaimed. "*Fuckin' probably killed them already! He's got a gun in there!*"

Kiani exited the house. "You guys shouldn't have came!" she shouted at Sofina and Ruby. "They're gone and you're next!"

"My *God! Nooo!*" Ruby fainted and fell to the ground.

Sofina threw her purse on the ground and screamed hysterically. She ran to the police cruiser parked in front of the house and threw herself on it. Pounding on the hood of the car, she sobbed, "It wasn't supposed to happen like this! It wasn't supposed to happen like this!"

"He's in the house! He's still in the house!" Louis said. "*He killed them! That's what happened!*"

Ruby was just regaining consciousness. "*Go get my baby!*" she screamed.

A police officer approached Sofina.

"What did you hear? What did you see?" he asked.

"I didn't see anything," she replied. At that moment she heard the sound of two gunshots coming from inside the house. Again she became hysterical.

Doreen Sanchez was just sitting down to watch *All My Children* in her living room when she first heard the women shouting across the street at the Wesson house.

During the trial, Sanchez testified that she heard two gunshots shortly after 2:00 P.M. and went outside. When asked by the defense attorney if she could have heard the shots later in the afternoon, Sanchez said she knew she heard the sounds between 2:00 and 3:00 P.M. because she was watching *General Hospital*. Other neighbors made similar statements about hearing gunfire. Oddly, not one police officer reported hearing a single gunshot.

Sergeant Jackson was just a few feet away near the front door and was crouched down with his gun drawn. He was pointing it inside the house. Sofina joined Ruby behind the yellow school bus parked in the driveway. The police told them to get away from the house. Sofina and Ruby clung on to each other and crossed the street.

3:47 P.M.

Police cars surrounded the house. The SWAT team was on its way, and several officers were positioned in the front yard with their weapons drawn. A crowd of interested neighbors was gathering in the street, and officers created a perimeter around the house with yellow crime tape to keep the onlookers a safe distance away. A large police RV pulled up to the house, the words "Mobile Command Unit" written on the side. Officers escorted the female family members into the vehicle, including Sofina and Ruby, who were both crying and still holding onto each other. Kiani and Rosa were also inside the RV. About twenty minutes passed and a female officer came by to ask the women what the children were wearing.

"Is my daughter alive?" Ruby asked the officer, her face wet with tears.

"We don't know yet," the officer replied.

In the front yard, Fresno police officer Wynn Mooney had the best view into the house. He stood next to a tree just a few feet from the front door. His K-9 was at his side.

Mooney could see most of the living room and the hallway that led to the back of the house. The door to the back bedroom was shut. He called out, "Marcus! Marcus! It's the police department! Just come on out and talk to us!" There was no answer. The SWAT team arrived. Officers dressed in black and carrying automatic weapons surrounded the house. More than an hour went by, and for Mooney it felt like an eternity. He continued to call out, "Marcus! We just want to get your side of the story. You're not in any trouble!"

Then Mooney saw a shadow moving inside the house. It was dark inside but the afternoon light shone into the front room through the open front door. He saw the shadow move toward the back of the room in the hallway. Officer Mooney thought his eyes were playing tricks on him, but he saw the movement again, and this time he realized someone had emerged from the back bedroom.

4:47 P.M.

"I have movement in the house," he whispered into his police radio.

Mooney called out to the shadow looming inside.

"Marcus! Just please come on out here and talk to us. We just want to talk to you. Come on out!"

Mooney saw the shadow move back farther into the hallway, out of his view. Moments later the shadow reappeared.

He called out again, "Marcus! Let's get this over with! Just come on out!" Walking into the afternoon light reflecting into the front room, Marcus Wesson emerged from the shadows. His expression was emotionless and his clothes were covered with blood. Wesson would not take his eyes off Officer Jimmy Ray Passmore, who was off to Mooney's left near the front door.

"Step on out here where we can see you," Passmore advised Wesson.

Wesson complied. He raised his hands near his head and stepped outside.

"I'm going to pat you down," Passmore said, approaching him slowly. He told Wesson to turn around and place his hands on the side of the house, and again Wesson complied. Passmore patted his hands on Wesson's bloody clothing and removed a leather knife sheath from his right front pocket. Passmore tossed it onto the ground. The empty knife sheath hit the cement, and Officer Mooney, who was just feet away, wondered where the knife had gone. Passmore placed handcuffs on Wesson, who stood expressionless in the light of the afternoon sun.

THREE

I am Happy To Be Home
with my Father In Heaven,
and to see my whole family
Together Again,

This world is not made
for us, we are like fish
out of water, can't happen.

Jesus, the love of my life,
without him, we would be
lost. At last, we go home and
are more than happy, to preserve
our souls.

We've lived for Christ now we
must die for Christ.

The Wesson Family

—*Diary Entry of Kiani Wesson*
dated December 14, 2003,
which she read from the witness stand.

Officer Eloy Escareno was the first to enter the
house. He was followed by officer Howard Tello.

"It's okay, kids! You can come out!" Tello called out.

Escareno made his way down the dark hallway and slowly approached the door of the southeast bedroom with his shotgun drawn. The door was slightly ajar, and with his free hand he pushed it open. The room was pitch-dark and silent. Escareno went in. He panned his flashlight across the room, but his eyes hadn't adjusted to the darkness of the room and all he could see were the outlines of shapes beginning to form. Three large coffins were leaning up against the wall to his immediate left and blocked his view of the northeast corner of the room. Officer Tello entered the room and found a light switch along the wall. He flipped it on. Escareno gasped. He dropped his shotgun, fell to his knees and began yelling.

"Oh my God! We need an ambulance! Code three! Code three!"

The bodies were stacked on the other side of the coffins in the northeast corner of the room. The oldest victims were near the base of the pile, and a large pool of blood had formed on the floor. The victims appeared to be stacked deliberately; 25-year-old Sebhrenah and 17-year-old Lise were the most visible and covered the bodies of the children.

The bodies were still warm to his touch, and Officer Escareno frantically began to search through the pile for any signs of life. He checked pulses and felt none. Trying not to move the bodies, he continued to search for someone breathing, a pulse, a gasp for air, anything. He came to an infant. Like all the others, the baby had been shot in the eye. He held the child to feel for a heartbeat but there was none. Then with his hands covered in blood, Escareno broke down and cried.

"We need an ambulance for these kids," he said as he wept.

"Okay, but we have to finish searching," Tello replied. But Escareno couldn't go on. Tello helped him up and Escareno left the room.

Tello continued to check for signs of life, with no success. When he reached the bottom of the pile, he had counted five victims. A subsequent search by another officer concluded with a count of seven victims. It wasn't until the crime scene investigators came into the room that they discovered the total number of those deceased was nine. Some of the youngest and smallest victims were at the bottom of the pile and had initially been overlooked.

Aboard the police RV, Sofina and Ruby sat together praying they were caught in a nightmare. They continued to ask the police about their children but they still hadn't received any word. After what seemed to be an hour or so, the same female officer who had asked what the children were wearing boarded the RV and said she had some bad news.

"Some of the children are deceased," she said.

Hearing those words, Sofina, Ruby, and Rosa became hysterical, while Kiani sat expressionless. Ruby and Sofina started to scream.

"Quiet down . . . Calm down," an officer told them.

Sofina gathered herself as much as she could. "Which ones?" she asked, sobbing.

"We don't know yet," the female officer answered, shaking her head.

Sofina hugged Ruby and they continued to weep.

"Sofia and Ruby, it's your guys' fault. You guys should have never came here in the first place," Kiani said.

The female officer turned to Kiani. "You know what? Go in the other room," she said. Kiani left the room.

Officer Passmore guarded Marcus by the school bus in the front driveway. He had called for a large transport vehicle, reasoning that Wesson's 300-pound frame would not easily fit in the back of a police cruiser. Wesson's hands were cuffed behind his back because of his protruding belly. He stood calmly waiting with Officer Passmore and did as he was told. When the police wagon arrived, he stepped on board.

The police chief had arrived at the scene and was about to make a second briefing to the large group of reporters who had gathered just beyond the crime scene tape. Initial reports were that police had responded to a "multiple homicide," but there were no specifics. Chief Jerry Dyer choked back tears as he announced the latest number of murder victims was up to seven.

"What's making it so difficult is the bodies are not only intertwined, but stacked on top of each other," Dyer told reporters. When asked about a motive, Dyer shrugged his shoulders but said there might have been some kind of ritual involved.

Inside the house, crime scene investigators began their work. Identification Bureau technicians Leslie Forshey and Janet May methodically photographed the southeast bedroom and then immediately focused their attention on the first victim, 25-year-old Sebhrenah Wesson. She lay facedown on top of some of the younger victims. Her right arm was bent at the elbow and her left arm was out to the side, across the body of her sister, Lise. Forshey and May photographed Sebhrenah, naming her Victim 1. They noted she was wearing a black print dress and brown boots and she had been shot in the right eye. Under Sebhrenah's body investigators found the murder weapon, a .22 caliber handgun containing a live round of ammunition. It was void of fingerprints. They emptied the gun and bagged it as evidence. Later at the morgue, gunshot residue tests of Sebhrenah's hands produced negative results. The GSR tests on Wesson himself also came back negative, and a blood test determined that he was sober and drug-free at the time of his arrest.

Once Sebhrenah's body was moved off to the side, IB technicians examined and photographed Victim 2, 17-year-old Lise Wesson. She also lay facedown, her head turned to the side. She wore a pink top and a black skirt and had been shot twice in her right eye. The coroner would later determine that the first shot was fired at close range and the second from farther away. Investigators found a bloody knife with a five-inch blade just under her right arm on the floor. Police later discovered that the knife fit perfectly into the leather sheath Wesson had in his right pocket at the time of his arrest.

Lise's body was moved off to the side of the pile of bodies toward the door. Victim 3 was the youngest. Kiani's daughter, 1-year-old Jeva, lay faceup wearing jeans and a long-sleeve shirt. She, too, had been shot in the right eye. Beneath her, police found a red binder, and on top of the binder an expended .22 caliber shell casing.

Sedona Wesson was on her left side. The 18-month-old was wearing a white onesie and had also been shot in the right eye.

Eighteen-month-old Marshey Wesson was the fifth victim and the only one who had been shot in the left eye. His little body lay facedown and his left calf was crossed over his right ankle. He wore a white shirt and a diaper. He was the only son of Victim 1, Sebhrenah Wesson.

Victim 6, 4-year-old Ethan, was facedown, and like almost all the others, suffered a gunshot to the right eye. Investigators also found a bullet wound on the side of his abdomen. When he was moved from the pile, a spent bullet fragment fell out of his blue coveralls and rolled onto the floor.

Eight-year-old Illabelle, Victim 7, was on her left side, her head facing to one side and her feet facing in the opposite direction. She, too, suffered a gunshot to the right eye. Under her, investigators found three expended bullet casings and an empty Ruger handgun magazine leaning against her right shoe.

The last two victims were the children at the center of the dispute. They were at the bottom of the pile of bodies and it appeared they had been the first to die. Both had bullet wounds to their right eyes. Seven-year-old

Aviv lay on her left side, and 7-year-old Jonathan was on his back. A live .22 caliber cartridge sat on his left leg, and beneath him was a live .22 caliber cartridge. Rape tests were performed on all the victims and it was determined that none suffered from any recent sexual abuse.

Three large coffins were lined up against the north wall of the bedroom nearest to the door. Oddly, IB techs found no latent fingerprints on any of the coffins, which was strange because several officers admitted to opening the coffins to check the contents.[13]

Once the IB techs had finished their preliminary work, forensic expert Dr. Venu Gopal and Deputy Coroner Joseph Tiger entered the southeast bedroom. Their first order of business was to perform liver temperature tests on the two oldest victims. The tests would ultimately show that Sebhrenah and Lise died after the seven younger victims.[14]

As night fell, a huge crowd gathered outside the house. The news of the nine murders dominated live television coverage throughout the evening, and hundreds of curious onlookers had shown up to see the scene for themselves. The public would eventually learn that the victims were all Wesson's children with six different women, including his wife, two of his daughters, and three of his nieces, but at the time those who lived in the neighborhood had little knowledge about the family or how the murders could have happened.

"I never even knew there were kids living there," one man in his forties admitted. "I'd never seen them. That's why this is such a shock."

---

[13] Nothing of significance was found inside the coffins. They were primarily being used to store clothes.

[14] Dr. Gopal ultimately reinforced defense attorneys' claim that Sebhrenah and Lise probably died about an hour after the seven younger victims.

Sixty-one-year-old Barbara Alec, who lived next door to the Wessons, made reference to "strange odors" that came from their backyard almost every night.

"It would kill you to smell it. It would gag me. Whatever he was cooking, it was not food," she told reporters.

Rumors of missing cats in the neighborhood fueled misguided speculation that the Wessons sacrificed animals. Some reporters postulated that the murders were part of some kind of demonic ritual. In the front yard a group of police chaplains held hands and prayed. Many of the officers who had witnessed the gruesome murder scene were shaken by what they had seen.

The coroner placed the victims in body bags and removed them from the house. The commotion created by neighbors and reporters outside the house abruptly gave way to silence as the smallest victims were carried out in white body bags. Subsequently, police officers removed the ten mahogany coffins from the house, claiming them as evidence. By the end of the night a tow truck had arrived to take Wesson's renovated school bus to the county yard.

The next day the yellow crime scene tape that surrounded 761 West Hammond Avenue came down. The driveway had been transformed into a shrine of balloons, candles, cards, and flowers. Live trucks from every local television station still hadn't moved from their spots on Hammond Avenue from the previous night. Larger satellite trucks from Los Angeles and San Francisco had arrived overnight, as did CNN.

It was amidst this fury of activity that Serafino Wesson returned home. Surrounded by reporters, he shook his head. "He's the best dad anybody could ever have," he said. "He looks really dangerous . . . but he's such a gentle guy, I can't believe he did it."

FOUR

The headline on the front page of *The Fresno Bee* the day after the murders read, 9 DEAD IN FRESNO HOME: *Bodies of seven children age 8 and younger are discovered after Marcus Wesson, 57, surrenders and is arrested after a 2-hour standoff.* The front page photograph showed a panic-stricken Elizabeth Wesson being comforted by her sons. The article emphasized a "two-hour standoff with police" (in reality the standoff lasted eighty minutes) and the fact that Marcus Wesson had emerged from the back bedroom with blood on his shirt. The article quoted a family member named Mike,[15] who said Wesson "thought he was God" and that police were looking into the possibility that the family was involved in some kind of cult. Another front-page article was dedicated to the subject of how the murders affected police officers who had witnessed the grisly murder scene.

The morning after the killings, Police Chief Jerry Dyer appeared on network television. Dyer agreed to the interviews on NBC's *Today* show and CNN, reasoning that he didn't want Fresno to be known for the wrong reasons and to assure the general public that the mass murder in California's Central Valley was an anomaly. Dyer granted a phone interview with CNN just fourteen hours after the

---

[15] The source was likely Miguel Solorio, Elizabeth Wesson's brother.

killings and then spoke live via satellite with CNN's Bill Hemmer on March 15, 2004. During that interview, Dyer said that Wesson was cooperating with police but had not revealed everything investigators wanted to know. Dyer confirmed the cause of death for all nine victims, saying they had all been killed by gunshot wounds to the eyes.

When asked if he believed that Wesson had fired the shots, Dyer did not directly answer the question but said, "We believe that Marcus Wesson is the person responsible for the nine murders. That doesn't mean that as an agency we have ruled out the possibility that any other suspects may be involved. We don't want to become too narrowly focused in our investigation to exclude anyone. But we do believe, absolutely, that he is responsible for the murder of all nine victims." On NBC's *Today* show, Chief Dyer referred to the killings as "Fresno's worst mass murder." That same day, he held a news conference in front of police headquarters in downtown Fresno and addressed a group of reporters from all over the state. When asked if the district attorney would seek the death penalty against Wesson, Dyer paused. He looked at the dozen or so TV cameras that surrounded him and said with determination, "If this does not qualify for the death sentence, then there is no case that would."

Wesson spent more than ten hours over two days being interviewed by police. Detectives described his demeanor as "cooperative," adding that he was "very intelligent, very articulate, and very well-spoken." After his interrogation, Wesson was led from police headquarters to a transport vehicle that took him to the county jail. His hands were handcuffed behind him and his graying dreadlocks trailed down his jail-issued orange jumpsuit. It was Wesson's first and only "perp walk." Photographers were lined up snapping his photo, and a reporter asked him if he had anything to say.

"I love you," Wesson responded.

* * *

Wesson remained in isolation at the Fresno County Jail and was not allowed visitors or phone calls. The Sheriff's Department took the precaution after receiving an anonymous tip that Wesson would order surviving family members to commit suicide. During the trial, Wesson's daughter Gypsy explained that she had also expressed concern to Fresno police that other family members might kill themselves:

Q. Why did you think they would harm themselves?
A. Because they would see no reason to live anymore, you know, without their kids. And they would just be so, you know, devastated. I felt that none of them would want to live anymore 'cause there was nothing to live for. Like the family was our whole lives.
Q. Was there anyone in particular you were concerned about?
A. Mostly Rosie[16] and Kiani, 'cause they were really, really depressed. On the day—March the twelfth, um, I think Detective Reese[17] had asked me if I thought if they were to visit my dad would they—would they, um—would they harm themselves if he asked them to. And I said I believed they would.
Q. Why would you believe that?
A. Because they were really, um, really depressed. And, um, I felt that they were really vulnerable. And they would just do, you know—they won't want to live anymore. 'Cause even though I was not living in the house at that time, I felt that way, too. I felt I had nothing to live for.

Under the guidance of the County Counsel's Office, jail officials decided to impose restrictions on Wesson's visitation privileges, reasoning that the county would not be

---

[16] A nickname for Rosa Solorio.

[17] Detective Doug Reese was the lead homicide detective on the case.

responsible if something happened to any of the surviving family members. Those restrictions stayed in place for several weeks, until Wesson's court-appointed attorney argued successfully to have them removed. But concerns that Wesson would order other family members to commit suicide persisted long after his arrest. The following September, Gypsy Wesson confessed to a teacher that she feared her father might signal to her mother, sisters, and cousins to kill themselves. The teacher notified the principal and the principal called the police. This time, however, Wesson's jail visitation rights remained intact.

Wesson's elderly mother, Carrie Wesson, granted only one interview on the subject of her son's arrest, to the *Los Angeles Times*. About a week after the murders of her grandchildren, she told reporter Mark Arax from her home in Washington State, "The Marcus Wesson on TV I don't recognize. That's not my son. The Marcus Wesson I raised was a brilliant, loving, God-fearing child." She continued: "To make him do this, there must have been some big trauma. Something that pushed him over. This is a Christian family. This is not a cult."

Two days following the killings, the coroner still had not successfully identified all nine victims because the mothers of the children had not come forward to claim their bodies. Fresno County coroner Lori Cervantes made a public plea for relatives to help in the process. One woman called the Coroner's Office and claimed to be one of the mothers, but when asked to supply her name, she hung up.

Eventually all of the young mothers contacted the Coroner's Office and the victims were identified. A memorial fund had been set up for the victims, but it immediately invoked controversy when Miguel Solorio (Elizabeth Wesson's brother) warned the public that the money could end up funding Marcus Wesson's defense. Elizabeth Wesson was given $1,400 to cover funeral expenses. She spent $400 on groceries, and when she learned of her brother's public comments, she returned the remaining $1,000 to the Fresno Police Department. The decision was made to let Elizabeth keep $400 of that sum, and the remaining $600 was put into a bank account for Sofina and Ruby.

Elizabeth avoided public appearances and comment but issued a written statement through a spokesperson to thank the public for its generosity:

> *Thank you for the help and support that the community has given our family in our time of need. We greatly appreciate all the support that is spiritually, emotionally and financially given to us by the community. At this time we wish that you would give us time to mourn in peace. From the bottom of our heart, we would like to thank you for all your prayers.*

The family division was apparent when the bodies of seven victims were delivered to one funeral home, while Sofina's and Ruby's children went to another. A local funeral home had heard that the Wesson family was in financial dire straights and volunteered to offer funeral services at no charge. Jesse E. Cooley Jr. Funeral Home held funeral and burial services free of charge for seven of the victims: Sebhrenah, Lise, Jeva, Illabelle, Ethan, Sedona, and Marshey. The bodies of Jonathan and Aviv went to the Yost and Webb Funeral Home, and a private funeral service was held at a Seventh Day Adventist church in a neighboring town. Media attention focused on the funeral services of the other seven children, primarily because family members had allowed a television camera inside the funeral chapel. The service quickly became a public spectacle. Seven white coffins lined the front of the room, and the televised event showed mourners passing in front of the open caskets. The officiator, Elder T. J. Caldwell,

admitted the services were "eerie" and "traumatic," because of the number of dead children. Television cameras
also caught the conclusion of the service outside the chapel: the flutter of nine doves taking flight in the cool spring
air.

FIVE

"I don't want to talk about my past," Elizabeth told the detectives. She had been in an interrogation room for hours and was becoming despondent. Two officers were in the room engaged in a game of "good cop/bad cop," in hopes that Elizabeth would eventually break down and reveal something valuable about the murders. Officer Michelle Ochoa was playing the "good cop" role. Ochoa had the sensitivity of a social worker, but there were few officers as tough or resourceful.

"I think what you've done . . . you've done the best with what you were presented," Ochoa told Elizabeth. "I respect you."

Elizabeth said nothing.

"It's in the newspaper, Elizabeth. Your family is talking about this," Ochoa said.

Elizabeth remained silent, then finally whispered that she was afraid of her husband and began to cry. In between sobs she said, "What am I going to do? I don't have no skills! All I know is how to take care of my babies! Please don't take them away . . . please don't arrest me! I promise, I didn't know! I didn't know!" Elizabeth became hysterical. "I didn't see no babies! I just saw my daughter! I just ran and collapsed! Oh *God*!" Elizabeth sobbed. "I'm

tired of crying. I've been crying all day. Can I see my babies? I just want to see them. I want to hold them. They
weren't supposed to take them away from me!"

Officer Ochoa shook her head empathetically. "Elizabeth, he's kept you under his feet for so long. You're a great
person. You're a very strong woman. You can do what you
want. We're here to help you. If you committed a crime,
you would go to jail. At this point I'm not aware that you
committed a crime."

Detective Doug Reese played the "bad cop," a role
those who knew him would have found ironic; in reality,
he was polite and magnanimous. "What made you scream
when you ran out of the house?" he asked Elizabeth.

"I don't remember screaming," she answered. Several
witnesses had reported that she had yelled, "They're all
gone!" while running out of the house. She told police that
as she ran out she saw her 25-year-old daughter Sebhrenah
in the living room.

"Why did you walk out without your daughter
Sebhrenah?" Ochoa asked.

Elizabeth didn't answer.

"You're blocking this out," Reese said. "I know what
you saw. It was a horrible sight. I know you saw more than
just Lise because you made a comment when you came
outside."

"I can see in your eyes what you saw," Ochoa told
Elizabeth. "I can tell you know."

"I didn't see anything," Elizabeth insisted, shaking her
head.

"Did you have something to do with the death of your
children?" Ochoa demanded.

"No."

"Then you'd better start talking," she said.

"You're changing your stories and you're not being
truthful with us," Reese added forcefully. "Did you kill
those babies?"

"No," Elizabeth replied.

"Then who did?"

She didn't answer.

After a long period of interrogation, Elizabeth finally admitted that when she looked into the back bedroom on the day of the murders, she saw Marcus holding their 17-year-old daughter Lise. She said her daughter turned to her. "He was touching her shoulder, I think. When he saw me he called my name," she said. Elizabeth explained that Lise was crying. "I felt scared," she admitted.

"What scared you that day?" Detective Reese asked.

"It was so quiet and I didn't see any of the children. When he called my name, that's what scared me the most. I just knew I had to run."

Elizabeth told the detectives that Marcus considered their niece Ruby his wife, and said she disagreed with her husband on the subject of polygamy.

"Did Marcus have any other wives besides you and Ruby?" Detective Reese asked.

"I don't want to talk no more," Elizabeth replied.

"Don't shut down on us now, Elizabeth," Reese urged.

The detectives remained persistent, and Elizabeth eventually told them that Marcus had instructed the women to "send the children to God" if anyone ever tried to separate the family.

"What did he mean by 'sending them to God'?" Reese asked.

"Put them to sleep," Elizabeth replied.

"What did he mean by that?"

Elizabeth shook her head. "We've been talking about it for so long. I don't know. He's never hurt anyone. I trusted him. I didn't think he would harm my children."

Detective Reese asked Elizabeth about her daughters having children with Marcus. Elizabeth replied, "I was against it. But when they gave me the babies, they were mine."

Detective Ochoa asked Elizabeth if she worried about

any of her surviving children, and if there was a danger that some family members might commit suicide. Elizabeth wouldn't even acknowledge the question.

"I commend you, I think you're a great woman," Ochoa said, trying not to sound patronizing. "But you can't suppress this. If you don't tell us, shame on you. Hasn't this gone on long enough, haven't enough people died?"

Elizabeth sat silently, looking at the floor.

Detective Reese realized they were getting nowhere and decided to play a portion of the tape that was recorded at the murder scene, thinking it might spark some kind of response. The tape was cued to the point at which Elizabeth came running out of the house announcing that the children were "gone." He pressed the Play button and the sounds of hysteria came blaring out of the speakers. The room filled with the screaming. Reese stopped the tape.

"What made the women on this tape so excited?" he asked. Elizabeth did not answer. He asked Elizabeth if she felt guilty about what happened.

"I do feel guilty. I feel sick to my stomach," she said, raising her voice.

Reese suggested that she was trying to protect her husband.

"How could I protect him? Tell me!" Her voice grew louder. "You try to be in my shoes! Have all your children taken from you! You expect me to say something that I did not see. I don't even know what I feel anymore! I can't sleep and I can't eat! You guys have no right to say anything to me! My children were taken away from me and I couldn't do anything about it!" She paused and lowered her voice. "I don't care about myself. Everything is gone."

"We aren't blaming you for what happened," Reese said. "We are saying you know more than you are saying."

"It's too hard for you to say it so we'll say it for you,"

Detective Ochoa said. "You saw the pile of children and they were dead."

"I don't remember seeing that." Elizabeth began to cry.

"Should we show you a photo so you can remember?" Ochoa asked.

Abruptly, she stopped crying. "Show me the photo," she said.

"Is that going to help you remember?" Ochoa asked.

"Let me see it! I want to see it," Elizabeth pleaded.

"Are you able to handle the photo?" Ochoa asked skeptically, and shook her head. "Not right now, not like this."

"I want to see it! I want to see it!" Elizabeth insisted. Ochoa refused. Elizabeth became inconsolable and then hysterical, and it took her several minutes to calm her down.

As the interview ended, Elizabeth admitted that her 17-year-old daughter Lise had still been alive when she saw her with Marcus in the back bedroom. She explained that Lise was facedown and Marcus had his left hand on her right shoulder and appeared to be praying.

"How did you know she was still alive?" Detective Reese asked.

"Because she turned over," Elizabeth replied. "She lifted her head. She was crying."

PART TWO:

LIFE ON THE *SUDAN*

ONE

Marshall, California, 1998

"Are you sure this is what you want to do?" Marcus asked Sofina. "There's no turning back," he warned.

"Yes," Sofina replied as she stood in darkness on the deck of the family's boat that was anchored just one hundred feet off shore. A gust of cold wind lashed against her face as she looked out onto the dark bay. She folded her arms. She and her uncle had been talking for hours and it was late. At the age of twenty-four, Sofina had finally gained the courage to tell her uncle she wanted to leave. She had just admitted that she'd kissed a man she worked with, and Marcus was furious. He ordered her not to talk to the other girls, and Sofina decided she couldn't live in such close quarters with her sisters and cousins without being able to speak to them. It would have been torture; she would rather have died. Sofina told Marcus she wanted to go live with her aunt in San Jose. Marcus agreed to take her there and descended into the cabin of the inoperable tugboat the *Sudan* to tell his wife Elizabeth that he was going to drive Sofina to her new home.

Sofina knew she only had a matter of minutes. She hurried belowdeck and ran to her bunk. She pulled a turtleneck shirt over her head, grabbed her jacket, stuffed what belongings she could into a bag, and returned abovedeck.

Then she and Marcus boarded the *Sudan*'s small rowboat and Sofina paddled to shore.

She sat nervously in the passenger seat of the family's run-down van, clutching her bag. Marcus was behind the wheel, and as they began the trip, he interrogated her about her relationship with Oscar, a sous-chef at the nearby Marconi Conference Center where Sofina worked.

"What else did you do with him?" Marcus asked. "Who else were you messing around with up there?"

"Nothing! No one!" she replied.

Marcus told Sofina she could never come back to the *Sudan* or speak to her sisters ever again. The angrier he became, the faster he drove. He pressed his foot on the accelerator and sped through the hills on the rural stretch of Highway 1. Frightened, Sofina held onto the dashboard. She sat in silence, praying they would make it to San Jose and that her uncle wasn't bluffing about taking her there. After about twenty minutes they reached Petaluma and Marcus flipped a U-turn. The tires screeched.

"What are you doing?" Sofina asked. "I want to go to my aunt's, Marcus! Take me there!"

"No!" he said, raising his voice. "We have to talk about this!"

Sofina had almost led the others in the family in a murder-suicide pact just weeks before, but Marcus had told them it wasn't time.

"You are unworthy to kill my children!" he told her as they drove in the darkness.

The two sat in silence during the twenty minute ride back to the boat. When they arrived at Tomales Bay, Marcus pulled the car into the very same spot where they had been less than an hour before. He turned off the ignition. Sofina began to cry. Marcus leaned forward with his right arm reaching over his lap, his hand resting near his left hip, gripping a knife. He was no longer angry. He spoke calmly.

"Do you love the Lord?" he asked Sofina.

"Of course!" she said, crying. "You know that I do!"

"Did you ask God to forgive you of all your sins?"

"Yes, I do every day," Sofina replied.

He paused, then with all his force he swung his right arm across the front seat of the van. The blade of the knife struck Sofina just above her right breast. She screamed. With the other hand Marcus covered her mouth.[18]

"Shhh. Don't let anyone hear," he whispered.

The force of the blow knocked the wind out of her and her chest stung. Her world went to black.

Minutes later Sofina came to and felt a burning sensation in her chest. She was still in the van and Marcus was still in the driver's seat. She looked down and saw a tear in her jacket where the knife had entered her skin.

"Are you ready to go to the Lord?" Marcus whispered in her ear.

"What?" Sofina said, disoriented and just regaining consciousness. "What are you talking about?"

"Are you ready to go to the Lord?" Marcus whispered again.

"No! I'm not ready!" Sofina said, realizing that he was about to take her life. "No! I'm not ready!" she protested.

Marcus paused. Then he broke down and cried. Hugging Sofina, he said, "I'm sorry, Fia. I thought you said you were ready. You said you loved the Lord and had asked for forgiveness!"

Sofina told Marcus she wasn't ready to die. Marcus made her promise she would never tell anyone what had happened. She agreed.

It was early morning and the sun had not yet come up. Marcus helped Sofina onto the rowboat and rowed back to the *Sudan*. Once they boarded, Sofina went straight to her bunk. The pain was almost too much to bear. The wound stung, but she knew what she had promised her uncle. She

---

[18] These are the events as described by Sofina from the witness stand.

couldn't breathe a word of what had happened. Marcus woke his wife Elizabeth.

"You did what to her? What's wrong with you?" Elizabeth exclaimed. She rushed to Sofina's bed.

"Let me see," Elizabeth said.

Sofina pulled back her jacket and lifted her shirt. Muscle tissue protruded from the skin just above her right breast, and Elizabeth dabbed the blood with gauze she had retrieved from a first aid kit.

"Are you sure you don't want me to take you to the hospital?" Elizabeth asked.

"No, I'm just so tired," Sofina replied.

Sofina lay in bed that night feeling a sharp pain radiate through her chest. She thought about her then 2-year-old son Jonathan. She thought about what it would be like to be ignored by the other girls. She knew Marcus regretted stabbing her, but she also knew he would not forgive her for kissing another man, what he considered to be a sin of "adultery." As she drifted off to sleep, she knew it wouldn't be long before she would have to make her escape.

TWO

Just fifty miles north of the bright lights of San Francisco, nestled near the quiet waters of Tomales Bay, is the town of Marshall, California. The sign just outside town reads, POPULATION 50, but according to the U.S. Census Bureau, the true population is 394. The town has its own post office, but since it is not an incorporated municipality, there is no local government to speak of: no mayor, city council, police, or fire department. The townspeople will proudly announce to any outsider who happens to pass through that cell phones don't work in Marshall and that's the way they like it. Marshall's remoteness is something revered by its inhabitants, and it's a quality that attracted many of its citizens. Such was the case when Marcus Wesson began living there with a family of fourteen in the late 1990s.

The only notable structure in the town besides the post office is the Marshall Store, where a sign outside reads, "Best Oysters on the Planet." Inside, the store's owner, Kathryn Krohn, wore large rubber gloves and split oysters open with a knife, placing them delicately on the grill. "They just kind of moved around with no emotion," Krohn said of the Wesson girls, who would come into the store on a daily basis. "The boys seemed more real, more animated." The Wesson girls would wander around the store and not buy anything or they would purchase inexpensive items like Ramen noodles or chips, offering Krohn their loose change. They would also periodically come into the store to use the phone, Krohn added. She said the family would row ashore from the *Sudan* in a small rowboat every evening to empty their toilet waste into the Porta Potties in the boat yard and to fill up large jugs of water.

"The girls always appeared to be nicely dressed in skirts and blouses," Krohn said, cracking open another oyster. "Then one day I noticed that Sebhrenah looked pregnant, and I knew they didn't have social lives. That's when I started wondering." When the girls bought a package of diapers from the store, Krohn's curiosity grew. "I never saw any babies," she said.

The family made frequent trips back to Marshall after moving to Fresno, and two of the Wesson girls came into the Marshall Store just a few days before the murders.

"As they were leaving they turned to me and said, 'Kathy, Marcus says hi and that he loves you,'" Krohn recalled. "It was very strange. I thought it was very out of character for them."

Wesson owned at least five boats, and all were in some form of disrepair and moored in proximity to one another in the waters of Tomales Bay. The *Sudan,* a sixty-five-foot retired tugboat, provided the family's main living area. A forty-foot boat called the *Raven* was anchored just fifty feet away from the *Sudan*; the family used it to store their clothes and large jugs of water. The third was a boat the townspeople referred to as "The Ark" because of the strange ornate decoration along its hull. Wesson used wood furniture to decorate the boat and had planned to launch a business venture, giving tours of the bay. The idea was never realized.

"It was so top heavy, the slightest wave and that thing would have flipped," Marshall resident Chris Rainsford observed. Rainsford lived in a house on the bay and noted that Wesson and his family would only come ashore in the very early morning or late at night. "I almost thought they were like vampires because they only came out in the dark," he said.

Wesson also owned a small sailboat, *The Abejas,* and a fifth boat, *Phoebe,* that came apart in a bad storm. He wasn't around at the time so Rainsford and a friend rescued it. Just four days before the murders, Wesson was back in Marshall. He was furious and accused Rainsford of letting *Phoebe* sink.

"He nutted up on me. I thought I was going to have to hit him or something," Rainsford said. He explained to Wesson that he tried to save the boat, and immediately Wesson's demeanor changed. "It was like flipping a light switch," Rainsford recalled. Wesson said it was a shame about *Phoebe* and then out of the blue asked Rainsford if he wanted to have the small sailboat, *The Abejas.* Befuddled by Wesson's quick mood change, Rainsford said he would have to think about the offer.

Wesson purchased the boats with money from welfare checks, despite his conviction for welfare fraud and perjury in 1990 for which he was jailed for defrauding the Santa Cruz County Human Services Agency of $24,441. At that time, he was living with his family in Santa Cruz and had purchased a boat in Marin County that he planned to convert into a living space. He bought the vessel for $14,000 from a man named Kenneth Nelson, to whom he paid the entire amount in monthly installments of $500. Wesson paid Nelson with money orders and travelers checks, and the sale of the twenty-six-foot sailboat was finalized in October 1987. Wesson paid a marine surveyor to sail the boat from Paradise Key in Marin County to the Santa Cruz harbor. He knew that if the Welfare Department discovered his purchase, he could lose his government benefits. According to court documents, he asked Stoney Burnett, a friend, to register the boat in his name. Burnett, who attended church gatherings with the Wesson family, agreed to the scheme, and Wesson promised to pay him one percent of the sale price of the boat when he decided to sell it. While the boat was registered in Burnett's name, Wesson had already signed the vessel owner's report, and when the Welfare Department was informed of the purchase by the tax assessor's office, it took action against Wesson, (only a home or a car would have been exempt from the classification of "excess property"). When investigators contacted Burnett, he initially claimed the boat was his, but later admitted he had never even seen it.

A fierce court battle between Wesson and Santa Cruz County followed. Wesson defended his actions, saying that the boat was his family's residence but he had lied on his welfare application by failing to notify the government of the purchase. The district attorney was quick to point out that the boat could not accommodate a family of ten and could only sleep a maximum of four people comfortably. In addition, the welfare investigator had discovered the family was living on a plot of land in the nearby Santa Cruz Mountains. It was never discovered where Wesson obtained the $14,000 to purchase the boat.

Former juror Glenda Logan recalled that Wesson appeared very "straight-laced" during the trial, often wearing a tie, vest, and a suit to court and a short haircut. Despite his outward appearance, Logan characterized Wesson as "cagey," saying there was no question as to whether he had broken the law.

"It was a clear-cut case," she said. "Only one of the jurors was holding out, because she didn't want to send anyone to jail. But we all knew he was guilty."

It took the jury a single afternoon to decide that Wesson was guilty of two felonies: welfare fraud and perjury. He spent three months in jail, and according to the court record, while incarcerated wrote an obsequious letter to the judge in the case, William Kelsay:

June 15, 1990

I have never missed any of my court appointments. I did not appear at the two probation meetings because I was afraid that I would be hurt in the sentencing with the information.

But I talked to a man named; "Otis Hunt," a black fellow 48 years old. He said, " he knew you well, from the time he tricked you when you were a D.A." (smile). The following of what he told me hurt me deeply because I know it was the father in heaven speaking through the man to me: He told me that you wanted to protect my family, that you did not want to separate me from my children. He said that "you wanted to give me a little probation," that I would play the "game" and eventually it would be over. He said that I was being "stubborn" and that I made you angry because "you were trying to help while I was trying to get off 'scott free.'" He said, "You will probably let me 'simmer' in here three or four days and call it contempt to court." He told me that you were really a "easy going man inside with a hard shell on the outside but inside was compassion." He said "you were bound by the law but will always help a man." He told me with sincerity; " he respects you for this."

My father in heaven showed me that he puts his agents here on earth to carry out his work here on earth.

In his guidance in my life, he has shown me that; all that happens to me is for my good. This hurt me deeply.

Please forgive me for not trusting you as a judge. I am so very sorry for going against your judgment in my motions.

I apologize deeply for questioning your integrity. I will not fight anymore. I realize that; I was not trusting in God, but myself. I want a chance to prove; I trust your judgment. By denying trust in you I also denied trust in the father in heaven. I want a chance to prove; I am a man of honor, sincerity and integrity. Please release me, let me go on my own and apologize to Jim Vaughn. I will be at the probation interview. I will not miss my court date. This is my promise, my word. I want to start all over again by trusting in the people God puts in care of me and I want you to trust me.

My wife is with a lady whom is taking care of her until I get out.

God bless you. Marcus.

In addition to his jail time, Wesson served five years probation. He appealed the conviction but an appellate court upheld the sentence in 1992.

Following his arrest, Wesson's modus operandi involved not placing his name on any official documentation, including the birth certificates of the children. This way, the government would be unable to track him, leaving the women in the family still eligible to be on the government dole. The same logic applied to the boat; Wesson pointed out in one of his many appeal motions in the welfare case that there was no documentation to prove that he was, in fact, the boat's owner. He accused the judge and the all-white jury of misconduct and accused his lawyer of misrepresenting him. In one handwritten motion, Wesson wrote a letter addressed to

"Servants of the Law," in which he explained his life's philosophy:

> *A man is within the jurisdiction of equity, ethics and legality when he takes advantage of loopholes in the law for the betterment of his family. But the reason of this conviction is* not *the essence of equity when a government agency such as Human Resources can seek to tear down and destroy a family for spending prudently and wisely the monies they gave them for the exact same reason of shelter and food.*

Wesson concluded the letter by saying that the boat gave him "the needed leverage" to get off welfare, and he told the judge that the jury's decision was going to force him "to start all over again." He signed the letter, "With respect and love, Marcus Wesson."

Wesson also typed hundreds of pages of court motions, memorandums, and letters to the judge in which he misused legal jargon, alleging among other things that he was misrepresented in the welfare case by the public defender. The judge called at least one of the motions written by Wesson "gibberish." In one letter Wesson wrote, "My lawyer did not use the defense I had prepared long ago." In another, Wesson declared, "My lawyer did not file any of my pretrial motions during the entire nine months I begged him to do before trial." Wesson even tried to file a written Marsden motion.[19] He also filed a thirty-eight-page motion to dismiss the case against him in which he alleged juror misconduct, instructional error, prosecutorial misconduct, and insufficient evidence, among several other things. Wesson might have taken his legal strategies from a book called *How to Dust the Pros-*

---

[19] A motion made by a defendant in an effort to have his lawyer removed from the case.

ecutor, which gives criminal defendants tips on how to
beat the system. That book was among the reading material confiscated from the Wesson home following the
murders.

Criminal defense attorney Jim McMillin eventually
tried to remove himself from the case after Wesson
signed McMillin's name to several court motions.[20]

"I was quite angry he signed my name," McMillin recalled. Despite Wesson's repeated criticism, McMillin
sympathized with Wesson's predicament.

"Of course, the D.A. made out like he was living the life
of luxury there at the harbor and he really wasn't," McMillin said. "It was pretty meager." (The family did not reside
on the sailboat after all. Instead, while at the harbor they
slept aboard a bus Wesson had converted into an RV.)
McMillin remembered Wesson as a caring father whose
primary concern was to educate his children, and as someone who truly believed he was being wronged by the government.

"He was eccentric and a lot of the eccentricities were
around raising the family, but no more so than you would
see with the local home-school-type movement. There's
an isolationist approach but it's not that uncommon,"
McMillin said.

But there was nothing common about Marcus Wesson.
One of the odder strategies he employed was his repeated
impersonation of the actor Richard Widmark when calling government agencies. Wesson admitted in one of his
letters to the court:

> *I knew that the welfare department had illegally
> received the information because I, posing as the
> actor Richard Widmark called the tax office just
> three days before I had received the notice ... I*

---

[20] As for Wesson's claim of "inadequate representation," McMillin said
he wasn't bothered by the accusation.

*posed as the actor Richard Widmark because I
wanted to find out why the boat was in Marcus
Wesson's name instead of my wife's name; Elizabeth Wesson.*

Widmark starred in many classic film noir roles in the
late 1940s and 1950s. The 1947 film *Kiss of Death* contained one of the more terrifying moments in American
film history: a scene in which Widmark's psychopath
character pushed a helpless wheelchair-bound woman
down a flight of stairs and cackled as she plunged to her
death. Wesson often invoked Widmark's name. After a
tax lien was placed on the $14,000 sailboat, Wesson
again called the tax assessor, identifying himself as
Richard Widmark to inform the tax collector that Marcus Wesson could not pay the lien because he was on
welfare.

He also had an ongoing feud with the harbormaster
over unpaid docking fees in the amount of $2,300. After
Wesson's arrest in 1990, the boat was sold and a portion
of the proceeds went to pay his outstanding debt.

There were not many places as liberal and accepting as
Santa Cruz in the 1980s, but even there, Marcus Wesson
stood out. Residents recalled him walking around town
and on the beach followed by his wife and children. At
times he wore a long brown cloak and carried a staff.
One neighbor said he thought Wesson was trying to be
a "Black Jesus." The family scrounged for food and dug
through Dumpsters, often recovering half-eaten ham-
burgers from McDonald's. He walked the streets espous-
ing a spiritual belief that God created human beings in
a perfect state. One resident called Wesson "a frustrated
cult leader" who no one would listen to. Some Santa Cruz
residents complained to the harbor office about the Wesson children rummaging through the trash cans on the
beach. Harbor officials also received complaints that

the older girls would bathe the children in the public rest-
rooms and clog the sinks. Wesson often sent his children
on a quest to find aluminum cans in the upper harbor
area; he said he was trying to teach them humility.
Neighbors expressed concern that the children were evi-
dently not attending school. Those concerns prompted a
visit from Child Protective Services, but because the
family moved around so much, the agency was unable
make a follow-up visit. Wesson himself had been ordered by the court to find regular employment, but he
had decided long ago he could not hold a regular job.

Seeking to continue his life's philosophy of "[taking]
advantage of loopholes in the law for the betterment of his
family," and following his court battle in Santa Cruz,
Wesson moved his family to Tomales Bay, where his
daughters and nieces and at least one of his sons found
employment at the nearby Marconi Conference Center.
Each morning, the women rowed ashore from the *Sudan*
in a small rowboat. They either walked in a group or Wesson would drive them about a half mile up the road to the
conference center, where the girls worked ten-hour days
in the dining facility. Like many of the citizens of Marshall, those who came to the Marconi Conference Center
did so to escape the sounds and pressures of the city and
to be surrounded by the quiet and serene wilderness. Up
on a steep hill, the center overlooked the still and pictur-
esque waters of Tomales Bay. High-powered Bay Area
executives would schedule retreats at Marconi to reinvig-
orate their employees.

"They always received compliments," administrator Pa-
tria Mole recalled of the Wesson children. "They were
very good workers. Always reliable, always on time." At
the end of their shifts, the girls would have to turn in paperwork to Mole, and it was during these times in the late
evening that the generous woman with an Australian accent befriended them. "I thought maybe I'm one of the few
friends they had," Mole said. She knew the family didn't

have much, so Mole would leave snacks in her office in anticipation of the girls' arrival. Some of the girls were more willing to socialize; Sofina was "the chatterbox," while Mole recalled Sebhrenah as more reticent to trust an outsider.

As their relationship developed, the girls became more comfortable and open with Mole and willing to share their thoughts. "They never talked to men," she recalled. As the year 2000 approached, the girls grew excited. They told Mole they were all getting baptized at a Seventh Day Adventist church, and Mole considered attending the baptism services to show her support. "They said they wanted to be ready because the world might end," Mole said. On one occasion, she recalled the girls asking her what she thought of several women having the same husband. She said it wasn't for her. The girls told her they believed in polygamy and were all married to the same man. Mole said she didn't press the issue but suspected they might have been referring to Marcus. On another occasion she couldn't contain her concern. The girls often talked about the end of the world, and in the context of one of those conversations they revealed that Marcus had purchased coffins for them.

"I remember they said they each had one," Mole recalled. "Please tell me you're not going to sleep in them," she remembered telling the girls. The girls said they did not sleep in the coffins but they were planning to use them to store clothing. "They said they were going to gut the inside of their bus and use the lids of the coffins as seats." Mole could not shake the oddness of the conversation. She remembered the girls talking about the mass suicide of the Heaven's Gate cult in Southern California. "They were very impressed by that," Mole recalled.

As a home, the *Sudan* was neither convenient nor accommodating, but it provided something Wesson sought for his family: isolation from the outside world. Marcus dreamed of sailing around the world, but the *Sudan* was in poor condition. The turn-of-the-century tugboat had been reinforced with concrete but dry rot had set in. Wesson commissioned a local by the name of Malcolm Chase to do some repair work on the boat, but when it became clear that Wesson would be unable to pay him, Wesson made a strange offer. "He said something like, 'I should set you up with one of my girls,'" Chase recalled. "I almost considered it to be a joke." Chase did not take Wesson up on his offer.

The living quarters were impossibly small for Marcus, Elizabeth, and the fourteen children. A long hallway led from the location of the rebuilt diesel engine to a room with three bunk beds on both the port and starboard sides where the girls, the babies, and Marcus slept. The boys slept at the other end of the boat in a room that had one large bed. A staircase near the stern led to the deck and the area of the boat where the shower was located. The *Sudan* was also equipped with a refrigerator and a portable toilet. The bathroom facilities didn't provide much privacy, so the girls would use the bathrooms at the conference center when they arrived at work. For those who used the bathroom on the boat, a single bedsheet provided their only shield from other family members.

Each morning Marcus would row ashore with the three boys to empty the toilet's receptacle into the Porta Potties on shore and return with jugs of water that the family would use for cooking and for showers. The method of showering was also regimented: Each person received a gallon jug of water. The water would be heated on a small propane stove and each family member took a turn standing in a basin, covering themselves with water and soap and then rinsing themselves clean. Laundry was done in the salty waters of the bay. The women also used the propane burner to cook the family's meals. Their diet was determined by both necessity and Marcus's homespun doctrine. While Wesson himself occasionally ate meat, his family almost exclusively consumed beans. Neither Marcus nor his wife Elizabeth worked while living on the *Sudan*. Elizabeth also did not cook, leaving most of the daily chores to the children.

Wesson's daily trips ashore were a nuisance to David Harris, who lived in a house along the rocky shores of Tomales Bay. Every morning around five o'clock Marcus would drag the rowboat across the rocks, waking Harris's dogs. It caused such a ruckus that it woke Harris up. It led to several confrontations in which Harris repeatedly asked Wesson to cease his early morning trips ashore. When Wesson refused, Harris threatened to put up a fence. Wesson threatened to sue Harris, even though he was the one trespassing on private property. Harris eventually lost his patience and called the Marin County Sheriff's Department. Those complaints along with others would eventually prompt the Wessons to leave Marshall.

The young women worked at the Marconi Conference Center to support the family, and Marcus continued to meet weekly with the females (excluding his wife) for "girl talks." The meetings happened in the boys' sleeping area toward the back of the boat, while the rest of the family stayed on the other end of the vessel. During these talks, Wesson taught the fundamentals of his family tenets: mainly, that the girls were to stay away from all men, including their brothers and male cousins. For those who worked, he would ask how they were acting at their jobs and if they had any contact with men. Wesson encouraged snitching, and many times his daughters would tell on each other, reporting to Marcus that one of the girls had been acting inappropriately at work by talking to male coworkers. After determining who was at fault and spanking the offender, Marcus would then excuse the youngest girls from the room and discuss the idea of having more children with his older daughters and nieces.

In that back room of the *Sudan*, Wesson also continued the practice of "loving"—having sex with the young women in the family. Wesson's jealousy was particularly intense when it came to his niece Ruby, then in her early twenties. He would often hit her in the face for talking to other men. Ruby would deny her uncle's accusations but Wesson insisted he didn't believe her.

"There was one incident where he had all of us girls in the back room," Ruby recalled. "He was talking to all of us about, that he feels that some of us are hanging around men. And he asked Kiani if she had noticed if I had been talking to men. And she told him that she did see somebody talking to me. And he just . . . he like back-slapped me, like with the back of his hand across my face." The blow to her face left a bruise under her right eye. "I just started crying," Ruby said. "And then that day I remember just thinking that I was going to leave." Ruby often wore long skirts and blouses to cover up her bruises.

In addition to "girl talks," Wesson had private one-on-one sessions in the room at the back of the *Sudan* with each girl. Despite the smallness of their living quarters, it left many of the women ignorant to what Wesson was doing or saying to the other women in the family. "Each one of us girls had a different life with him," Sofina explained. "He worked on every psyche. He knew each girl individually. Some were stronger than the others, some were weaker in some ways, and that's how he worked." At the trial, Sofina testified that it wasn't until after the murders that she learned that Marcus had forced Ruby and Kiani to perform sex acts on each other and that he had performed a ceremony in which the two girls were "married." A love letter written to Kiani from Ruby was introduced into evidence:

To my Wonderful Sweet Wife,

Always remember that I love you and with all my heart. You are a sweet girl and I don't ever want you to lose that beautiful spirit that surrounds you. Please never forget that I love you. May the Lord always bless you.

Love Always,
Ruby

"The more you gave yourself to him, the more free he felt doing all of those things," Sofina explained. Wesson had a sadistic personality, and Sofina recalled that he enjoyed hitting the girls in a "playful" manner in front of the entire family. "He would slap you, or pull your hair, and the more you resisted, the more he would do it." After he had finished and the girl was in tears he would beckon her and say, "Okay, now kiss me."

THREE

While the family lived aboard the *Sudan,* Wesson began work on his book, a partly autobiographical work entitled "In the Night of the Light for the Dark." He had set out to depict some of the events of his life, but more importantly, he was taking on a task of immense proportions: He hoped to compose a bible that would be the foundation of a new religion mixing vampirism and Christianity. He wrote obsessively for days on end while listening to trance music to inspire him.[21] He made several mix tapes and would attempt to enter a trancelike state while composing the manuscript. The music also appeared to fuel his obsession with vampires. He began the writing process in the late 1990s and continued writing even after his arrest in 2004.

Wesson used a typewriter to type the book's nearly one thousand pages, and wrote it in three sections: "The Dark," "Of the Light in the Dark of the Night," and "The Manifestation of It All." He continued to write a fourth section, called "The Lost Seed of Righteousness," and explained in a letter from Death Row that the final section would clarify much of what the book set out to accomplish.

---

[21] A musical genre that became popular in dance clubs in the 1990s characterized by a repetitive techno beat.

Some of the prose is traditional in its narration, but most is written in a kind of free-form, free-verse poetry such as this early passage from the first section of the book:

```
The birth of the great being;
Vampire, as told by that being
      to his fallen angel;
```

```
JEVA MPYRCVS SUSPI RE' VLADENSPHERE
```

```
MARSHAY
```

```
THE ONLY WAY TO ETERNAL LIFE VMPYR
```

```
VMPYR
```

```
THE MASTER, HIS BEGINNING
            VMPYR
PATH TO LIFE ETERNAL
```

Later passages would reveal a more violent and descriptive narrative. In the proceeding passage, Wesson introduced "Marshay," who is one of the main characters in the story. At times, Wesson referred to himself by this name, and it was also the name of one of the infants killed on March 12, 2004. Wesson clarified that he had named many of the murdered children after the characters in his book: Marshey, Sedona, and Jeva, to name a few.[22] The following passage demonstrates the autobiographical nature of the manuscript:

```
Tessa sat at the piano in the vessel
knitting a sweater for her little
girl Sedona C~e year eight months is
her age The laws concerning children
have gone crazy in the name of C P A
```

---

[22] Wesson explained this in a letter written from Death Row that appears in the final section of this book.

```
Child protection is what it means so
as the gypsies of old they stay in
the hold of the vessel down below

Sedona sees the night as her day for
the day she sleeps as her parents do
for this is the way the gypsies
taught now it is the vampire way to
do

Marshay wrestled his sons Tahla his
rmm watched in laughter at him as
the son of Shedanie tussled with him
a tussle or two Kina her daughter
had to be fed while Rahni combed her
little girls hair

All was fair in the ships lair
```

Wesson used vampire names for everyone in the family. Sofina's vampire name was "Tahla," Ruby was "Rahni," Sebhrenah was "Shedanie," and Kiani was "Kina." His misuse of the acronym for Child Protective Services (CPA) was intentional; he said it stood for "Child Protective Abductions." In interviews with police following the murders, many of the surviving children referred to the agency as CPA or even the SPCA. In his writing, Wesson views "CPA" as the embodiment of a government gone wrong: "The main objections of CPA is to re-assimilate the minds of children of the poor in to their own devise for the power it brings in military might for power and money."

It remains unclear if Wesson actually believed himself to be a vampire in the literal sense, but it operated as a powerful metaphor in his manipulation of his family;[23] he

---

[23] In a letter written by Wesson from Death Row, Wesson says that he believes that he is a vampire, in a spiritual sense. The letter appears in the last section of this book.

was the Master, the *Sudan* was his lair, and the women were his "fledglings," or his concubines, who did his business and served his every whim. Wesson spoke as both "The Master" and referred to himself at other times by his vampire name, "Je-vam-marc-sus-pire," a combination of the words Marcus, Jesus, and vampire. In the first volume of his book, Wesson made an ominous prediction:

```
I Vampire of the dark will not fail.
My spiritual bite must deceive all.
My pretense of love must convince
all of right. I must live love itself
and be love to perpetuate my evil
among man. I will triumph in my
quest for it is my essence.
```

While most of his writing contained misspellings and grammatical and punctuation mistakes, there were still some moments of poetry:

```
Our last child we had was born in a
   raging tossing storm
But this time with our love of the sea
   still those sails
They hit the air to the call of the
   gypsy flair
When we see our masters face we will
   be free
```

The *Sudan* was not a working sailing vessel, but in his mind Wesson had conquered what he called "the freedom of the sea." In a chapter entitled "The Escape" in the third section of his book, he clearly referred to the *Sudan*: ". . . our ship sixty-three feet of cement wood and steel." He refers to his "humble wife" and his fourteen children and their collective dream to sail around the world. He makes reference to an encounter with "CPA," saying that they "heard the cry of a child . . . but had to give up their search." Wesson says the government agents were so impressed with the "vessel's decorative dress" that it "took their breath away." He then makes an eerie prediction: "It will not be long when they will have a reason to say their laws are designed that way to take of their children away."

Describing a subsequent encounter with the harbor police, Wesson explained that the officers had heard laughter and the sounds of someone playing a piano coming from the boat. The sounds of music were not in his imagination. Behind the rebuilt diesel engine of the *Sudan* sat an upright piano left by the previous owner, a character locals referred to as "Buddha Bob." In his narrative, Wesson said the harbor police ticketed him for not having an adequate number of life jackets aboard the boat. That, too, really happened. The Marin County Sheriff's Department cited the family for illegally living aboard the boat because it failed to meet two requirements of a watercraft residence: It had to move on its own power, and had to do so every five days. The family was ordered to evacuate the vessel in 2003. Eviction notices were posted on all four boats, but Wesson and his family continued to come and go, using the *Sudan* as a temporary living space until the day of the murders.

Wesson's story continued to parallel reality. After their eviction from the *Sudan,* he wrote that he left under the cover of night with his "fledglings" and expressed concern that no one should see the babies: "tis the babies under eight that the vastness would hoard."

Chris Rainsford remembered the night of the family's frantic departure from the *Sudan.* He observed the children rowing back and forth between the *Sudan* and the *Raven*, where the family had stored many of its belongings. When the family left, as was customary, Wesson rode in the stern of the rowboat while two of the women, one on each side of the boat, paddled him to shore. "Those girls were like slaves," Rainsford said. "He was like the king."

In the chapter titled "The Escape," Wesson described loading the children into the van and mentioned the inadequate number of seat belts. According to his story, the family decided to return to the boat to "think things over" and perhaps to leave in "a week or two." He depicted himself as the character Marshay, saying, "Marshay held the steering wheel and shook his head having children is dangerous these days this is the reason for our fear we cannot last another year."

Wesson worried that the authorities would eventually come back and find the younger children. At this point in the story, he made one of his only overt written statements about a possible murder-suicide pact:

```
They had waited till the time was
   right to the risk of his predict-
      able flight
They knew he might run they are
   confident in the gun
```

It's possible that Wesson was referring to the officers being "confident in the gun," but the reference could have also implicated the children. Ultimately, Wesson denied that the statement "they are confident in the gun" had anything to do with a murder-suicide plan. The story reached its climax with the officers' return to the boat the following night. Wesson's persona said he feared that the government might succeed in the "reassimilation" of the children, and he concluded the scene with the officers leaving the boat after not being able to find them. The chapter ends in a tearful reunion between Marshay (Wesson) and his children:

```
His face wet from their tears and
theirs from his he kissed the tears
from their salty cheeks their
wonderful face
```

```
His tears had nothing over them They
fill on the floor right where they
stood in tears and in love

For an hour they held him and kisses
and cried Never will we part again
our master thee from our side

Thou art our aims of love
```

These passages paralleled Wesson's life, while others did not. In the third section of the book, entitled "Of the Light for the Dark of the Night," Wesson depicted a violent murder committed by one of his narrative personas. He described snapping the victim's neck and the "jugular blood gushing . . . spewing blood." The victim's head dangled from its body, but Wesson said, "Still alive the head looked on in agony." As the victim took his last breaths, Wesson's literary persona drained the man of the rest of his "precious fluid." The scene ended with an eerie scene of Marshay (Wesson) lying on the floor next to the "headless body." Marshay's clothes were soaked with blood.

While some passages depicted clear narrative events, most of the book was written in the abstract. Wesson offered some of those abstractions as spiritual explanations to justify polygamy and incest, as in the following passage:

```
The master's first wives had to be
daughters to purely reproduce
himself in an evil generation;
the deep. They came from his body
in spirit.
```

In a section entitled "The Premium of Incest," he wrote:

```
Thus in incest one produces the seed
of perfection of one's self, though
```

```
the resulting appearance or defor-
mity must be shared. One must wait
for the manifestations of seeds of
perfection to appear within down the
bloodline.
```

While Wesson seemed to use his spiritual writings as a way to justify his unorthodox lifestyle, the main thrust of his literary project was to establish a new brand of religion, to trace (or invent) its origins and to justify his place as the leader of that new spirituality. In 2003, Wesson sent the manuscript to a New York publisher, which rejected it as incoherent.

FOUR

As Wesson continued to work on his manuscript, he shared more and more of his doctrine concerning vampires with his family. Elizabeth Wesson admitted to her own interest in vampires and frequently read Anne Rice novels and watched Dracula movies. Many family members wore black clothing, and 25-year-old Sebhrenah Wesson began to apply a white powder to her face and bright red lipstick in an effort to look more vampirelike. Many of the girls kept daily journals and wrote love notes to "their Master, Jevamarcsuspire." Take this poem written by Ruby to her uncle:

Marriage Prayer from the Lair

May our blood lines cross.
May our sex lines cross.
May we be one for eternity.
Let our blood stone give life eternal.
Let us serve our master,
Jev Am-Marc Suspire,
Le roi Le veut.[24]

---

[24] The French phrase *Le roi le veut* translates in English as "The King wills it." The poem was entered into evidence at trial, and Ruby identified it as her writing from the witness stand.

Most of the entries in the journals of the young women in the family referred to mundane daily chores; none speak overtly of sex with Marcus. A good example is an entry written by Kiani Wesson on January 30, 2001:

> We all woke up at 5:00 am to go to *Sudan* and some people got ready for work. Well, we lefted to *Sudan*, there were bits of snow everywhere, the road was very icy. We started working on the boat. After working on the boat it was around 6:00 we went down the hill, we bought some peanut butter and bread and some apples, Dad and I made a bet on the price of apples. Well, we had enjoyed our dinner in the car where it was warm and cozy.

During this period, Kiani's journals painted an idyllic family portrait. The family regularly ate ice cream together and watched a prodigious number of videos, sometimes as many as five feature films in one day. Marcus preferred the violent thriller genre and he even went as far as to put hundreds of videos on layaway at Wal-Mart. A typical entry in Kiani's journal read, "Tonight we watched *Knock Off*, *Universal Soldier* and *Aliens 2*." Kiani Wesson recorded the family's viewing habits in her diary: "Well, another special night, we watched Jet Li's movie again and we also watched *Anti Trust* very good movie. We also watched *Twister*. We went to bed late." On January 22, 2002, she wrote, "Today was a special day, Jet Li's movie came out on VHS. We all been waiting for his movies to come out." A few days later she wrote, "The special thing about today is that *The President's Man* came on at 9:00 P.M. starring Chuck Norris, we were all looking forward to seeing it, cause we had not heard from him since he quit *Walker Texas Ranger*." Kiani seemed to speak in code when it came to the sexual contact with her father. Frequently she wrote in her journal, "Daddy was sweet today," and decorated the words with small hearts.

* * *

The boys remained ostensibly clueless to the sexual relationships between their father and the girls in the family. While living on the *Sudan,* several of the girls gave birth to Wesson's children, and he had instructed the women to tell everyone that they had been artificially inseminated. It was a story the Wesson boys claimed to believe even after their father's arrest. After the murders, Wesson's son Dorian recalled, "It's hella weird but I just like you know okay, I just sort of played dumb you know . . . I didn't want to go there. Until the third one came I was getting a little suspicious because they all had the same nose. All the babies had the same nose, they had like, my nose. I'm like, 'Dang, they look like me almost!'"

Wesson spoke of artificial insemination in spiritual terms, as he did with polygamy and incest. He explained in the first section of his vampire bible, called "The Dark," that the goal of artificial insemination was "to end up with a new strain of being that is void of all universal principle and laws."

As naive as they may have been, the Wesson boys clearly understood their father's beliefs about polygamy. "He said Moses had seven wives, King David had thousands of concubines, just the usual Bible stuff," Adrian Wesson told the police. Some of the boys also had a vague knowledge of the family's murder suicide plan; Adrian Wesson told police that the family would never be separated. "We would all go up to Heaven or something like that," he explained.

Wesson moved the family to Fresno after several confrontations with the authorities and the family's eviction from the *Sudan.* Sofina stayed behind with Kiani, Sebhrenah, and Almae, and they continued to live aboard the boat (in spite of the eviction notice) and to work at the Marconi Conference Center. When Marcus left, he took all of the children, including Jonathan, to Fresno. Sofina missed her son and longed to be near him.

Marcus returned to the *Sudan* a couple times a week and continued to collect the paychecks of the older children. He also checked to make sure they had enough propane and food. The periodic visits also included "girl talks," in which Wesson made sure the girls were not having inappropriate contact with men and that they were obeying the rules. This continued until the winter of 1999, when Wesson moved the remaining family members to Fresno.

Nearly two years after the murders, the *Sudan* was still moored off Marshall's shore. Neighbors had complained they wanted it removed because it was an eyesore and a reminder of the unwelcome notoriety the town had received since the killings. The Sheriff's Department had made repeated promises to remove the vessel, but in December 2005, Mother Nature gave the residents of Marshall their wish. A winter storm brought torrential rains to Northern California. The *Sudan* couldn't withstand the elements and sank to the bottom of Tomales Bay.

PART THREE:

EARLY YEARS

The boy's voice boomed from his imaginary pulpit, calling out to the lost souls he was trying to save. His brother and sisters listened attentively to the crescendo of his voice as he invited them to turn from evil and begin a new spiritual life. Playing church was serious business, and as the oldest, Marcus Wesson filled the role of the preacher. Asking the choir to sing, his sister Detri sang out of tune and loudly. Cheryl, just two years his junior, emulated the grown-up ushers in church: She stood with her head held high and her right hand behind her back. The youngest child, Michael, filled the imaginary pews of the sanctuary.

This was the favorite game of the Wesson children and a large part of their spiritual routine growing up. Every night their mother, Carrie Wesson, led her children through family worship that included prayer time and a Bible reading before bedtime. The family attended a Seventh Day Adventist church every Saturday without fail, and a young Marcus frequently answered altar calls, making his way to the front of the church in search of healing and forgiveness from the Almighty.

Marcus Wesson was born in Kansas City on August 22, 1946. He was the oldest of Carrie and Ben Wesson's four children. His siblings included his sister Cheryl (two years younger), Detri (three years younger), and his brother Michael (four years younger). The family moved frequently, making homes in Kansas City, Missouri, and several cities in California, including Los Angeles, Milpitas, and San Jose. The reason for their repeated relocation was not always clear, but Wesson's sister—now Cheryl Penton—recalled that the moves were often unexpected and a result of being evicted. Ben Wesson had no career to speak of; he worked odd jobs and received a pension after being injured during his service in the U.S. Army during World War II. Carrie Wesson worked as a nurse.

Carrie Wesson was the disciplinarian in the house, and according to family members, often used a switch, a belt, and an extension cord to punish her children. She was a religious fanatic, conducting family Bible studies throughout the week, and composed volumes of her own spiritual writings by hand. Her project was to make the Bible easy enough for a 12-year-old to understand. She focused on the New Testament Book of Revelation, and Daniel in the Old Testament, and spent ten to fifteen years postulating on what to expect in the End Times. Carrie Wesson also voraciously read the writings of a prophet of the Seventh Day Adventists, Ellen G. White. White's teachings emphasized the End Times and the Second Coming of Christ.

Along with his siblings, a young Marcus Wesson was baptized in the Seventh Day Adventist Church. As a boy he had a severe stuttering problem that he eventually overcame. Despite his speech impediment and awkwardness, the young Wesson maintained a caring and thoughtful nature, according to his sister. His good deeds included making sure his sisters opened their Christmas presents first. "I'm kind of ashamed to say but Marcus would make sure I had the doll with the pink dress because I liked pink," Cheryl Penton remembered. She also recalled Marcus's fascination with animals, which resulted in the family's ownership of several pets: "They were stray cats or stray dogs or stray amphibians . . . or anything. He'd bring it home and try to rub it and wash it up and nurse it back."

In her only public interview following the murders, Wesson's mother told the *Los Angeles Times* that as a boy Marcus once nursed a dog back from the brink of death.

"I told him, 'That dog's dead,' but he wouldn't believe me. 'Mama, I can hear a faint heartbeat.' He fed it milk all day and night and brought it back to life," Carrie Wesson told the newspaper.

Childhood friend Gregory Bledsoe told an investigator from the Fresno County District Attorney's Office that as a boy Marcus had mated two dogs that were dissimilar to see what kind of breed would result. "He showed me some puppies. And he told me that they were from two dogs that he had put together and mated. And it looked like a strange little dog to me," Bledsoe said. He also told the investigator that as Marcus grew, he came to love the "adulation of others." Bledsoe said, "I told him that Marcus was a person that used to work with the children. All children seemed to be around him. He used to fix their go-carts and things like that." At a young age, Wesson built go-carts from scrap parts, exercising his keen mind and his ability to fix things.

"His entertainment was the Church. He wasn't running around seeing what little girl he could catch," his mother told the *Los Angeles Times*. "Instead, he'd be at the table eating food, always stuffing his face. That's why he got that big."

Wesson's family left the Midwest and moved to California when Marcus was ten years old. He attended school until the twelfth grade, and although he participated in a graduation ceremony at Samuel Ayer High School in San Jose, he never received a diploma.

Wesson's father was mostly absent from his son's life. In his teens, Marcus excelled in track and field, but his father never attended any of his track meets. "I don't recall him going to nothing of Marcus's at all," Penton recalled. She testified during the penalty phase of her brother's trial that Ben Wesson was a neglectful and sadistic alcoholic:

Q. And when you were growing up, did you become aware that your father had any personal problems?
A. He was an alcoholic.
Q. Do you remember when you might have realized that?
A. Probably a good portion of my life, you know. We were small.
Q. What do you remember as some of the family problems that resulted because of your father's alcoholism?
A. I would say for the most part probably financial, meaning, we thought we had some money during the month when we didn't.

Penton said her father didn't show at her eighth grade graduation because he was drunk. She testified that his drunken rages would often end in violence and recalled an instance in which he had his neck slashed in a fight. As a girl, she remembered her father bloody and near death after being brought home by a stranger. The wound was seven inches long and covered the width of his neck.

In addition to his propensity toward alcohol, Ben Wesson also frequently crossed the line of appropriate behavior when it came to his children and other young relatives. "He was a super mean alcoholic," Penton testified. "He would just hug and kiss all the time. You'd have to kind of run up the stairs or something." She stopped short of calling her father a child molester.

In the late 1960s relatives from Alabama, including Marcus's grandmother, his cousin Larry Morgan, and his niece Patricia, came to live with the Wessons in San Jose. According to court testimony, Ben Wesson subsequently began a gay relationship with his nephew, 18-year-old

Larry Morgan. Penton described the relationship between her father and Morgan as "suspicious" and "not normal." Ben Wesson raised eyebrows by leaving his wife and moving in with the young man. The two shared a cottage in San Jose.

Gregory Bledsoe testified during the penalty phase of the trial and recalled that as a teenager he had been propositioned by Ben Wesson. "He said if I let him suck my big dick, he would give me a fifty dollar bill," Bledsoe told the court. "At first I didn't, but then I did. It's something I'm not proud of," he said. "Mr. Wesson often talked about the size of [Morgan's] genitalia. Then he would say to me, 'I bet yours is even bigger than his. I can tell by what's hung down in your pants that you're a winner,'" Bledsoe testified. Bledsoe recalled an incident when he was sleeping over at Ben Wesson's apartment: "To my surprise, Mr. Wesson was trying to pull my pants down. I said, 'Look man, I don't ever want you to touch me again.'" After testifying, Bledsoe said outside the courthouse that he didn't believe that Marcus deserved the death penalty: "I'm not sure his father didn't also molest him."

Ben Wesson was absent from his wife and family for ten years and eventually moved to Los Angeles. In the late 1970s he returned to his wife, and the couple moved to Washington State to be near their daughter Cheryl. Ben Wesson died from prostate cancer just two weeks after his son's arrest in April 2004.

There is no indication Marcus Wesson even experimented with homosexuality, but it appeared his father's bisexuality had an effect on him. Rather than rejecting it, Marcus appeared to embrace the idea of same sex unions. In his writings, he described the first human relationship as a "homo marriage" between the Creator and the first man. In the first section of his book, Wesson wrote: "The gays and lesbians of today join together physically just as the master and man joined together spirit-metaphysically in the past and society accepts them." Wesson even seemed to think of gays and lesbians as spiritually superior. He wrote, "Thus; the gays, lesbians, bi-sexual, could be the master's true people yet; weaker to the master himself."

Childhood friend George Hudnall met Marcus Wesson in 1965 at the Ephesus Seventh Day Adventist church in San Jose. Hudnall was in his early twenties, and Wesson was nineteen. Hudnall described Wesson as a "real nice guy" despite his need to convince others of his point of view. "Even as a teenager, Marcus was kind of controlling and tried to kind of brainwash you or something into believing what he believed," Hudnall said from his home in San Jose. Although it went against Church doctrine, Marcus believed in polygamy and told others that he would have a lot of children someday, Hudnall recalled. He remembered Wesson as a loner and "not real popular," although he did have a few friends. Marcus sang in the church choir and sang bass in a male quartet. Hudnall said Wesson was "very smart," recalling his impressive talent for repairing bicycles and for building things.

At any early age, Wesson had already developed his own thoughts on polygamy, despite the fact that it went against the teachings of the Seventh Day Adventist Church. He continued to attend church gatherings, although the Church disputed Wesson's official membership after the murders occurred. A statement on the Church's website read simply: "We cannot find any record of Mr. Wesson's being a member of any Seventh-day Adventist Church." The lengthy statement went on to say that both of Wesson's parents were Seventh Day Adventists but that his contact with the Church over the years was "sporadic." The statement also said that Wesson attended the Central California Adventist Camp Meeting in Soquel a few times and that he worked as a janitor there in the late 1980s and early 1990s. The Church did, however, admit that many of the Wesson children belonged to a Seventh Day Adventist Church in the Fresno area.[25]

Perhaps the reason the Church was so quick to disassociate itself from Wesson had not only to do with the killings, but with Wesson's fascination with David Koresh.[26] Koresh led the Branch Davidians, a cult that had its origins in the Seventh Day Adventist Church. The sect broke away from the main line denomination when its founder decided that Christ could only return to a small group of "purified" believers. The sect's founder, Victor Houteff, believed he was the one chosen by God to accomplish this cleansing. Marcus Wesson did not follow the doctrine of the Seventh Day Adventist Church nor any of its breakaway sects, but he maintained the Church's dietary restrictions and observed the Sabbath on Saturday.

On June 22, 1966, a 19-year-old Wesson joined the U.S. Army and spent the next two years as a Specialist 4, Medic, in the 695th Medical Ambulance Company. He trained for ten weeks as a medical corpsman, then drove an Army ambulance in Europe during the Vietnam War. Wesson was honorably discharged in June 1968 and returned to San Jose. He attended college classes with money he received from the GI bill but never received a degree. Upon his return to the states, he moved in and began a relationship with a woman thirteen years older than him, Rosemary Solorio. Solorio was separated from her husband and already had several children. Wesson did not have a job and the family lived on welfare. Rosemary Solorio gave birth to Marcus Wesson's first child, Adair, in March 1971; Marcus was twenty-five at the time. The

---

[25] Sebhrenah and Kiani Wesson, Ruby Ortiz and Sofina Solorio, were all registered members of the Seventh Day Adventist Church.

[26] Wesson idolized Koresh and felt the government was unfairly interfering with Koresh's leadership of the Branch Davidians. This was discussed at length during the trial.

family dynamic in the three-bedroom home was anything but harmonious.

"He tried to take control of the family," Rosemary's son Jessie recalled of Wesson. Jessie said he was ten years old when Wesson punished him for teasing his brothers. Testifying at the trial, he told the court that Wesson hit him across the face with a belt and chased him through the neighborhood. Wesson sometimes stole what he needed, he said, recalling an incident when Marcus took him to Montgomery Ward and stole hardware from the store, telling him to keep an eye on the security guard. Wesson also controlled what the family ate, imposing new rules that favored a vegetarian diet. Jessie told the court that after Marcus began to physically abuse him, he would occasionally stay with his biological father. The conflict between Marcus and Rosemary's sons infuriated Jessie's father, and on cross examination by defense attorneys, Jessie admitted that his father would call Marcus Wesson derogatory names in Spanish and English.

Q. You've called Marcus Wesson a "nigger," haven't you?
A. I sure did. I've used that word ever since I met Marcus Wesson.
Q. Where did you learn that word?
A. I learned it from Marcus Wesson.

Although he had just fathered Rosemary's child, Marcus had his eye on her 14-year-old daughter Elizabeth. He began a sexual relationship with Elizabeth and eventually asked Rosemary for her permission to marry the girl. Rosemary agreed but tried to keep it a secret from the rest of the family. When Elizabeth became pregnant, Jessie, who was a teenager at the time, confronted Marcus.

"How are you telling me what to do when I know you're fucking my sister?" Jessie demanded. Marcus would not tolerate backtalk, and he whipped Jessie mercilessly across the back with an electric cord. The abuse was so severe Jessie refused to shower with the other boys on the high school football team because he was embarrassed about the marks on his back. A family member called the police to report the abuse, and when Marcus realized he could be arrested, he agreed to leave the family if Jessie agreed not to tell the police about what had happened. "I thought it was a good deal," Jessie said.

Before leaving, however, Marcus insisted on taking the family's van and he threatened to take his son Adair with him if the family didn't agree to let him have the vehicle. This incited one last fight between the teenage Jessie and Marcus that ended when Jessie, holding a screwdriver in his hand, told Marcus, "If you try to hit me again, I'm going to kill you." Marcus backed down and eventually left with the van and Elizabeth, leaving his son Adair behind.

Marcus Wesson married Elizabeth Solorio in 1974. She was fifteen, he was twenty-seven. Later that same year they had their first child, Dorian. In the subsequent four years, they had four more children: Adrian, Kiani, Sebhrenah, and her fifth child, Stefan, who died at birth. The couple moved in with Marcus's parents for a time, but while Elizabeth was pregnant with Adrian, she and Marcus moved into their own home in San Jose. Elizabeth dropped out of James Lick High School to care for the children. She began to home-school them, reasoning that public schools were "too dangerous."[27]

During this time the family patriarch worked as a commercial bank teller for Wells Fargo Bank.[28] Friend George Hudnall recalled that Wesson wore suits to work

---

[27] Elizabeth Wesson made this statement from the witness stand.

[28] Marcus Wesson told a probation officer that he worked at the bank for three years.

and maintained a well-groomed appearance. According to Hudnall, Wesson soon became tired of the conservative work environment, quit his job and started to grow dreadlocks.

Judy Hardin was only eleven years old when she lived across the street from the Wesson family in San Jose in the late 1970s. "Marcus was a very strict person," Hardin said. "Those children never cried. They were like little robots. They were programmed and manipulated." Hardin, who testified during the trial, said of Marcus's biblical teachings: "It was twisted. Men are kings of their households . . . that kind of thing. It was just loony. Marcus loves himself. And the only thing about respect was 'You will respect me.'"

Four years after Marcus and Elizabeth were married, a woman named Illabelle Lee came into their lives. They were an unlikely threesome; Lee was a pregnant white teenager with long blond hair. Lee first met the Wessons in October 1978 near Santa Cruz at a Seventh Day Adventist church, and she soon developed a deep connection with Marcus Wesson.

"It was my first visit to the church and I got off the bus stop and I remember arriving at the church and I remember them greeting me," Lee recalled. She began to attend church services with the Wessons. Lee had run away from her parents' home because her pregnancy had caused a rift in her family. "I was basically alone," she said. "They were just friends, somebody to spend time with, joke with, eat with. [Elizabeth's] friendship with me was on a different level, my friendship with [Marcus] was deeper. He's very good at listening and building trust."

Lee listened to Marcus espouse his beliefs about the benefits of polygamy. "At the time when I first met [Marcus] I was under the delusion that the father of my child would have a relationship with the child I was carrying. I realized that wasn't going to happen, and at that point I am looking for someone to depend on, someone to trust, and Marcus was someone I could trust, I could confide in," Illabelle recalled.

A sexual relationship developed between Illabelle and Marcus toward the end of 1979. "It wasn't discussed or decided upon, it just happened. He likes to hug. And people need hugs. And then he would hug and it would be a hug and a squeeze. Eventually you begin to cross lines," Illabelle recalled. "I remember he came to my apartment and he kissed me and I remember he was touching me and we had partially disrobed. I don't remember if this was our first sexual encounter, it might have been. There was oral intercourse."

The sexual relationship between Marcus and Illabelle continued until her departure from the California coast in 1983. Illabelle admitted to being in love with Wesson, and Wesson also appeared to have strong feelings for her. "He told me that he loved me. I knew he loved Liz as well," Illabelle said. "It was my understanding that [Elizabeth] knew about it. The word used to describe me during our relationship was 'mistress' not 'wife.'"

On May 14, 1982, Wesson wrote a love letter to Illabelle, inviting her to become his second wife. He invoked scriptures to justify his position that it was natural for a man to have several wives, telling Illabelle, "My marriage to you was one of acceptance through Christ for there is no Bible appointed ceremony. Yet my conformance to Romans 13:1-7 is not in breach. For God said, 'Be fruitful and multiply.'" The letter concluded:

> *Illabelle, you, Liz and all the children are my kingdom. Christ has many individual marriages but together they are his kingdom.*
>
> *Many use the adage that if God wanted man to have more than one wife he would have more than one for Adam and that "They twain shall be one flesh," not three or four or five.*

*I say this. For the same reason he put one tree of
life. Or Jesus did not marry is the reason he gave
Adam one wife. He knew the woman would sin and
then give four or five.*

At some point Elizabeth became uncomfortable with
the relationship between Illabelle and Marcus. Illabelle
explained that she and Marcus only engaged in oral sex
because Elizabeth was unwilling to let her bear Marcus's
children. "He cherished her and he didn't cherish me. I
felt like she was a 'nine' and I was a 'three.' I didn't feel
like I could ever measure up," Illabelle said. Not willing
to give up on the idea of having more than one wife, Marcus made the suggestion to Illabelle that she should be
Elizabeth's "handmaiden." "I was supposed to be Elizabeth's servant or something," Illabelle said. "I took that
as I was not a threat to their relationship, that my relationship with him was secondary. I don't think it was
meant that I was supposed to be doing errands or her bid-
ding. It's fine that Liz was a 'nine' but I wanted to be an
'eight' or an 'eight point five,' and I was never able to
reach that level. So combine that with being handmaiden
to Elizabeth and that's why it ended."

Illabelle feared withholding her money or physical in-
timacy from Marcus because she was afraid he would
end their relationship. "He was a father figure, a confi-
dant, a husbandlike individual," she testified. "I was psy-
chologically dependent on him."

Ultimately, Illabelle wanted more of a commitment
than Marcus was willing to offer. "I came to a point
when I realized that was not going to happen, so I realized it was Liz who had the control over my relationship
with him," she said. Her brother, who lived out of state,
helped her buy a car. Within a week of getting her driver's license, she left the central California coast and the
Wesson family behind. Years later she would discover
that Marcus had named one of his daughters after her

and that her 8-year-old namesake[29] was one of the nine murder victims. Twenty-five years after they met, Illabelle Lee took the witness stand at Marcus Wesson's murder trial and called him one of the greatest influences of her life.

During the late 1970s, Wesson's friend George Hudnall realized Wesson had "gone off the deep end." Hudnall said Wesson became overly protective of his family, not allowing his children to socialize. He forced them to stay indoors. Yet according to Hudnall, every year, Wesson attended camp meetings sponsored by the Seventh Day Adventist Church. At one of those meetings, Hudnall confronted his friend about his overbearing behavior, and Wesson told him to mind his own business. By the early 1980s, Wesson's eccentricities had grown. "There was just no reasoning with him," Hudnall said. Wesson espoused the importance of a vegetarian diet and forced his family to live on beans, but ate meat himself. From all appearances, he did stay faithful to one personal vow: He never drank alcohol or took any kind of drugs.

By the end of the 1980s the Wessons had a total of eleven children. Two of those children had died; Stefan was stillborn in 1979, and Donovan Wesson died of spinal meningitis at six months of age in 1981. After leaving his job at the bank, Wesson vowed to never work again, although he told a probation officer that he had worked "under the table" in telemarketing in the four years prior to his arrest (there was never any evidence to substantiate this claim).

These were not the only calamities to befall the Wesson family in the early years. On the witness stand, Elizabeth Wesson related an accident that sent their son Adrian to the Intensive Care Unit. According to her, the

---

[29] Illabelle Wesson was one of the children Marcus Wesson had with his daughter Kiani.

family was driving down the road, and Adrian, who was just a boy at the time, fell out of the car and onto the road, where he was run over by an eighteen-wheeler:

A. The time that Adrian fell out of the car on the freeway, he was just laying on the freeway. We saw a big old eighteen-wheeler pass right over him. Just ran right over him. And he ran and picked him up.

Q. Who ran?

A. My husband. He ran and picked him up.

Q. And then what happened?

A. I thought he was dead. But my—my husband was crying, and he said he's still breathing.

Q. And what happened next?

A. And we took him—we went to the hospital. We just drove to the hospital. And he was in intensive care for two weeks. He had a fractured jaw.

Q. So he got hit? Adrian was hurt in some way?

A. Yes. Yes. His face was really swollen.

The defense brought the story out at trial as an example of a time that Marcus Wesson had cried. Wesson's attorneys were rightfully concerned that the jury had not seen any evidence that Wesson was a compassionate human being. Elizabeth told the court her husband had also cried when the couple's daughter Kiani was born prematurely, and when he learned that his father had cancer and was dying.

Marcus Wesson's parents and siblings remained virtually invisible from public view at the time of the murders and in the months that followed. Wesson's father died shortly after the killings, and his mother's debilitating health prevented her from testifying during the penalty phase of the trial. Wesson's sister Cheryl was one of two witnesses to take the stand on his behalf. She wrote to him during his incarceration, offering advice on how to "correctly" interpret the Bible. Cheryl worked as an accountant near Seattle, and Wesson's brother Michael worked as a restaurant manager in Michigan. Defense attorney Pete Jones made the point through his questioning during the penalty phase that Michael had suffered a mental breakdown in the early 1980s.

In her interview with the *L.A. Times,* Wesson's mother insisted that all of her children had grown up in a loving, religious family. "If Marcus is guilty, I would really feel disappointed in my country if it didn't make him face the penalty," Carrie Wesson told the newspaper. "But I'm a biblical person, too, and I don't believe in capital punishment. What I would like for Marcus to do is sit in prison and think about what he's done and read the Bible. I think he will come back. Spiritually he will come back. Because I want to see my son in heaven someday."

PART FOUR:

ESCAPE TO THE MOUNTAINS

In the 1980s, Wesson purchased land in the remote Santa Cruz Mountains. He built a prefabricated house on the property northeast of Watsonville, but after failing to stay up to date on the mortgage payments, he lost both the land and the house. The following decade, the Wesson family traveled between the Santa Cruz harbor and the mountains, where Wesson had arranged a deal with a landowner that allowed the family to stay on a remote plot of land along Summit Road, tucked deep in the wilderness. According to Elizabeth Wesson, Marcus had reached a rent-to-own deal with the landowner, A. J. Wheeler. She testified that she and Marcus paid Wheeler a down payment of $500 from their welfare check, to secure promised ownership of the quarter acre of land. Part of the deal with Wheeler included a promise not to place Wesson's name on any documents, in order to not interfere with the family's receipt of government aid. The Wessons converted the plot of land into a campsite and lived there periodically during the late 1980s and early 1990s.

In 1995, Wesson decided to move the family to the campsite on a more permanent basis. During that year, Kiani, Ruby, and Sofina all became pregnant with Marcus's children. Kiani's pregnancy had begun to show, and some of the men on the Solorio side of the family started asking questions. Elizabeth's brother Jessie surmised that Marcus was fathering the children and angrily confronted his nieces. During the trial, Elizabeth Wesson denied knowing that it was her husband who had impregnated their daughter:

Q. Were you aware that Kiani was having intercourse with your husband?

A. No.

Q. And after Kiani became pregnant, isn't it true that Mr. Wesson had the family move to the Santa Cruz property?

A. It was—no. It happened—it happened before that, I think. Because, um, my brother Jesse got very physical and verbal toward me and the girls. He was threatening us, so we left my mom's.

Q. Isn't it true that you and Mr. Wesson moved the family to the Santa Cruz Mountains because you became concerned that Kiani was beginning to show her pregnancy?

A. No, we left because Jessie threatened us.

Q. Isn't it true that all the Solorios, your side of the family, was concerned that the girls are getting pregnant?

A. There was a big old argument. Jessie was calling Ruby the "B" word. He was cussing her out. He was cussing out Sofina, telling them that they were—he was calling them the "B" word. He was getting aggressive with them.

Q. Isn't it true he was concerned that his nieces are getting pregnant, and they're at such a young age?

A. I don't know if he was concerned or not. But he was more vulgar. He was more verbally vulgar toward the girls.

Q. And isn't it true that Jessie was concerned 'cause he believed that your husband was impregnating all the girls?

A. I don't know if my brother was concerned or not. If he

was concerned, he would have probably handled it differently.

In fact, Jessie Solorio had confronted his sister Elizabeth about the idea that Marcus had impregnated his own daughters and nieces. Elizabeth told Jessie the girls had been artificially inseminated. "I said to her, 'Do you think I am as stupid as you are?'" Jessie recalled. "And she said, 'Do you think I would let happen to them what happened to me?'" Jessie told his sister she was an idiot.

For her part, Kiani felt she was performing the role of surrogate mother because Marcus had explained that Elizabeth was beyond her childbearing years. Despite this, Kiani testified that it was something she never talked about with Elizabeth:

Q. Why didn't you tell your mother that you were having your father's children?
A. Because I was a surrogate mother and I didn't want to tell her. I didn't want her to know. I felt she would have stopped me.
Q. Because you thought it was wrong.
A. No, I didn't think it was wrong.
Q. Is it wrong in any case to have a baby with your father?
A. I was a surrogate mother. Other cases, I don't know.
Q. Why do you think your mother wouldn't have wanted you to have a baby with your father?
A. Because I didn't want her to know, she wouldn't have wanted me to do it with my dad.
Q. Did you feel disloyal to your mother by having sex with your father?
A. No, because I was a surrogate mother.
Q. You were more than a surrogate mother. What did Illabelle[30] call you?

---

[30] Illabelle Wesson was the biological daughter of Kiani and Marcus Wesson and was also one of the murder victims.

A. Mom. She distinguished, she called [Elizabeth] Mommy and she would call me Mom.

Q. Like she was a puppy. You're having her and saying, "Here, Mom." What was the difference between you having Illabelle and someone picking out a puppy?

A. What do you mean?

Q. These are human beings you gave birth to. Don't you think there should be a formal process owed to the child?

A. There was. I had a child. I gave it to my mom.

Viewing his brother-in-law's discontent as a harbinger of a dispute that could involve the authorities, Marcus decided to move the family into full seclusion—so they packed up and escaped to the mountains. Wesson had done what he could to make the desolate plot of land livable for his wife and the thirteen children, installing a foundation for a huge army tent that served as the family's living quarters. There was no running water, so the family filled gallon jugs on its way to and from Santa Cruz. The campsite included an open-air bathroom that sat on top of a five-thousand-gallon septic tank just down the hill from the tent.

The long, rectangular tent's square footage rivaled that of most two-bedroom apartments; each of the children had their own bunk. The tent was divided by zipped flaps into three sections: one for the boys and the other for the girls, while Marcus and Elizabeth slept in the large middle section that served as a living room and a kitchen, equipped with a sink and an icebox. When the family left Fresno, Kiani and Sofina both knew they were pregnant. Ruby discovered her pregnancy shortly after moving to the campsite.

"I discovered it just because I started missing my period and I was feeling nauseous," Ruby recalled. While Elizabeth took the other two girls into town for their prenatal visits to the doctor, Ruby didn't see the inside of a clinic until she was eight and a half months pregnant. On September 16, 1995, Kiani gave birth to Illabelle Wesson. Six months later Sofina gave birth to Jonathan. Both women delivered the children at a hospital in town and returned to the campsite with their children. Three months after Jonathan was born, Elizabeth and Marcus drove Ruby to Watsonville Community Hospital, where she gave birth to her daughter Aviv. Marcus remained in the car, and as with the other girls, he had ordered Ruby not to identify him as the father. After Ruby gave birth, a social worker asked the inevitable question. On the hospital form, Ruby had written that the father was "unknown." The social worker insisted that Ruby divulge the information, explaining that Medi-Cal wouldn't cover her medical expenses unless she completely filled out the form.

"Just forget it, then," Marcus advised his niece. "You don't need to get [those benefits]." Ruby obeyed and left the hospital with her newborn daughter and without settling her hospital bill.

"We all agreed that when we have the children . . . that, on the children's birth certificate, we would just put 'unknown,'" Ruby testified. "That was our plan. Because a lot of teenagers have kids and they don't know who the father is. That was just our game plan."

When the family was living aboard the *Sudan,* the children had contact with people outside their immediate family circle, but in the mountains there was little to offer even a glimpse of the outside world. They were miles from the nearest town and surrounded by thick wilderness and steep terrain. Brandi Solorio was seventeen years old when the family lived in the mountains and she had seen the other girls become pregnant with Marcus's children. She had even taken part in the "marriage" ceremony between her uncle Marcus and her sister Ruby. According to Brandi, the children took part in the ceremony while the older Elizabeth Wesson watched TV in another room.

"I was supposed to be Ruby's mother. One of us was the preacher and I was the mother and acting out like a mother. Drama, you know. They walked down the aisle," Brandi testified. Like her sisters, Brandi had been molested by her uncle. She testified that the touching began at the age of seven and that she lost her virginity to Wesson at the age of fourteen or fifteen. Like with the other girls, Wesson had explained to Brandi that she was to have "babies for the Lord."

While growing up in the Wesson household, no one recognized that Brandi had a slight learning disability that prevented her from learning as fast as her sisters, brothers, and cousins. Since the children were home-schooled, Brandi hadn't learned to read. When Wesson discovered that his niece was illiterate at the age of twelve, he spanked her.

"A month later he would test me, and I would pretend I could read. But I couldn't," Brandi testified. While on the witness stand, she recalled an incident when she was eight years old, sitting next to her uncle on the couch. Brandi explained that she had a blanket on her lap and that Wesson had his hand under the blanket. He began to penetrate her with his fingers while many other family members were still in the room.

Brandi had also learned about the family's murder-suicide pact. "That we should take poison or something so we wouldn't be separated," she testified. When the prosecutor asked how they had planned to carry out the plan, Brandi replied, "I guess I really didn't think about it, I just know I was willing to die."

When the family moved to the mountains, Brandi had not yet become pregnant with her uncle's child, but she knew she was the next in line. Worried that her sisters' fate would become her own, she decided to run away. "I was very depressed. I could see no hope. I did not want to be there anymore," Brandi said. She woke up before dawn and made her way to a clearing not far from the tent that the children referred to as "Girls Land." She wanted to say goodbye to her sisters and cousins but knew it was too risky so she decided to leave a message for them another way. With rocks, she began to spell out I LOVE YOU on the ground, but halfway through her message she heard someone coming and ran off. She had a couple of biscuits in her pocket and she knew the walk would be long and difficult. She walked all day. Finally, she reached a road and was able to hitch a ride with a nice couple who drove her to a market. From there, she walked all the way to Santa Cruz. Brandi thought of going to the McDonald's in Santa Cruz where her male cousins worked to tell them that she had run away, but then decided they might force her to return to the campsite. She stopped at a grocery store and called her mother, who lived in Fresno. According to Brandi's testimony, on the phone, her mother scolded her for running away and threatened to take her back to the Wessons.

When the other children woke up that day, they quickly realized that Brandi was gone. Her sister Ruby found the incomplete message written in rocks and feared that her sister had been kidnapped. "We didn't think she would run away," Ruby said. "And there was somebody walking around the tent at night. We could hear someone. We didn't know who it was. So we would always say there is a pervert lurking around there somewhere. We just thought maybe he took her." The family looked everywhere for Brandi but could not find her. Two days later Elizabeth called her sister Rosemary and discovered that Brandi was with her mother. Marcus convened a meeting with all the women (excluding his wife) to find out why Brandi had run away. None of the girls offered an explanation.

"Marcus said that he believed that the reason why she ran away was because she wanted to have a baby. And he was not . . . he did not give her a baby," Ruby recalled. This time, Marcus did not persist in an attempt to bring

Brandi back to the campsite, because he had other problems: there were infants to take care of and the family was running out of money and food. Even water for showers had become scarce. In her diary, Kiani Wesson wrote: "Us girls did not take showers. We had to save the water because we couldn't go down the hill 'cause we had no gas money." On June 30, 2003, Kiani wrote, "We are in a money crisis . . . We had no propane this morning, so we cooked the oatmeal on the heater. Everyone felt tired." The situation became so desperate that Wesson would take the girls to town and equip them with metal poles to scour through Dumpsters for food. From the witness stand, Kiani Wesson explained how the family searched for their meals:

A. At a bakery, all they throw is just like breads in [the garbage]. So we would get it.

Q. So the family would go through the garbage by a bakery to get bread?

A. Yeah. 'Cause they throw like fresh breads out there. And they said we could go out there sometimes to get it. So we would get it.

Q. Would the family go other places and look through the garbage for food?

A. Um, only on other, um—at a fruit stand. Like they would—they put out fresh fruit, so we would—we would get it.

Q. And how about the back of Safeway? Did the family ever dig behind the back of Safeway to dig for vegetables?

A. Um, yeah. Because the manager had talked to us and said that he puts out fresh fruit all the time, and we would feel free to go and get it.

The adults in the family struggled to feed themselves and the three newborns. To make matters worse, the owner of the land the Wessons were living on, A. J. Wheeler, died

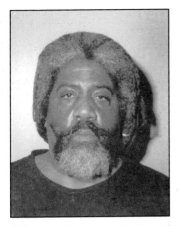

Marcus Wesson on the day of his arrest.

Wesson's mug shot the day he entered Death Row, a year-and-a-half later. He lost almost half his body weight during his incarceration.

Wesson in court with defense attorney Pete Jones (in foreground).

The tugboat named *Sudan*, where Wesson lived with his wife and fourteen children.

Taken on the deck of the *Sudan*. *From left to right:* Gypsy, Brandi, Rosa, Sebhrenah, Lise, and Sofina holding Jonathan.

Taken belowdecks of the *Sudan*. *From left to right:* Sofina holding Jonathan, Kiani holding Illabelle, and Brandi.

From left to right: Jeva (1), Aviv (7), Sedona (1), Illabelle (8), Marshey (1), Ethan (4), and Jonathan (7). Wesson fathered all seven children with his daughters and nieces. All seven died in the massacre on March 12, 2004.

From left to right: Murder victims Sedona, Jeva, and Marshey.

Sebhrenah Wesson with 8-year-old Illabelle. Sebhrenah wore white powder on her face to look like a vampire.

Kiani holding Jeva, the second child she had with her father. Taken on the campsite where the Wessons lived in the Santa Cruz mountains.

The girls rowing the dingy, the family's only way to get from the *Sudan* to shore.

761 West Hammond Avenue, where the murders occurred.

Pile of bodies in the back bedroom of the Wesson house. Several of the family's ten antique coffins were standing on their ends against the bedroom walls.

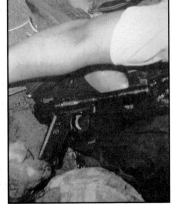

The murder weapon, a .22 caliber handgun, was discovered under the body of 25-year-old Sebhrenah Wesson.

Elizabeth Wesson being comforted by two of her sons, shortly after running out of the bedroom where the killings took place.

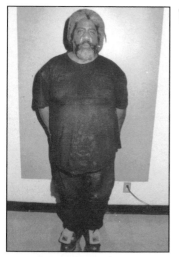

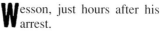

Wesson, just hours after his arrest.

Bloodstains covered Wesson's shirt and pants.

Sofina holding her daughter Alyssen, standing next to her son Jonathan's casket.

Jonathan Wesson, the son of Sofina Solorio and Marcus Wesson.

Wesson being transported from the Fresno County Jail to San Quentin's Death Row.

One of the letters Wesson wrote to me from Death Row.

Marcus Wesson's mug shot, taken shortly after his arrival at San Quentin Prison and after having his dreadlocks cut off in accordance with prison policy.

in 1997. Wheeler's son inherited the plot of land. There was no written record of the deal the elder Wheeler had reached with Marcus Wesson. Wheeler's son sold the land and once again the Wesson family was forced to leave the place they had considered home. Wesson decided to move the family back to Fresno, where the women could start working again to support the family. He knew it was a risk, but he didn't have a choice. Fresno didn't offer the seclusion the mountains had and he knew that people would start talking if they saw the babies. Wesson worried that someone might discover the secret he had worked so hard to protect.

PART FIVE:

FRESNO

ONE

When the family returned to Fresno on a more permanent basis in 1997, in truth, they had lived in California's Central Valley off and on for many years. Wesson came to Fresno to find jobs for the women in the family and set up interviews for Sofina, Ruby, Kiani, and Sebhrenah at a McDonald's restaurant on the northwest side of town. They all were hired. Marcus drove them to and from work, and they turned over their paychecks to him. As part of their uniforms, the girls were required to wear pants. They objected, and with some convincing, the restaurant manager permitted them to wear skirts. Soon the area supervisor took notice of how polite and efficient the young women were and decided to split them between several McDonald's around town. Ruby and Kiani were transferred to another McDonald's, where they were trained as managers.

The older boys did not move back to Fresno with the rest of the family. Dorian and Adrian stayed in Santa Cruz and lived on their own. According to Wesson's family rule, they were obligated to send him money for the first two years of their independence. The rest of the family moved into the upstairs section of a duplex on College Avenue in Fresno. As the family was accustomed, the living quarters were small and the children slept in the living room. In a bedroom of the duplex, Marcus continued his "girl talks," warning the women—now in their early to mid-twenties—not to socialize with people in the outside world.

"Our family life was supposed to stay private," Ruby explained. "Because everybody would not understand why we lived the way that we lived." Wesson became increasingly distrustful of his daughters and nieces and would beat them with a small wooden bat for socializing with men. He would make the offending woman lift her skirt and administer twenty-one strikes of the bat for each determined offense.

Despite her uncle's warnings not to socialize with others, Ruby made friends with a woman by the name of Emma and with one of the managers at McDonald's. As she became acquainted with her newfound friends, Ruby began to see that she didn't have to stay under her uncle's control. She realized that like other young women her age, she could have a life of her own. She knew that Marcus had made it clear she couldn't leave; she was his "wife" and had no choice but to remain at his side. A couple of months went by and Kiani was no longer working at the same McDonald's, so before Marcus came to pick her up from work, Ruby decided to run away. She got off early and left with her new friend Emma. She spent the night at Emma's house.

It didn't take long for Elizabeth to figure out where Ruby had gone; Emma's family owned a store in town, and Elizabeth found Ruby there the following day.

"You need to come outside and talk to Marcus," Elizabeth urged her niece.

"I don't want to talk to him," Ruby said. "I'm not going back there."

"*Mija*, you have to come out and talk to him," Elizabeth pleaded. "You just need to tell that to your dad. Just come out and talk to him."

Ruby went outside, and Marcus was sitting in the driver's seat of the family's van. She peered through the open window on the passenger side. "What do you want to talk about?" she asked.

"Come inside so we can talk," Marcus said.

"No, we can talk right here. I don't want to go back," Ruby said.

"I promise . . . just come inside the van. I promise we're just going to sit right here and talk."

Reluctantly, Ruby got into the van. Elizabeth jumped into the car and slammed the passenger's side door. Marcus sped off. He drove fast all the way back to the family's apartment without saying a word. He pulled into a back alleyway, parked, and motioned for Elizabeth to get out of the car. "Okay, Bee," he said to his wife. "We're going to talk."

Remembering the stabbing incident with Sofina, Elizabeth looked concerned.

"Marcus, don't do anything," she said.

"Don't worry, Bee. I promise we're just going to talk."

"Okay," Elizabeth said, exiting the van.

Marcus asked Ruby why she had run away. Ruby said she just didn't want to live with him anymore.

"Let's go upstairs and talk," Marcus said.

He and Ruby got out of the van and went inside. He took her into his bedroom. Elizabeth was there, and he asked her to leave the room. She agreed, and Marcus closed the door behind her. Alone in the room with her uncle, Ruby explained that she wanted to eventually get married and start a family of her own.

"You are already married," Marcus told her. "If you leave me, you will be committing adultery."

"I don't want to live here anymore," Ruby said, shaking her head. "I don't want to be your wife anymore."

"Well, you are my wife," Marcus replied. He made a fist and punched Ruby's head. He avoided her face and struck her repeatedly on her scalp. She coiled in pain and gasped for air.

"I'm doing this because I love you," Marcus said. "I'm

not going to just let you go out there and be in the world
and let the world destroy you."[31]

He told Ruby she'd better think about their daughter
Aviv.

"I could just take her with me. You know, she doesn't
have to stay here," Ruby pleaded, holding her head and
trying to hold back tears.

"No," Marcus said emphatically. "You already know
that you had that child for the Lord, that you can't take her
with you. She's not your child."

Marcus kept Ruby in the bedroom all night, and after
twelve hours her spirit was depleted; she finally agreed to
stay. Marcus was glad, but told her he would still have to
punish her for trying to run away. He decided to beat her
for ten days in a row. By the end of the ten days, Ruby
couldn't even sit down. Marcus struck her mercilessly
with the miniature bat and she was covered with bruises.
He did not permit her to return to work at the same
McDonald's, fearing she would be influenced by her new
friends. He arranged for Ruby to work at another fast
food restaurant in a neighboring town.

Not long after Ruby's attempt to run away, Wesson purchased the *Sudan* and began to travel back and forth between Fresno and Marshall. The abuse became more
severe and unpredictable. On one occasion he backhanded
Ruby in the face. "He would tell me stuff like, 'I know
that you're talking to men. I don't know why you want to
keep talking to them,'" Ruby recalled. "And he would say
things like, 'You're not even that pretty. Just because you
have a pretty face, that doesn't mean that any man is going to want to live with you and love you.'"

Between 1997 and 1999, Marcus traveled back and forth
between Fresno and the *Sudan*. The women continued to
work seasonal jobs at the Marconi Conference Center near

---

[31] These events, including the actions of Marcus and Rosemary, are as
described by Ruby from the witness stand.

Marshall and then returned to Fresno in the winter months to work their fast food jobs. Shortly before the near murder-suicide attempt on the *Sudan* in 1998, Ruby tried to run away a second time. Marcus was in Fresno and Ruby was staying on the *Sudan* with Sofina and the others who were working at the conference center. That day, it was one of those rare occasions that Ruby was on the boat alone. Sofina, Kiani, and Almae had gone to work.

She rowed herself to shore and walked four miles along the road. She hitchhiked her way to the San Rafael bus station, and when she arrived she realized that she had no money. She started to cry. An elderly lady approached and asked Ruby what was troubling her.

"I'm running away from somebody," she replied. The woman could see the desperation in Ruby's eyes.

"Where are you going, honey?" the lady asked.

Ruby said she was going to Fresno. The woman told Ruby to stop crying and that she was going to help her. She took Ruby to her apartment and let her spend the night, and the next morning she bought her a bus ticket. She told her the bus would take her to the Amtrak station, where a train ticket to Fresno would be waiting for her. But when Ruby arrived, she went to the counter at the Amtrak station and there was no ticket waiting under her name. Again she began to cry. The man behind the counter had compassion on her. "Well, let me see what I can do for you," he said. He told her to sit down and wait. Several minutes later the man walked over to Ruby and told her it had all been taken care of and handed her a ticket.

Once she arrived in Fresno, Ruby went straight to the McDonald's where she had worked and found Emma. Emma sympathized with her friend, but her cousins were staying with her and there wasn't enough room at her house for Ruby so she arranged for Ruby to stay with a friend. For the next several days Ruby stayed with friends, but she was penniless so she reluctantly went to her mother's house. Rosemary encouraged her daughter to return to

Marcus. "That's what made you happy, so you need to go back," Rosemary told her daughter. Ruby told her mother that Aviv was Marcus's biological daughter and that Marcus had been hitting her. Rosemary initially had no reaction. Finally she said, "Well, Ruby, you made a choice that you wanted to marry him." Ruby cried. "Please, Mom! Just listen to what I'm saying," she pleaded. Rosemary would not budge. She told Ruby she should go back to Marcus.

Ruby knew her mother would contact Elizabeth and Marcus, so she left her mother's house. For the next two days she stayed with her brother and his wife, but it didn't take long for Elizabeth Wesson to find her. Again Elizabeth told her she needed to talk to Marcus, explaining that she couldn't just run away. Ruby had been through it all before and knew that he would just try to convince her to stay. But Elizabeth was persistent, so Ruby agreed to meet Marcus at a nearby Denny's restaurant.

Sitting at a table in the crowded diner, Ruby told Marcus she wasn't happy and didn't want to be married to him anymore. Marcus insisted the real reason was that Ruby had run away with one of the men she worked with. She denied it.

"Well, what about Aviv?" Marcus asked her, referring to their baby girl.

"What do you mean?" Ruby asked. "You always said I can't take her with me."

"Yes, but you still have a responsibility to her and to the other children," Marcus replied. He told Ruby that she needed to stay with family to help raise the children "for the Lord." The conversation went on for about four hours, and Marcus told her he was leaving the next day to go to the family's boat, but that they would continue their talk when he returned. Meanwhile, he told her to stay at her mother's house. Grudgingly, Ruby agreed.

When Marcus returned to Fresno, he had four of the children with him: Illabelle, Jonathan, Ethan, and Ruby's daughter Aviv. He brought them to Rosemary's house and told Ruby he was leaving the children with her. For the next three weeks Ruby cared for the children. She fed and bathed them and she taught the older children their ABCs. At the end of the three weeks, Marcus returned and told Ruby she should sacrifice her own desires to raise the children "for the Lord." She felt that she couldn't abandon her daughter or the other children, so she stayed. About a month later the family was evicted from the *Sudan* and Marcus returned to Fresno with the whole family. Like her first attempt, Ruby's second attempt to run away had failed.

TWO

Upon the entire family's return to Fresno, the Wessons stayed in the upstairs portion of the College Avenue duplex and then moved to an apartment on Huntington Avenue. Marcus moved between the two locations and made periodic trips to Marshall, but he had already decided on his next big purchase: a historic home on Huntington Avenue, near Fresno City College. The two-story Tudor had been gutted by fire in 1999 and needed major repairs. Marcus negotiated the purchase of the house with the help of a realtor, but his name did not appear on any official documents; the women were named as owners. The exterior of the house retained its impressive beauty. The home had once belonged to a former mayor and a secretary of state, but due to the extensive fire damage, Wesson negotiated to buy it from attorney Frank Muna for just less than $100,000. It would have taken more than $250,000 to renovate the house to its original state, and Wesson had vowed to do the work himself. Using money saved up from his daughters' and nieces' earnings, a down payment was made for a third of the sale price and Wesson arranged to make monthly mortgage payments directly to Muna.

Like the boats and vehicles Wesson had previously purchased, the house was a fix-up project of major proportions. While it had an acceptable exterior, the fire damage to the interior made the home uninhabitable. In early 2000 the family moved into a toolshed just behind the main house that had been untouched by the fire. When the women came home from working their full-time jobs, Wesson had them perform repairs to his new dream house. They swept as much of the soot out as they could, emptied the house of debris, and cared for the lawn. They even painted the wrought-iron fence in the front yard. But the family would never get the home into livable condition. The city filed countless code violations, complaining that it was taking too long for the new owners to make the needed repairs. Wesson had told Muna that he was the women's financial advisor, but Muna soon realized the relationship between Wesson and the women was much more than professional.

"It was really disturbing," he recalled. "When they were all together, the women would just step back into this subservient position. It was like total control."

At first the Wesson women came to Muna's office each month to make their mortgage payments, but soon they were behind with their payments and had not made the promised improvements to the house. In 2001, Muna sued the five women named on the deed, alleging in his lawsuit that the family had illegally occupied the house before escrow opened and that the Wessons stole property from his garage. That property, Muna claimed, included possessions he was able to salvage from the house after the fire: furniture, glassware, clothing, and other items totaling an estimated $15,000. Wesson told authorities he thought the items were abandoned property.

Their legal problems aside, the women continued to work diligently as banquet servers to finance Wesson's latest project. Their long hours working at the Radisson Hotel provided the family's only sustenance. But the time the women spent at work only made Wesson more paranoid that they were flirting with other men. The "girl talks" continued, as did the discipline.

"He would usually discipline Sofia first," Ruby recalled. "Because usually we both got in trouble. And then he would send all the girls out of the room."

By this time most of the girls were in their mid-twenties, and according to Ruby and Sofina, Wesson had taken to hitting them with a full-sized wooden bat. The scenario was all too familiar for Ruby: Marcus would accuse her of talking to other men and she would deny it. He would say he didn't believe her and hit her on her butt, legs, and arms with the bat. Ruby's work uniform covered the bruises on her arms; she took to wearing black stockings and long skirts to hide the marks on her legs.

She hid her bruises from the outside world, but Ruby was also guarding a secret: She had fallen in love with a coworker, and she thought if Marcus found out, he would kill her. She decided to run away from Marcus for a third time, but this time she vowed she wasn't coming back, even if it meant leaving her daughter behind. Again she decided to make her getaway while she was at work. She got off work early and her new boyfriend hid her at his mother's house. Ruby decided to sever all ties with her past. She didn't even return to her job at the hotel. She stayed with her boyfriend's mother until the young couple could find an apartment together.

After she was gone for a while, Ruby called her aunt Elizabeth to tell her that she was okay. Elizabeth scolded her for leaving and put Marcus on the phone.

"You need to come home," Marcus told Ruby. "You're my wife and you need to come home to your husband."

Ruby said she wasn't going back and that she had married someone else. Marcus became furious. He told her that the Lord would not recognize her marriage because in God's eyes she was already married. Ruby said she didn't care and that she wanted Aviv to come live with her.

"You know I can't do that," Marcus said. "These are children for the Lord, and I'm not going to let my children be raised out in the world."

Ruby became angry. For the first time, she raised her voice at her uncle.

"You don't understand what I'm trying to tell you!" she yelled. "I don't want to be with you and I'm not your wife!" She slammed down the receiver.

Eventually the Wessons were forced to leave the burned-out house on Cambridge Avenue. They had lost their court battle against Frank Muna and were ordered to pay him $30,000 to cover the items in his garage and the unpaid mortgage payments. According to county records, the Wesson women sold the Cambridge house in July 2003 for $149,500. They used part of the proceeds to pay Muna the money they owed him, and Marcus immediately started looking for a new place for the family to live.

THREE

Sofina was more miserable than she had ever been. Since the stabbing incident and her fling with Oscar, Marcus had ordered the other girls not to talk to her, fearing her "bad influence" would rub off on them. While working at the Radisson Hotel, she befriended an older man named Milton, who worked as a cook in the hotel's restaurant. At work, the other girls saw Sofina talking to Milton and they told Marcus. Sofina was twenty-six years old now, but in Marcus's eyes she was not too old to be whipped for her indiscretions. She was still "married" to her uncle, and in his way of thinking she was committing adultery. Sofina didn't care. At the time, Milton was the only one in her life treating her with respect and kindness, so she decided it was worth enduring the beatings to continue to talk to him.

During their talks, Sofina began to open up to Milton and a few times she broke down and cried. "I just had a bad day," she would explain, without being specific. He was a good listener and never pressed her to say more than she wanted to. Sofina finally let her guard down after Mother's Day. Her sisters and cousins were ignoring her, and Marcus forbade her to have contact with their son Jonathan, who was five years old at the time. She stayed in the Wesson home in part to be near her son even though she knew she couldn't even hold him. It broke her heart not to be able to laugh and play with her little boy. Marcus had promised her she could spend time with Jonathan on Mother's Day, but when that day arrived, he did not keep his word. All of the other children had made something for their mothers, but Jonathan's homemade gift was given to Elizabeth. Sofina was overcome with sorrow.

The next day she went to work and was still beside herself with anger and sadness. Milton gave her his car keys. "Go sit in my car and chill out for a while," he told her. She agreed. Several minutes later Milton came outside and got into the car with her. Sofina cried. "You just don't understand," she said. "My dad is very strict. If he knew I was even talking to you right now, I would get in so much trouble."

Milton was incredulous. "What kind of family are you from?" he asked.

"You don't understand," Sofina replied. "You shouldn't even get involved with me."

"I like you and I want to help you out," Milton said.

"Really? If I tell you some things, you won't tell anyone?" Sofina asked.

Milton assured her he would not tell a soul. Sofina told him everything, and though he was surprised, he vowed not to abandon her or their friendship.

The other girls continued to snitch on Sofina for talking to Milton, and Marcus continued to punish her with beatings. After a beating that was particularly bad, she arrived at work and Milton greeted her with a hug. Sofina winced from the pain; her back was sore and covered with bruises. At that moment she had a realization: Milton was old enough to be her father, but she loved him. With his support, she thought, maybe she could conjure the courage to leave her uncle's house.

She went home that day and told Marcus, "I don't want to live with you anymore. I want to live with my mom."

"No, you can't go," Marcus replied.

Sofina became angry.

"You know what, Marcus, I really don't care anymore. I'm not happy here. If Milton's willing to love me, then I'm going to be with him."

Sofina hugged her aunt Elizabeth and left the house expecting never to return. She left all her personal effects behind with the exception of her purse and ran to her mother's house, thinking Marcus might try to follow her and bring her back by force. Minutes after she arrived, Elizabeth pulled into the driveway. She told Sofina that Marcus wanted to talk to her and handed Sofina her cell phone; Marcus was on the line.

"We have to do this the right way, Sofia. I have to let you go. Come back," he said.

"You're going to let me leave?" she asked with a hint of skepticism in her voice.

"Yeah. Let's just talk about that," he replied.

Sofina got into the car and returned to the Wesson house with her aunt Elizabeth. When she arrived, Marcus told her if she left she would still have to abide by his rules. That meant she would still have to turn over her paycheck to him for the next two years. Sofina agreed. He also said she could sleep at her mother's house, but during the day, when she wasn't working, she would stay with the Wessons.

For the next couple of months Sofina did as Marcus had told her. He had ordered the other girls not to talk to her, and she spent much of her time just sitting in silence. Soon afterward, Sofina discovered she was pregnant with Milton's child. She was afraid to tell Marcus and she became depressed. In a dairy entry she wrote, "Dad says there's a bad spirit in the house. Could it be me?" She was unhappy and she longed to be with Milton. "I just felt my whole world was gone," Sofina recalled. "They were my family and I loved them. I just wished I was dead."

Sofina feared her uncle's reaction but knew her pregnancy would eventually show. She also didn't want Marcus to hear it from someone else. So one day she gathered the courage to tell him. She walked up to him and announced plainly, "I'm pregnant."

"What?" Surprisingly, Marcus's initial reaction was not angry. He hugged her. "Okay. Well, can I have this baby?" he asked.

"No!" Sofina replied. "This is Milton's baby. I don't think he'll let me give it to you.'"

Marcus's reaction immediately changed to disappointment. He told Sofina it was time for her to leave his house permanently. He told her she was a bad example for the other girls and he didn't want her rebellious influence to affect them. Again Sofina left the house, but her heart was heavy because she knew she had to leave her son Jonathan behind.

During the following year, Sofina moved to San Jose with Milton, but she would periodically return to Fresno to visit her son and bring the family money, food, and clothing.

"Marcus would call me and ask for money," she recalled. "He's like, you know, 'Jonathan needs a roof over his head. Can you give me $200? We just need around $200 to pay the rent.'"

FOUR

Given his legal struggle with Frank Muna, Wesson thought it best that he should make the next real estate purchase in just one of the women's names. In October 2003, Marcus finalized the purchase of 761 West Hammond Avenue, and Rosa Solorio was listed as the owner. Marcus was still traveling back and forth between Fresno and Marshall and some of the women were still working their seasonal jobs at the Marconi Conference Center. Shortly thereafter, Marcus's father, Ben Wesson, fell ill with cancer and Marcus returned to Fresno with the others and planned to make a trip to Seattle to visit his ailing father.

Sofina maintained a relationship with the Wessons and she often supplied them with money and food. Ruby, on the other hand, had cut off all contact with Marcus and the others. By December 2003, 19-year-old Gypsy Wesson had also run away from home. Kiani missed her sisters but remained faithful to her father. On December 14 she wrote in her diary:

Gypsy my sweet sister,
It is time for you to come home. I miss you so much.
Christ wants you back home Lu.[32] Don't let the world

---

[32] A family nickname for Gypsy.

use you, you are much loved in your home. Gypsy
the time is near.

On the same page, Kiani wrote:

Ruby, my love forever,
You know the time is here for you to return, come
home now, God has a mission for us. Ruby, I know
you feel it too. I love you, we will be together as a
family soon.

By this time Kiani had two children by her father: 8-
year-old Illabelle and an infant named Jeva. For the most
part, Kiani only wrote about the surface events of the
family's life, but there seemed to be an unspoken sadness
in much of her journaling. She rarely spoke of or envi-
sioned her own future. Instead, her biggest joys in life were
eating ice cream and watching videos. She complained of
being tired and spoke of her father's pampered lifestyle.
The women would often scratch his head and armpits as
he sat in the living room:

I woke up at 9:00 am, took a shower. Everyone else
got up too. I folded my clothes. And I called the bank
to see if the $280.00 was taken out yesterday. Well,
Bre[33] called and there was a little mistake. Well, we
scratched dad's hair, dad told me to stop scratching
his hair . . . We were deciding if we should make
another attempt to pay Frank Muna . . . [34]

Without Ruby there, Kiani became terribly unhappy.
She missed her cousin desperately and had been counting
the days since Ruby had gone. Jeva was only five months

---

[33] A nickname for Wesson's daughter Sebhrenah.

[34] Kiani spent hours on the witness stand reading these and other entries from her journals.

old when Kiani wrote the following in her diary: "What am I going to do? I feel no hope right now. Usually I would be cleaning up real good, but nothing is motivating me. I feel bla, well to keep myself occupied I made dinner, made tortillas. I also braided my hair." The young woman who would later state publicly how happy everyone was in the family despite their unorthodox lifestyle, had lost hope. In late 2003, Kiani wrote, "My thoughts are torn apart, they just don't know where to go. Lord, guide me. I know it's the end of time but my thoughts are always looking, searching on the outside and we don't need anyone to be thinking like this in the situation we're in. But Lord I feel like it won't go away."

Even after her father's arrest, Kiani couldn't escape those gnawing feelings. On one of her many visits to the county jail, she had told her father she wanted to move to Las Vegas with her sister Gypsy.

"I'm thoroughly disappointed in you. Ashamed really," Marcus told his daughter from jail. "You're not following the Lord. You know what you should do? You should get a bald head. If you can't be faithful to me, you can't be faithful to the Lord."

In many of her diary entries, Kiani refers to the "girl talks," but never said what was discussed. Many times the discussions would last all night long: "Well, dad had talks, we had talks until 5:30 am, we watched *Parent Trap* and *Love Bug*." Court testimony revealed that Wesson was teaching the murder-suicide pact to his daughters and nieces during those discussions, and warned them about talking to anyone in the outside world. It appeared a strange choice, therefore, that Wesson allowed his family to watch Disney movies such as *Love Bug* and *Parent Trap,* which espouse such syrupy sweet worldviews. Perhaps it explained the children's obsession with movies: They provided an escape from the dark and isolated world Wesson had created.

"Once in a while he would say, you know, is everybody ready to die for the Lord?" Wesson's daughter Gypsy recalled. She said her father would ask the women this question every other day, explaining that the world was turning bad and that they should be ready to go at any time.

While Wesson's sons enjoyed a freedom that was not afforded their sisters or female cousins, there were certain lines not to be crossed by the male members of the family. Wesson's 23-year-old son Almae violated that code when he began a relationship with one of Elizabeth's nieces by marriage.[35] Marcus issued an angry written tirade entitled "The House of Elizabeth" to his sons. The fourteen-page handwritten letter was addressed to "All ye men of my house of Elizabeth," and harshly rebuked Almae for violating Wesson's "commandments," namely that the younger Wesson had "dishonored" his parents and committed "adultery." Wesson explained that he had set his sons "free" and made it clear that they were to "stay away from the females of [his] house." Quoting scriptures to support his point of view, Wesson warned that Almae's failure to discontinue his relationship with Elizabeth Wesson's niece would result in "a family prayer" that would cause God to "remove the offending entity."

The idea that Wesson's niece by marriage was part of his own personal harem seemed far-fetched, but it was something he ardently believed. While saturated in spiritual language, the sentiment of his rant was clear, and best summed up by the last sentence: "Get a life! Find your own women as God has commanded." In Wesson's eyes, he had afforded his sons freedom and independence with one caveat: They could not touch his women.

---

[35] Almae Wesson began a relationship with a woman named Marsha, who was married to Danny Solorio (Elizabeth Wesson's nephew).

* * *

After returning to Fresno, Marcus made some odd purchases that included ten large mahogany coffins, a dilapidated limousine, and a yellow school bus he had equipped with a hot tub. He purchased the coffins from Dugovic's Antiques in Fresno, where owner Lois Dugovic is still haunted by the image of the Wesson women loading the coffins onto the yellow school bus. "The girls carried the coffins," Dugovic remembered. "He didn't lift a finger." Wesson bought the antique caskets for about $400 apiece. He told Dugovic he planned to use the wood from the coffins to decorate the family's houseboat. Wesson's daughters and nieces made payments on the coffins after he had negotiated a price. The store owner told Wesson the caskets could not be delivered, so Wesson showed up weeks later in the renovated school bus. "He said, 'I bought a bus just so I can pick up these coffins,'" Dugovic said.

"We had coffins in the home because at the time we were looking into [buying more] boats," Rosa Solorio explained. "We were going to have some as armoires, like as closets for hanging clothing, and our furniture that we were going to build on the boat."

Despite that explanation, the coffins sat in several rooms of the Hammond house and were converted into beds for the youngest children. This was accomplished by placing a sleeping bag on top of each closed coffin. A piece of inch-thick plywood went on top of the sleeping bags so as not to damage the wood's finish. A cushion rested on top of the plywood. The children slept like that up until the day of the murders.

While testifying at her father's trial, Kiani Wesson said the idea that the coffins were related to her father's obsession with vampires was just playful in nature:

Q. And do you recall all of you girls writing your names—
   your vampires' names in the dust on the coffins?

A. Yeah. 'Cause we were just playing around. And we were just following Fia and Ruby. They start writing their names. And they said, "Hey, you guys, let's write our name on there." So we were just playing around.

While they remained seemingly ignorant to the sexual abuse happening in the Wesson home, Wesson's sons were well aware of their father's idiosyncrasies, including his fascination with vampires. Then 22-year-old Marcus Wesson Jr. told police following the murders that his father claimed to have "special powers," including mental telepathy, and that he claimed to be in spiritual contact with all of his relatives. "He knew when I was suffering," Marcus Jr. recalled. " He says the Lord tells him everything."

To those on the outside, the Wesson family seemed eccentric, but to those with a closer perspective, the concern for the youngest Wesson children only grew deeper as time went on. In a letter that was not dated but written to Elizabeth Wesson while the family lived on Hammond Avenue, Marcus's father, Ben Wesson, expressed an urgent concern about the children and encouraged the family to relocate to Seattle:

> Hi Liz—
>
> Just a few lines to let you know how very much we love you—and my (our) grandchildren. How is your mother? Give my love and regards to your brother and sisters—
>
> Why don't you and Marcus hurry and send your things and come here to Seattle? Investigate first and see what kind of business venture you want to do—

The elder Wesson went on to say that he could help find his son a job in Seattle and advised his daughter-in-law that the family should be faithfully attending church "regardless of [their] circumstances."

The letter concluded:

> Please *come here—and let us put those children in school—when the authorities find out how old they are—and the fact is—that they have never been to school—the fact is—Marcus does not realize it— but they will see his picture & yours—and the children in every newspaper—*
>
> *I will help him to put them in private school for a year or two (Adventist) until that can get a bearing—*
>
> *I don't want the problem to get any bigger—Please consider—*
>
> *Love,*
> *Ben*

Although he seemed aware of a potential disaster, it's not likely that Ben Wesson could have imagined that the growing problem he referred to would end in the mass murder of his grandchildren.

Just twenty-four hours before the killings, the family was preparing to make the trip to Seattle to visit Marcus's parents (the family was to evacuate the Hammond Avenue home by March 12). An employee of the storage facility where Marcus kept one of his two buses observed the women working frantically on the bus. "The girls were wearing dresses and working on the bus," Lisa Zamaripa said. "We thought that was kind of strange." The family was apparently using the older school bus for spare parts in an effort to repair the newer bus that was parked in front of the home. In the days that preceded the murders, neighbors reported that the Wesson women had worked on the bus in the driveway well into the late hours of the night; some of the women held flashlights while the others worked. More importantly, the secret Wesson had worked so hard to keep in Santa Cruz, Marshall, and in Fresno was still intact: No one on the outside had any idea there were seven children living inside the house.

PART SIX:

THE TRIAL

ONE

Television cameras were rolling as Marcus Wesson made his first court appearance during an arraignment hearing on March 17, 2004. The hearing took place in one of two courtrooms located inside the Fresno County Jail, where hundreds of inmates were shuffled through a revolving door to enter pleas to their alleged crimes and often to have a public defender assigned to their cases. Such was the order of business in Judge Brant Bramer's courtroom; he was fastidious, swift, and fair. But Marcus Wesson was about to bring the morning's court schedule to an abrupt halt.

The courtroom had filled with some of Wesson's family and was packed with reporters from every major TV network and from newspapers across California. Outside, photographers waited to chase down family members and attorneys, following the hearing, and satellite trucks with large round dishes lined the street.

"The court calls the case of Marcus Delon Wesson," Judge Bramer announced. Wesson entered the courtroom, and like the other inmates who had appeared in court that morning, he stood off to the side of the judge's bench in a small room visible to those in the gallery through a window. His arms and legs were shackled and he stepped forward into a small area surrounded by a four and a half foot wall. He wore a yellow jail-issued jumpsuit and his graying dreadlocks hung down his back. He was stoic as he glanced into the gallery; he seemed unfazed by the formality of the proceedings.

Wesson objected as the judge attempted to assign a public defender to the case.

"Please, I beg thee, I don't want a public defender," Wesson said. He explained that he had an attorney whom he was unable to contact because jail officials were not allowing him to make phone calls.

"What is your attorney's name, Mr. Wesson?" Bramer asked.

Wesson refused to answer. "Is that necessary?" he replied.

Bramer was losing patience. "Is there anyone here to represent Mr. Wesson?" the judge asked, addressing the courtroom.

A hand shot up from the gallery. "I am! I love you, Dad!" Wesson's 23-year-old son Almae blurted out.

"No, I'm looking for an attorney," Bramer advised. "Please sit down," he told Almae.

Almae refused. "I love you, Dad! I love you, Dad!" he shouted again.

Wesson seemed unaffected by the outburst. Almae would not quiet down and continued to proclaim his love for his father as two bailiffs escorted him out of the courtroom.

After the commotion was over, Wesson told the judge, "I have a lawyer, sir, I just can't contact him." Bramer agreed to allow Wesson twenty-four hours to contact his attorney.

"We have to proceed one way or another," Bramer warned Wesson. "At that time, you need to have a lawyer here or we will appoint one to you."

Ultimately, Wesson would not get his wish to have the attorney of his choice. A week later, Fresno attorney David Mugridge refused the case once he discovered Wesson had no means to pay for his defense. An attorney from the Public Defender's Office was assigned. On March 25, 2004, with public defender Pete Jones at his side, Wesson pleaded not guilty to nine counts of murder and what would eventually amount to fourteen sex charges ranging from forcible oral copulation to rape. District Attorney Elizabeth Egan announced that her office would seek the death penalty.

Outside the courthouse, Wesson's children defended their father. They deflected questions about incest and polygamy but said they wanted the right to visit Wesson in jail.

"Nobody knows Marcus," Wesson's daughter Kiani told a group of reporters who had chased her into the street. "I just wish everyone would stop telling lies out there. We're dealing with a man's life."

TWO

The following chapter includes excerpts of conversations that occurred at the Fresno County Jail between Marcus and Elizabeth Wesson. The majority of dialogue is taken from a visit Elizabeth made to the jail on December 10, 2004. Audio recordings of these conversations were played for the jury.

Elizabeth Wesson climbed the stairs outside the Fresno County Jail. She signed in, passed through security, and waited patiently to see her husband. He had been in jail for nine months, and since his arrest Elizabeth had found it hard to find her way in the world. She didn't have a job and claimed not to have a permanent place to stay. On this visit she came to ask her husband what she should do about all of their mounting unpaid bills.

Marcus walked into the small room divided by a thick pane of glass, sat down and picked up the telephone receiver hanging on the wall.

"Hi," he said.

"Hi," Elizabeth replied.

"Everything okay?" he asked.

"Yeah. I tried to come and see you Wednesday but they wouldn't tell me how long I would have to wait."

Marcus laughed. "Oh, shoot. Yeah. They told me you came."

"Oh, they did?"

"A couple of days ago. And they said, Marcus, sorry, but she said she couldn't wait. And I said okay."

"No. He . . . he wouldn't give me an answer," Elizabeth insisted nervously. "I . . . I . . . I told him, I go look. I could be an hour to two hours, he said."

"So everything's okay?" Marcus asked.

"Yeah, yeah."

"You sure?"

"Uh-huh. I just wanted . . . I didn't want to waste this week. I wanted to see you."

"Oh, okay."

Elizabeth told Marcus that she had received an envelope in the mail from him with no letter inside.

"Oh, no. You gotta be kidding," Marcus said. "Why would they do that?"

"I don't know. No . . . no . . . I thought I'd let you know about that, and, uh . . . Marcus, um . . . we need to sell . . . well, I need to sell some furniture so I can pay some bills."

Elizabeth explained that she needed to pay the taxes and that the county was threatening to put a lien on the house. (The family had already been evicted.)

"Yeah, but the lien is just a lien," Marcus reassured his wife. "They can't take the house. By the time they get through with the administrative paperwork and all that, and the hearing, uh . . . you'll have it. Those are just scare tactics."

"Did you go to court today?" Elizabeth asked.

"Yeah."

"What was it for? I didn't get to see the news," she said.

"To change a couple of things on a motion, that's all. How'd you know?"

"A friend called . . . called us on the phone. They said that you were on the news."

"I wasn't on no news," Marcus replied.

"Yeah, you were on the news," Elizabeth assured him.

"Oh, really? You saw me?"

"Well no. I didn't see . . . they saw you."

"Oh."

"Yeah. Every time they bring you out, you . . . you're news." Elizabeth laughed.

"Oh, my God. I didn't know I was on the news," Marcus said, shaking his head.

Elizabeth paused.

"Yeah. So, um . . . I thought I'd let you know that I'm basically living by myself," she said.

"What do you mean?"

"Well, you know Rosa is moving somewhere else, you know, that's safe. You know, it . . . it's okay. It's not gonna be far, you know. But, um . . . most likely, I'll . . . I'll be by myself. That's the way she wants it."

"No, the Lord told me that this morning," Marcus said.

"Yeah?"

"He was telling me all night last night that she's going to do that. Bee . . . He said . . . He said that she's doing it for love."

Marcus changed the subject. "I feel like I look old," he said.

"You look the same to me," Elizabeth replied.

"The same? There's no wrinkles here?" Marcus said, pointing to his face.

"No."

"Oh God, I feel like I'm . . . I mean, I haven't seen a mirror, but I've been feeling my skin, and gee, what do I look like?" Marcus laughed.

"You look the same, Marcus."

"I do, really?"

"Yeah. The same."

"I'm glad to see you," Marcus said.

"Yeah?"

"I'm glad you came."

Elizabeth continued to fret about the taxes.

"Forget about the taxes," Marcus told her. "You can go . . . you can go a year without paying the taxes."

"Well then it's just—" Elizabeth began.

"Lady, listen to me, please. Baby, listen baby. If you need money to go search for a house to live, you don't have to pay all of the taxes. You can pay part."

Elizabeth told Marcus that the children had all scattered and that she was worried about making it on her own. He told her that the Lord would provide an apartment for her to live in.

"Right now, the Lord needs to work," Marcus said. "Listen. He wants to work. That's what He told me. And then He wants to work on everybody. He said there are people in the house separating. Everybody. He says that's the way I wanted it. Then He's gonna bring everyone back together. And He says *you* are gonna bring all the kids back," he said to Elizabeth. Marcus laughed. "He knows what's He's doing. Baby, He's strengthening the family. That's why He let everything else happen. He's strengthening the family. And then, when everyone gets strengthened, He'll bring them back."

Marcus continued. "And you . . . He's working on you, *mija*. He said He's gonna get you. He's gonna work on you. He said He's gonna get you to confess." Marcus laughed.

"Confess?" Elizabeth asked, confused.

"Whatever," Marcus replied. "You and Him know."

"I—" Elizabeth began.

"I don't, but you know," Marcus interrupted. "He's gonna get you to do that. He's gonna work on you. He says that you're gonna leave me for about five minutes. You'll be mad for five minutes."

"Oh, don't believe that Marcus," Elizabeth said.

"No . . . you . . . no, no. You're gonna separate from me. You're gonna leave me for five minutes and then you'll get your head together."

Elizabeth nodded and moved on to more practical

matters. She told Marcus she needed to buy new tires for the car. He told Elizabeth the Lord had spoken to him about that, too, and that she should buy tires on Sunday.

"Babe, come on. Admit this," Marcus said. "When I was out there, everything I did had the Midas touch."

"Yeah," Elizabeth replied.

Marcus told his wife he had been feeling an electric current in his head since his arrest.

"I woke up laughing and I was shaking the bed. They're going to think I'm having convulsions." He laughed. "I was laughing so hearty I couldn't believe it."

"You always start laughing in your sleep," Elizabeth said.

"I'm not going to lie to you," Marcus replied. "You know that Indiana Jones movie where you hear that whip noise? When I wake up I hear static electricity. I turn my eyes each way . . . I feel shocked. I feel like I am getting shocked. I've been hearing this for four to five months. It's real. The Lord says He's never seen that from the beginning of time since man was mixing with angels . . . the Lord said I have this angelic brain."

Marcus told his wife that the Lord had put him in jail for a single reason: to lose weight. Once he reached his goal weight and had lost 190 pounds, the Lord would set him free, he said.

"Because I'm not here to cause trouble for people. I'm here to do what the Lord says. I'm here losing weight. Then I'm going to do something in court. I'll be done. You think I'm going to spend the rest of my life for a stupid little stunt? Forget it. No, I'm here to do my job. I done it. I'm here to show people kindness, respect. And I'm here to model inmates to do in the Lord. I'm in God's jail."

The conversation shifted between talk of spiritual matters to more practical subjects without transition. The couple discussed the current price of gasoline and politics.

"Republicans are mean-spirited, they don't care about

welfare and all that," Marcus said. "But Democrats want to make government bigger. That's why I'm not a Democrat . . . I don't want the government in my life."

Wesson continued his political commentary: "So they put Rush Limbaugh on Clinton's butt and then after eight years it paid off. Republicans are destroying the world at ninety miles per hour and Democrats are doing it at forty-five miles per hour."

Seconds later Marcus referred to the End Times. He then described a conversation he claimed to have had with the Lord in which he asked the Lord why his children had to die.

Marcus quoted the Lord saying, " 'They weren't ready, they would have been in darkness.' And to hear some crap like that scared me," Marcus said. "Finally I said, why didn't you take me? 'Because you weren't ready' [the Lord said]. So He wants me to do some serious work for Him."

Marcus spent much of his time in jail working on the fourth part of an autobiographical work entitled "In the Night of the Light for the Dark." Several reliable sources in and around the jail would confirm that when Wesson wasn't writing, he spent much of his time isolated in his cell masturbating; he would then smear his ejaculate into his dreadlocks. Local media found the development too unsavory to report.

Marcus told his wife he had also been composing songs while in jail. One was a country western song about his dead children. He sang some of it for her:

> *"This is a guitar blazing in my campfire,*
> *wondering why they took them from me.*
> *Tears made my eyes see blurry as I sat and drank*
> *   my coffee.*
> *I can see my wife, the one who used to light*
> *   my candle.*
> *But when I ride, I can see my children with me."*

At this point in the song Marcus began to cry. "I can't sing no more, baby," he said.

Elizabeth asked Marcus if he was comfortable in his cell. He told her that he was toughening himself and that he hadn't brushed his teeth, washed his face, or shaven in more than a year.

"Honest," he assured her. Elizabeth laughed.

"If you don't stay tough, *mija,* you're gonna lose. If a world hates you, you gotta be tough. So please, get your booty to the apartment," he said, and then laughed. A serious look came over his face. "'Cuz God is so angry at our family for what happened. He is mad. I mean really. I haven't heard the Lord use words like He has. I'm serious. He's telling me some stuff you don't even want to hear."

Elizabeth began to cry.

"What's wrong baby? What?" Marcus asked.

"Nothing. It's just . . . it's . . . I don't have it in me, Marcus."

"Well then get it," Marcus replied. "You're the mother, *mija.* You know your spirit will dictate how they feel. Look here. If Mama ain't happy, who's happy? You're the head of the house. Look at me. Don't I have a reason to feel downtrodden? And what am I doing? I'm spirit for you and everybody."

THREE

On a cool January morning more than five hundred people lined up outside the Fresno County Plaza building,
having received jury summonses for what had been
dubbed the trial of "Fresno's worst mass murder." Since
the district attorney had decided to pursue the death penalty against Wesson, and because of the high profile nature of the case and the number of potential jurors, the
ballroom on the first floor had been transformed into a
makeshift courtroom. The room had been set up theater
style, with more than five hundred seats facing a stage
built with risers. Two fold-up tables sat on either side of a
podium from which the judge would conduct the hearing.

The line of potential jurors stretched from the door of
the ballroom across a courtyard and down the sidewalk.
Some already seemed annoyed at being called as potential panelists, while others were curious to get a glimpse
of the man accused of orchestrating the mass killing of
his own family. It took two and a half hours for all the
potential jurors to make their way through metal detec-
tors and to have their belongings searched, and then another forty-five minutes for the jury commissioner to take
roll call once everyone had been seated. Potential jurors
chewed gum and glanced at their watches. Some complained that this was cutting into a personal errand or
a job commitment they had scheduled that morning. But

the murmur of all those concerns fell silent when Marcus Wesson walked into the room.

Unlike at his arraignment, Wesson's feet were not shackled. He walked on stage wearing a black shirt and pants; his dreadlocks were tied behind his head in a pony-tail. Mesmerized, the crowd watched as he took his seat between two defense attorneys from the Public Defend-er's Office, Pete Jones and Ralph Torres.

Superior Court Judge R. L. Putnam was known for his meticulous nature. He appeared strangely out of place behind the ballroom podium and the proceedings seemed more like a convention at a Las Vegas hotel than a court hearing. The judge explained to those gathered in the ballroom that they could choose to fill out a jury question-naire or a hardship form, explaining why they were un-able to serve as jurors on the case. But first, Putnam said, he was going to let the attorneys introduce themselves and the defendant. Putnam turned to the defense table and Pete Jones stood up.

"My name is Pete Jones and this is my colleague Ralph Torres. I'd like to introduce you to our client, Marcus Delon Wesson," Jones told the crowd. Wesson rose to his feet and bowed. The room remained silent.

Putnam turned to his right, where Deputy District At-torney Lisa Gamoian sat alone. She introduced herself in a confident, clear voice.

Judge Putnam then read out loud the complaint against Wesson, which outlined the accusations he faced. As Putnam listed the charges, Wesson buried his face in his hands.

The attempt on the part of Wesson's attorneys to have the trial moved out of Fresno County failed, and by the end of a one-month jury selection process, twelve panelists were selected to decide Marcus Wesson's fate. They included a retired soccer coach, a stay-at-home mother of three boys, a security guard, and a domestic violence educator for the

Health Department. The panel was made up of seven women and five men, and represented a diversity of backgrounds except in one glaring regard: There were no African-Americans on the jury.[36] The trial would get under way just days before the one-year anniversary of the killings.

On March 3, 2005, the mass murder trial of Marcus Delon Wesson began with opening statements, and prosecutor Lisa Gamoian was first to address the jury. She had earned the nickname "Go-go Gamoian" and "Lisa the Lioness" from her colleagues for good reason: She took her job seriously and pursued her cases with persistence and a rare tenacity. Her demeanor was businesslike and direct, and she was focused on seeing that Marcus Wesson was convicted on all counts and that the jury would return with a verdict to have him executed. The D.A. had decided against pursuing conspiracy charges against any of the surviving family members, and seemed to be focused solely on Wesson as the perpetrator of the crimes. For months Gamoian had lived and breathed the case. She had memorized family histories and facts of the case and could regurgitate them at will. She had familiarized herself with thousands of pages of evidence, and there was so little time to spare in her sixteen-hour workdays that she often ate her meals out of a vending machine.

Promising a "road map for the journey," Gamoian outlined the People's case against Wesson for the twelve jurors. She pointed to a huge family tree on a corkboard that measured eight feet long and four feet high positioned awkwardly in a corner of the courtroom. She explained Wesson's polygamous relationships with his daughters and nieces and spoke of the evidence: the feud that lead to the murders, the position of the bodies, and the nature of

---

[36] According to the 2000 census, African-Americans made up 5.3 percent of Fresno County's population.

the victims' wounds. There were no identifiable fingerprints on the gun or on the magazine inside it, but the
prosecutor said Sebhrenah's DNA had been discovered on
the weapon. Gamoian pointed out that the site mark of the
gunshot wounds was pointed in an upward direction on
all the victims except for the oldest. The sight mark on
Sebhrenah Wesson's wound was pointed down, Gamoian
said. The prosecutor would later argue that it would prove
an awkward way to kill oneself.

Gamoian gave the jury a short family history explaining
the Wesson family's nomadic lifestyle and Wesson's inadequate attempts to home-school his children. Gamoian
said that Wesson would discipline his children by hitting
them with a stick wrapped in duct tape or with a baseball
bat. She described intense Bible studies that would happen
three times a day in which Wesson would offer his interpretations of the scriptures, effectively brainwashing them
with his teachings.

"In the Wesson family, there was something called
'loving,'" Gamoian said. She explained it was Wesson's
term for the sexual abuse that happened in the home, saying the abuse began when the girls were as young as
eleven years old.

"The defendant would rub the girls over their clothing
on the vagina and breasts, and then moved to rubbing and
touching them under their clothes," Gamoian explained
matter-of-factly. She said the touching would progress to
Wesson forcing the girls to perform oral sex on him and
then forcing them to have sex with one another. It would
then ultimately lead to Wesson raping and impregnating
his own children.

Gamoian described ceremonies conducted by Wesson
in which he exchanged marriage vows with his daughters
and nieces. He presented the girls with rings, and with
their hands on the Bible, he made them swear their faithfulness to him. When the girls turned eighteen, Gamoian
said, they were sent out to find jobs, and many of them

worked at fast-food restaurants. Wesson collected their paychecks and distributed allowances to the women; he alone controlled the money.

When the girls were in their teens, Wesson began periodic "girl talks." Gamoian said at these talks, Wesson instituted a family murder-suicide pact, teaching the older girls to kill the children and then themselves in order to "be with the Lord."

Gamoian finished by asking jurors for their patience; it would be a long trial and it would take months for her to make her case. But she assured the jurors that when it was over, they would have no doubt that Marcus Wesson was guilty as charged.

As Gamoian made her opening statement, defense attorney Ralph Torres sat on Marcus Wesson's right side. Torres leaned back in his chair, his head nearly touching Wesson's shoulder. Torres had a look of incredulity on his face. After Gamoian had finished, Torres stood and walked across the room toward the jury box. It had been decided that the more veteran lawyer on the team, Pete Jones, would handle the penalty phase of the trial, giving the younger and less experienced attorney the opportunity to defend the city's most high-profile case in more than a decade.

Torres was a confident and deliberate attorney, and if he had fears or doubts about his case, they would never manifest themselves in the courtroom. As he began his opening statement, the defense strategy became clear: They would argue that Sebhrenah Wesson had killed her siblings and then herself. Torres said Sebhrenah was fascinated with guns and that she kept bullets and folding knives in her purse. She talked about joining the Army, the public defender said. He spoke of a tape recording made by a family member on the day of the murders, calling it "a blessing in disguise."

"You will hear it," he promised the jury.

Torres said that at 2:10 P.M. you could hear Sofina on the audio recording trying to get her son Jonathan. You could hear women fighting and Sebhrenah calling Sofina a "fucking whore," Torres explained. Family members would testify that Sebhrenah was acting as if she was demon-possessed and spoke in the husky uncharacteristic voice of a man.

Torres told the jury that Marcus Wesson was the peacemaker on the day of the murders. Wesson was in disbelief and trying to calm everyone down. His voice could be heard on the recording at 3:23 P.M., placing him at the front door of the house, Torres explained. The public defender said he would present evidence that seven of the victims were killed before that time, before Wesson ever entered the southeast bedroom. Liver temperature tests performed on some of those killed determined that the children died at least one to two hours before the oldest victims, Lise and Sebhrenah.

"And the wound to Sebhrenah's eye is consistent with suicide," Torres added.

Torres also promised that jurors would be able to hear gunshots on the tape before Wesson's voice disappeared from the recording.

As for the sex charges, Torres admitted they were indisputable, conceding that Wesson was a "flawed man" who engaged in "deviant behavior." But Torres denied the existence of a murder-suicide plan instituted by the defendant.

"There was no plan," Torres assured the jury. He quoted Wesson's niece Ruby Ortiz, who said, "There was never a plan. It was just talk."

"Even Kiani Wesson said, 'About five years ago we all agreed that if the government ever came to take the children we would rather take their lives ourselves," Torres said. He paused then added, "But even she said, 'I could never hurt the children.'"

Torres painted the picture of a happy family.

"Friday was a family day to eat ice cream and watch movies," he told the jury. He said the Wessons owned almost two thousand movies on videotape, and Torres listed some of the titles: *Home Alone 1* and *2*, *Rebel Without a Cause*, *Gladiator*, *A Few Good Men*, *The Hand that Rocks the Cradle*, *Cannonball Run 2*, *Raiders of the Lost Ark*, and *Rocky*. He explained that many of the VHS tapes had been discovered aboard one of two school buses owned by the family.

Torres finished his opening statement by assuring the jury, "He didn't shoot them. The evidence will show you that Sebhrenah shot all the kids and then herself."

FOUR

"The People call Sofina Solorio to the stand," the prosecutor announced. The doors of the courtroom opened and Sofina, who hadn't spoken publicly since the murders, stepped forward. She seemed surprisingly unshaken, and she spoke confidently as she was sworn in. She swept her long straight hair behind her shoulders as she took the witness stand.

"I want to begin by drawing your attention to March 12, 2004," the prosecutor said. "On that day, did you come to Fresno?"

"Yes," Sofina replied.

"Why?" Gamoian asked.

"I came to Fresno to get my son. For one thing, I was off that day from work and we felt that if we didn't get them as soon as possible that they were going to flee," Sofina said. She explained that her sister Ruby was having the Wesson house watched.

"What did Ruby tell you that she had seen that led you to the belief that the Wessons were fleeing and you needed to go on March the twelfth to get your kids?" Gamoian asked.

"She seen Marcus with several of the girls working on the motor home or the bus late at night."

Sofina described the details of March 12, beginning with her arrival at the Wesson home and the ensuing cus-

BY THEIR FATHER'S HAND 165

tody fight. The prosecutor showed her photos of the interior of the house, and Sofina pointed out where she fought with her sister Rosa and her cousins and pointed out the southeast bedroom, where she last saw the children alive.

Sofina then described how she came to live with the Wesson family. She explained that when she was ten years old she was living with her mother and grandmother in a duplex on North College Avenue in Fresno. Her brothers and sisters and many of her uncles also lived with them in what she called the "front house." Among the uncles was Adair, the biological child of Marcus Wesson (Wesson had impregnated his mother-in-law, Rosemary Maytorena, before marrying her teenage daughter Elizabeth).

A year later, when Sofina was eleven, she moved to the back of the house with her mother and siblings. They lived upstairs, and that year the Wessons moved into the downstairs part of the duplex. Within months her brothers had moved downstairs to live with the Wessons, and the Solorios' lifestyle dramatically changed under Marcus Wesson's influence. Sofina could no longer eat meat or anything with sugar. Sodas were banned from the family's diet and the children were not allowed to watch TV. Sofina could no longer wear pants; the girls were mandated to wear skirts that came to their ankles. Her mother forbade her and the other girls from wearing clothes with any kind of print or pattern, and they wore long-sleeve shirts and scarves to cover their heads. At the time, no one in the house was working, Sofina told the court. Her mother received welfare and food stamps that she shared with Marcus Wesson.

The changes the family experienced were rooted in her family's newfound spirituality. Wesson held family prayer three times daily in the downstairs living room, at 9:00 A.M., noon, and 7:00 P.M., and would deliver sermons on his own biblical interpretations for about an hour per session. Evening prayer would sometimes last for two hours, and Sofina explained if the younger children fell asleep while Marcus was talking, they were taken into a back room and spanked.

Sofina stopped attending public school because Marcus had taken on the task of home-schooling the children. She testified that he would give them textbooks and without explanation tell them to write reports. If they performed poorly, he would hit them with a stick wrapped in duct tape.

More than educating the children, Wesson's primary concern was keeping the girls and boys away from one another. Sofina explained that Wesson didn't want the girls to develop "feelings" for any of their brothers or cousins. There were even two couches in the downstairs living room: one for the girls, another for the boys.

When Sofina and the other girls became teenagers, Marcus forbade them to go outside. He warned that there were boys in the neighborhood who would notice the girls and have "sexual feelings" for them. He also warned the girls that they could get in trouble with the police if someone discovered that they weren't attending public school. So from the age of eleven until fourteen, Sofina couldn't leave the house. She even had to ask permission to go into the backyard. The boys, on the other hand, could skateboard in the neighborhood after finishing their evening chores. The girls could only speak to the boys out of necessity—to tell them that a meal had been prepared or to pass along a message from Marcus—but under no circumstances could the girls joke around or play with their brothers or male cousins.

Sofina was still sleeping upstairs where her mother lived, but Rosemary Solorio had become disengaged from the strict family life commandeered by her brother-in-law. She no longer took part in prayer or helped home-school her children. She no longer cooked meals, and she refused to dress as the other women did. She began to slowly fade from her children's lives. One day Marcus explained to

Sofina that his rules were too much for her mother to handle. He told Sofina that her mother had handed custody of her children over to him.

With her mother out of the picture, and at the tender age of eleven, Sofina took over the role of home-schooling the younger children: Marco, Martin, Serafino, Lise, Gypsy, Marcus Jr., and Almae. Not knowing how to teach, she would tell the children to draw pictures while she did her homework. She was the teacher in the house, and along with the other girls, she cooked and cleaned.

"Now, did there ever come a time when you became familiar with the term 'loving'?" Gamoian asked.

"Yes," Sofina replied.

"Who explained what loving is to you?"

"Marcus," Sofina said. "He said loving is touching but he didn't really say it. He just did it and he called it loving."

"And how old were you when he first introduced you to loving?"

"Twelve," she said.

Sofina recalled the first time Marcus had touched her. He took her into a small room downstairs. He began to feel her inner thigh and between her legs with her clothes on, she explained.

"He's like 'Why are you so tense?' He goes, 'Somebody has touched you before.' And he goes, 'Who was it?' And I go, 'No one.' He goes, 'No, somebody's been touching you before.'"

For several hours Wesson persisted with his questions and Sofina kept denying the accusation.

"He told me, 'We're not going to leave until you tell me.' And I would get tired and I would, like, almost fall asleep. He said, 'Wake up. You know, the devil's in you.'"

For hours Sofina resisted answering. Finally Wesson told her, "We'll continue this tomorrow."

The next day Sofina gave in and admitted to Marcus

that one of her uncles had molested her. They were again alone in the same room.

"He said, 'What he did to you is wrong. He was molesting you. That was wrong. He had no, you know, right to be touching you like that,'" Sofina explained. Marcus told Sofina that he wanted to teach her the "right way" to have sex with a man.

"He says, you know, 'This is what I do to my girls.' He goes, 'I call that loving. You know, everybody else calls it molestation or the world will say it's molestation, but this is loving. This is teaching my daughters how to love their husbands when they meet their husbands.'"

Sofina said that Wesson began rubbing her back and her upper thighs and then started kissing her on the lips. He introduced her to French kissing, instructing her to stick out her tongue and then began to touch her between her legs. Sofina described the graphic sequence of events methodically.

"Then he would put my hand on his penis," she said. "And he was like, 'Okay. Just rub it.' He goes, 'Pinch it. Rub it.' And then once I was doing it he would go, 'Yeah, like that. Like that.'"

She explained that Marcus raised up her skirt and pulled down her panties and penetrated her with his fingers.

"He would just say things like, 'Oh, baby,' you know, 'It's nice.' You know, 'It's wet.' His penis was already out, out of his pants. He had me rub it and start kissing it," Sofina said.

"And how old were you when he had you first start kissing his penis?" Gamoian asked.

"Twelve and a half," Sofina replied.

She said Marcus began instructing her on how to perform oral sex on a man.

"He goes, 'Put your mouth on it.' He goes, 'Now just go down.' But I would just like, you know, go not all the way down because I would get choked up. He would say,

'No, take it easy. Now come up.' And he was just show-ing me how, you know, how to do him."

Sofina said that Marcus ejaculated in her mouth but she refused to swallow his semen even though he insisted on it. These sessions of oral sex happened three times a week, Sofina testified. At the age of fourteen, she said, her uncle Marcus used an asthma inhaler to penetrate her. Several jurors shook their heads in disgust as she re-lated the story from the witness stand.

As time went on, Marcus introduced other girls into his "loving" sessions with Sofina. She told the court that when she was thirteen he forced her and her sister to orally copulate him at the same time. She told the court of another incident in which Wesson had all of the girls in the back room of the house performing various sex acts on him.

"Now, did Mr. Wesson ever have the girls perform sex on each other?" Gamoian asked.

"Yes," Sofina replied.

"And how old were you when that first happened?"

"I was seventeen."

She explained that Marcus didn't want the girls to be-come jealous of one another if he showed more attention to any one girl over the others. He reasoned that the girls should love each other.

"He had Sebhrenah rub my breasts. He had Ruby and Rosie kissing, or else he'll have Kiani rubbing Ruby's breasts," Sofina testified.

"And what was he doing while the girls were doing this as he directed?" the prosecutor asked.

"He was just watching and telling who to touch who."

"How long would this session last?"

"A couple hours."

Sofina said she was nineteen years old when she first had intercourse with her uncle Marcus. The whole country had been watching a disaster unfold in Waco, Texas, as the Branch Davidians faced off with the federal government.

Marcus enthusiastically invited the children, who were not allowed to watch television without special permission, to watch the news coverage with him. Sofina and the other children sat and watched wide-eyed as the Davidian complex burned and as David Koresh's photograph flashed on the screen.

Sofina said that Wesson had the highest admiration for Koresh and called him a "man of God." She told the court that Wesson felt the government was unfairly interfering with Koresh's leadership of his own family.

"He's like, 'You know what? That's a shame that they have to go in there and enter into his home and disrupt that family.' He goes, 'David Koresh died because of what he felt was right,' " Sofina testified.

Sofina said that it was while the family was watching coverage of the disaster in Waco that Wesson announced that he wanted to have many more children. He told the girls that Elizabeth was getting older and had passed her childbearing years.

"He had said that he always wanted to have children for the Lord and that, you know, he didn't have enough. And that, um, us girls, you know, God's coming really soon and that we should have children with him," Sofina said.

"Did Mr. Wesson ever make any statements about why he believed David Koresh had all those children?" Gamoian asked.

"Yes."

"What did he say?"

"He said that David Koresh had all those children because he wanted to take them all to the Lord. Like when God came, he had like more abundance. He got more people for the Lord."

So the girls had agreed to have "babies for the Lord," as Wesson put it. It had been decided that Ruby would be the primary care giver and that the others would act as surrogate mothers for Elizabeth. Once the girls had all agreed they wanted to have Marcus's children, he called a family meeting with just the women in the house and announced the plan to his wife.

"Marcus had said that, you know, 'The girls would like to have a baby. They would like for you to be the surrogate mother,'" Sofina testified.

"And did Elizabeth Wesson respond?"

"Yes."

"What did she say?"

"She's like, 'What do you mean?' And he was just like, 'Yes, they would like to all have children.' And Elizabeth's like, 'Is that what you girls really want?' And we're like, 'Yes.' And she said, 'You know what,' she goes, 'I don't know.' She goes, 'We need to talk about this, Marcus.'"

If Elizabeth had any objections to her husband's plan to impregnate their daughters and nieces, they did not prevent the plan from moving forward. As always, Elizabeth acquiesced to her husband's demands.

When Sofina turned twenty-one she and Marcus took part in a private marriage ceremony. Sofina testified that Marcus took her into a room and had her place her hand on the Bible and swear her faithfulness to him. They exchanged marriage vows and he presented her with a wedding ring.

"The main thing that I remember was being faithful to him," Sofina said.

On March 14, 1996, Sofina gave birth to her uncle's child. She named him Jonathan Saint Charles Wesson. Shortly after he was born, Jonathan stopped breathing and had to be hospitalized. He recovered, and Sofina kept a journal to record his progress and recovery. One month after he was born, Sofina wrote, "Jonathan is perfectly fine. He eats well. He stays awake more often. He is aware of my voice. He is a very sweet boy." In a subsequent entry Sofina noted her son's senses waking to the outside world: "He tries to crawl. He likes to be talked to and his new name is 'Take Charge.' We went down the hill in [the car] and Jonathan loved it. He watched the trees go by and he stared around, enjoying the ride." Sofina's close observation of her son continued into his youth. On his fourth birthday Sofina wrote, "Jonathan is really tall and very smart. He was potty trained at three years old. Walked at one. He can reach the restroom faucet to wash his hands and turn the light on."

Marcus Wesson would eventually share wedding vows and also give rings to his daughters Kiani and Sebhrenah, and to Sofina's sisters, Rosa and Ruby. Wesson decided not to impregnate the girls until they were at least seventeen and a half. He explained if it happened too soon it could be considered statutory rape and he could get into trouble with the law. When the girls became pregnant, he told them to tell those who asked that they had been artificially inseminated.

But that was not the only secret Sofina and the other girls were guarding. According to Sofina, Marcus had taught the female family members that if the government ever found out how they were living they would be separated and would "lose [their] souls." So he instructed the older girls to carry out a murder-suicide pact if Child Protective Services ever came to take the children. Wesson met with the older girls about once a month, Sofina said, to discuss the method of a mass suicide.

"We decided the fastest way was to put the gun in our mouth and point it up. We were supposed to take our child's life and then ours," Sofina explained.

After Sofina "married" her uncle Marcus, they had sexual intercourse about three times a week. Sofina said that on one occasion her aunt Elizabeth walked into the bedroom while she was performing oral sex on Marcus. Wesson had instructed Sofina to leave her clothes on during their sexual encounters in case his wife Elizabeth ever walked into the room. She was on her knees and Marcus was lying on the bed. Sofina jumped up when her aunt Elizabeth opened the bedroom door.

"She said, 'Marcus, what are you doing?' And he covered himself. And he's like, 'Bee,' and she's like, 'I told you, you know, not to . . . I give you certain times for you to be doing this stuff,'" Sofina told the court.

Sofina pulled her skirt down over her waist and her aunt Elizabeth told her to get out of the room.[37] She went into the living room and sat on the couch. For two hours Elizabeth and Marcus were in the bedroom with the door closed. Sofina wondered what they could be saying. Were they arguing? Would her aunt treat her differently after this? Her fears subsided the next day. Elizabeth treated her no differently and Sofina's "marriage" to her uncle remained unaffected.

The prosecutor then asked Sofina tell the jury what led Marcus to stab her when the family was living aboard the *Sudan*. Sofina explained the situation: that Marcus was angry with her for developing a relationship with a man she worked with and that she was unhappy living on the boat. She told Marcus that she would prefer to live with her aunt in San Jose. Initially, Wesson reacted rationally and even began to drive her to her aunt's house, but then became angry when she admitted to having sex with her coworker. Marcus turned the van around, and when they arrived back at the *Sudan*, he approached her and asked, "Are you ready to go to the Lord? Are you ready?"

"No!" she screamed. Wesson hit her and she felt a sharp pain in her chest. She looked down and realized he had stabbed her. At this point in the story a female juror let out a loud gasp.

Sofina said she still had a scar on her breast from the stabbing. She testified that Wesson made her promise

---

[37] Sofina related this series of events from the witness stand. Under oath, Elizabeth claimed she didn't remember it happening.

never to tell anyone what happened and she never breathed the story to a soul until she was interviewed by police after the murders. She looked over in Wesson's direction at the defense table and for the first time during her time on the witness stand she began to cry.

Once Sofina had gathered herself, the prosecutor asked her if she could show her scar to the jury. She stood up, turned with her back to the gallery and unbuttoned her blouse. She turned around, holding her blouse open to reveal a scar on the upper portion of her right breast. The jurors leaned forward in their seats and nodded in approval as she passed in front of them. She returned to the witness stand and resumed her testimony.

"Now, after your baby Jonathan was born, was he disciplined at all?" Gamoian asked.

"Yes."

"When did disciplining your baby begin? How old was he?"

"He was couple weeks old."

Sofina told the court that Marcus forced her to hit Jonathan if he cried for no reason. She used a twig on his butt and legs but after a few strikes she couldn't continue.

"I couldn't hit him. 'Cause the more . . . like when I hit him, he'll cry more. And it hurt me. I couldn't do it. Marcus said, 'You know what, you're not doing it. You're supposed to, you know, do it right. If you don't do it right, I'm going to do it.'"

Elizabeth advised Sofina to discipline Jonathan herself because Marcus would be much less forgiving. Elizabeth even showed her what kind of stick she should use to hit her then 1-month-old son, Sofina testified.

"And why were you supposed to discipline him on this occasion?" Gamoian asked.

"'Cause he was crying for no reason. I was supposed to spank him and tell him be quiet and, you know, let him know he can't be crying, until he stopped crying. But he wouldn't stop."

Marcus said Sofina wasn't doing it right and retrieved a stick about half an inch in diameter. She watched in horror as Marcus struck their son on his butt and legs with the stick.

"And how many times did Mr. Wesson hit Jonathan?"

"He was just hitting him. I wasn't counting. He was just hitting him to stop crying. He just keep on doing it. And he'll stop, and Jonathan was just crying like a lot. Lot. He kept on. Kept on. Told him be quiet. And then at one point he quiet down, and he kind of like fell asleep."

"And did Mr. Wesson stop hitting him?"

"Yes."

Sofina saw bruises and welts all over her son's legs. A short time later Jonathan woke up and started crying again. Marcus told Sofina to bring the baby to him and she obeyed. She placed Jonathan in a playpen, where Marcus resumed striking the infant on his back, butt, and all over his legs and feet. Jonathan continued to cry and Sofina couldn't watch anymore. She left the room.

Later, Sofina returned to the playpen where her son lay, bleeding and bruised. When she picked him up he woke and began to cry again. She took the boy to her aunt Elizabeth.

"And she just telling me, 'You know what, *mija*,' she goes, 'you have to do it. If you don't do it, he's going to do it.'"

Tears welled up in Sofina's eyes as she told the story.

"And I go, 'I hate him. I hate him. Why is he hitting him? He's just a baby.' And she just saying, 'Well, you know, *mija*, it happened to my sons, too. My kids. I used to go in the other room.'"

Sofina said she bathed her son in warm water and took him to bed with her. At this point her testimony Sofina was crying on the witness stand, and Juror 2, a mother of three boys, also wiped tears from her eyes.

* * *

As the year 2000 approached, Wesson warned his family to prepare for the end of the world. Like other religious zealots at the time, he believed Armageddon would happen on what had been dubbed "Y2K." The previous year the family was traveling between Fresno and Marshall, where the tugboat was moored. During this period, the outside world began to open up to Sofina and she started to question her uncle's teachings. On August 11, 1999, she wrote in her diary:

> The Lord is speaking to me. He is calling. I shall be ready for him. Show me the way Lord. I am with you. I want you in my heart eternally. You have me here at Marconi for a reason. I pray I fulfill your will in every way. And that I will not fail thee. Hide me behind the cross. Show me the way. Help make everything right. I need the Lord Jesus Christ. Be with me and bless me.

Gamoian asked: "Now, during prayer times and during the girl talks with the defendant, Mr. Wesson, with regards to God, Jesus, how did he compare himself?"

"He compared himself . . . he was Jesus Christ," Sofina answered.

"How would you or any member of the family get eternal life if he was Jesus Christ?"

"I argued about it with him," Sofina said. "I'm like, 'No, no, you are not Jesus Christ.' And he would read from the Bible and show me, 'Look, Sofia, this is what he says that, you know, be as perfect as I am. And that's what I'm doing. So I can be Jesus Christ.'"

"And with respect to having babies with his own daughters, did he justify that by showing you anything in the Bible?"

"Yes."

"What did he say?"

"He was saying that the Lord's coming soon. And because we have no husbands and we probably won't have them before God comes, that, you know, we need to have children before we go to Heaven. Because that's one of the duties that we're supposed to do."

Gamoian walked toward Sofina and placed a notebook on the witness stand.

Q. Do you recognize this?
A. Yes, it's one of my journals.
Q. On the inside of the front cover it says, "I love my daddy." What did you mean by that?
A. That I love Marcus.
Q. And also, there's . . . it says on a Post-it note, "Vampiress Tahla."

"Tah-lah." Sofina smiled, correcting the prosecutor's pronunciation.

Q. And who's that?
A. That was my vampire name.
Q. And did the other girls in the family, did they also get vampire names?
A. Yes.
Q. Did Mr. Wesson ever make comparisons between Jesus Christ and vampires?
A. Yes.
Q. When Mr. Wesson would compare Jesus with vampires, what would he say?
A. He would say just as Jesus had died and rose back up, that's what vampires do. They die and they raise back up. But the vampires are more like without Christ, you know. That's why they come out only at night. And that's why they suck people's blood. Because you know, they're not like Jesus, whereas, he could go straight up. But [Marcus] compared it. Jesus died. He rose back up. The vampires die. They

rise back up. But they don't have a soul. Jesus does have a soul.

Several jurors squinted their eyes and appeared confused.

Q. And in the family, were the girls given vampire names?
A. Yes.
Q. Who gave them their names?
A. Marcus.
Q. And did the defendant have a vampire name?
A. Yes. It's Je-Vam-Marc-Suspire.
Q. Do you think you can spell that?
A. It's J-E. And then another word, V-A-M. Another word is M-A-R-C. And the other one is S-U-S-P-I-R-E.

Sofina repeated it slowly, emphasizing the pronunciation of the last part of the name (sus-pir-ray). She explained that Marcus's vampire name derived from three words: Jesus, Marcus, and vampire. Marcus designated himself the Head Vampire in the family, and some of the girls were his wives while others were his concubines, Sofina explained. In those roles it was the job of the women to protect the Head Vampire from the world, according to Wesson. That's why the women took care of Marcus's business affairs and worked to support him, Sofina explained.

"And the only time that he was to come out is if he needed to protect us."

"No more questions," Gamoian said.

Marcus Wesson did not have any notable reaction to his niece's testimony. He sat quietly at the defense table and seemed to be writing something on a yellow notepad. Torres stood and walked across the courtroom toward the jury box to begin cross examination of the witness.

"Do you recall testifying as to the events that occurred March 12 that you, in fact, heard gunshots?" Torres asked.

"Yes," Sofina replied.

Q. How do you know they were shots? Prior to March 12, had you ever heard gunshots before?

A. Yes, many times.

Q. And you described a gun that was in the Wesson household right?

A. Yes.

Q. Did you ever see anybody shoot that gun?

A. Yes.

Q. So you knew how it sounded?

A. I did.

Sofina said that her sisters Brandi and Ruby also heard gunshots that day. "It was muffled, but they heard it," she explained. Sofina admitted that she couldn't remember if she told the police that she had heard gunshots on the day of the murders. Torres opened a thick binder and began to flip its pages.

"So you don't remember telling police that in fact you didn't hear any gunshots?" he asked. He quoted the transcript of Sofina's interview with police on the day of the murders.

"Detective Reese asked you, 'So you think they were doing something to the kids?' And you said, 'Yes, I think they were hurting them, but I didn't hear no gunshot. I have to be honest on that part. I didn't hear them.'"

"Yes," Sofina said without hesitation.

"Could you describe for the jury what you mean by you didn't hear any gunshots?"

"When Sebhrenah and Elizabeth were in the room, I didn't hear them. Not until after Marcus went in did I hear them."

"You told the police that before Marcus ever got into

the room, Sebhrenah and Lise were doing something to the kids, isn't that right?" Torres asked.

"Yes."

"So you believed that before Marcus ever went back there, that the children were being hurt. Is that correct?"

"No."

"Well, did you tell the officer that Sebhrenah and Lise were doing something to the kids before Marcus ever went back there?"

Sofina admitted she told one of the detectives she thought Sebhrenah was smothering the children.

Torres asked Sofina about the fight between her and the other Wesson women on March 12.

Q. From how you lived with the Wessons, the daughters, and how you grew up, how is it that you had the courage to fight them if you believed your son was going to get hurt?

A. I was protecting myself.

Q. So you weren't thinking about I'm afraid my child is going to get hurt so therefore I better calm down, right?

A. I didn't want him to see, you know, the mothers fighting among each other.

Q. You weren't worried about your son being killed at that point?

A. I was worried about it before. When I first drove there, I already knew there was a possibility.

Q. Right. But the way you were acting, weren't you pushing Sebhrenah into hurting your child?

A. No.

Her answer was followed by a long silence.

Q. In your experience with Sebhrenah, you knew that she was easily angered, isn't that right?

A. No.

Q. She had a bad temper?

A. No.

Q. So she was your best friend, best sister, is that right?

A. Yeah.

Q. And you were close?

A. Yeah.

Q. So your testimony is that in your experience with her, she was not easily angered?

A. Yeah, she wasn't.

Torres paced back and forth behind the defense table.

Q. And you knew that Sebhrenah had a fascination with guns, didn't you?

A. Yeah.

Q. How did you know that?

A. We used to watch a lot of Army movies. And we used to go to the property. We used to act like we're hunting and stuff. She would collect little guns that the boys brought. Like fake things and stuff.

Torres launched into a series of questions about the day of the murders, while referring to a time log of the audio recording made by Louis Garcia.

"At nine minutes and forty-four seconds after you arrived, did you hear Marcus say, 'The police can do it rather than force'?"

"I don't remember," Sofina replied.

Q. You remember Marcus saying that, though, right?

A. No, I don't remember.

Q. At eleven minutes and fifty seconds after you arrived, did you say, "I'm not leaving. No. Even if it's death. Even if it's death"?

A. I don't think I said it that quickly. It was after a while or so. I did say it, but I don't think the timing is right.

Q. But you remember saying it?
A. Oh, yeah.
Q. And you said it to Marcus, right?
A. Yes.

Torres flipped through his notes and asked, "When Jonathan told you that day that he didn't want to go with you, how did that make you feel?"

"I understood," Sofina replied, not breaking eye contact with the public defender.

Torres continued to flip pages and asked Sofina about the ten coffins Marcus had purchased at an antiques store in Fresno. Torres found the page he was looking for and, with it in hand, approached the witness stand. The paper was a diagram of the interior of the Hammond Avenue home, and he pointed out the placement of the coffins in three bedrooms and in one common area.

"Do you know why he purchased the coffins?"

"He wanted to use them as furniture," Sofina replied.

"It had nothing to do with vampires, did it?"

Sofina paused.

"Well, we would jokingly act like one bed's for you, and one bed's for you, but no it didn't."

Torres read from a police report regarding the incident aboard the family's tugboat when Sofina was ready to carry out the murder-suicide plan she says was orchestrated by Marcus. Torres made the point that the plan was not practiced and therefore was not really a plan. He quoted Sofina's interview with police and her statement about the gun: "I didn't know how to load it, I didn't know nothing."

Q. Do you remember saying that?
A. I'm not sure if I told them that.
Q. But that was the truth, right, you didn't know how to load that gun?

A. Yes, I did. I loaded it.

Q. And in regard to what you told police about the murder-suicide plan. Talking about how you were feeling at that time when you told Detective Reese, "I listened. Only Rosie would say okay. I couldn't do it. And I know Ruby couldn't do it." So my question to you is: You had the free will to say I would never do that?

A. Yes.

Q. And you made it clear to Mr. Wesson that you wouldn't do that?

A. Yes.

Q. That's why you had talks, right?

A. I was unworthy to be a soldier for Marcus. I was unfaithful to him so I couldn't be a soldier for him.

Q. That's not the point. The question is, ma'am, when you told the police that you didn't tell them, "I was unworthy to be a soldier." You never told them that?

Sofina shook her head in frustration. "You guys wouldn't even understand all that stuff if I was to tell you. It was up to Marcus who he chose to be a soldier. It's not up to us. We could say we want to or we can't, but it was up to him. It's according to him, if he felt that we were worthy. And all of us girls all had been unfaithful to him one way or another and we had to show our worth to him to be a soldier."

"So you weren't the only one that was unfaithful, right? And when you say unfaithful, you are talking about the fact that you liked guys?"

"Talked to other men, yes."

Sofina explained that all of the girls had been guilty of some form of "adultery" except for Rosa, and that Marcus had chosen her as the "strong soldier" because of her devotion. Sofina explained that Marcus had considered her "unworthy" to kill the children.

Through his questions, Torres made the point that

Wesson had asked permission to continue the practice of "loving" after the girls turned eighteen. Sofina testified that before she lived with Wesson at the age of eleven, she had been molested by four other men.

Torres began to rehash Sofina's previous testimony, and many of the jurors lost interest. One juror yawned. Another scratched his head and looked up at the ceiling. Sofina was growing equally impatient with the public defender, supplying one-word answers to his inquiries. With Sofina's patience running out, Torres launched into a long line of questioning about what she was told to wear as a young girl.

"Now, with that attire, you didn't have to wear that attire up until you left when you were twenty-six, did you?"

"No."

"Okay. You were only eleven and a half years old, and you were told to wear a dress and a scarf. And that only lasted for what? About a year, ma'am?"

Sofina cracked a big smile.

"Why are you smiling at me?" Torres asked.

"Because you're asking questions, and you're answering them yourself," Sofina replied. Many of the jurors smiled.

"Let me ask you about your religious beliefs. Why did you believe Jesus was coming in 2000?"

Sofina said Marcus had convinced the family that the world would end in the year 2000, and she didn't believe she would live past the age of twenty.

"After Jesus didn't come in 2000, did some family members say, 'Hey this is bullshit'?"

"No," Sofina replied.

"I'm going to talk about some vampire issues," Torres continued, abruptly changing subjects. "When you were talking to the detectives initially you told Detective Ochoa, 'At one time we were . . .' And then you stopped.

You started laughing. You said, 'This is so stupid. He was like the head vampire and us women were his vampires.' And you start laughing again. Do you remember that?"

A. Yes.
Q. You knew it was stupid at that time that you were doing the vampire names, isn't that right?
A. No.
Q. Why did you laugh and say, "This is so stupid"?
A. Because I was already out of it and I couldn't believe the stuff that we were doing.

Torres asked Sofina about Wesson's book on vampires. Sofina said she had read some of it.

"Now, writing the book never changed Marcus's strong conviction that Jesus was coming for the second time, did it? This talk about vampires, that didn't change?" Torres asked.

"At that point he wasn't trying to claim to be Jesus Christ anymore. He was trying to claim to be God. So we weren't really talking about the Second Coming anymore. We already knew about that. He's evolving into being Jesus now, evolving into being God himself."

FIVE

Elizabeth Wesson covered her face with a newspaper, shielding herself from photographers as she made her way down the long hallway to Department 53 of the Fresno County courthouse. She entered the courtroom frazzled and confused. Her curly hair fell to her shoulders and she wore a shiny black vinyl jacket.

"I'll go ahead and execute this, Your Honor," Gamoian said, handing the judge a piece of paper. The prosecutor had offered Elizabeth immunity to testify against her husband. The district attorney wouldn't charge Elizabeth with a crime—of knowing about the sexual abuse and not reporting it, for example, or for being an accessory to the murders—if she testified as a witness for the prosecution. The court had provided Elizabeth with an attorney who reviewed the terms of the immunity deal. After discussing it, Elizabeth had agreed to the D.A.'s terms.

Court was in session and Judge Putnam asked Elizabeth to step forward with her attorney.

"So, Mrs. Wesson, you've had time to review the immunity agreement with your attorney. Do you understand what it means?" Judge Putnam asked.

"Not really," she replied timidly.

The judge let out a sigh. "It basically means the things you say in court cannot be used against you. However, you can be prosecuted for perjury, contempt, or failing to answer," Putnam explained.

The look on Elizabeth's face changed from confusion to dismay. After some discussion, and in spite of her confusion, she said she would accept the terms of the immunity deal.

"We can have your attorney present during your testimony, if you would like," the judge told Elizabeth.

"Yes," she replied, glancing down at the floor.

As Elizabeth approached the witness stand, she was breathing rapidly and she looked terrified. She glanced at her husband, who was seated at the defense table, but he did not look up.

Elizabeth spoke softly and slurred her words. She said that she had been married to Marcus Wesson for thirty years. During those thirty years, she testified, she was a housewife and Marcus held only one job as a bank teller in San Jose for two years.

"If neither of you were working for most of those thirty years, how did you support yourselves?" Gamoian asked.

Elizabeth said they received welfare. It was her job to care for the children and to do the housework, she explained.

"Then why didn't your husband work?" Gamoian asked.

"You can't work if you are on welfare," Elizabeth replied.

"Don't you think he should work, especially since he has to care for nine children?"

"I don't know," she said. "You have to ask him."

Elizabeth married Marcus when she was fifteen years old and he was twenty-seven. Marcus had already fathered a child with her mother, Rosemary, Elizabeth explained.

When asked to identify her husband, Elizabeth nervously pointed at Wesson, who was seated at the defense table.

"Who is Jonathan's mother?" the prosecutor asked.

"I am," Elizabeth replied, explaining that Sofina had given her Jonathan when he was born.

"And Aviv? Are you her mother?"

"Yes," Elizabeth said.

Gamoian asked who the biological mothers of the children were, and although she was reticent, Elizabeth identified Sofina and Ruby.

While living in Santa Cruz, the family owned a motor home and a boat called *The Happy Bottom*. Gamoian asked how the family was able to afford the boat and motor home if no one was working.

"We used our welfare check," Elizabeth answered.

The prosecutor addressed the day of the murders, asking Elizabeth how she felt when she discovered Sofina and Ruby had gone to her house to retrieve Jonathan and Aviv. Elizabeth said she was surprised.

"They had no right going to my home," she said. "They had no right taking the kids." She denied having a conversation with Sofina two weeks prior to March 12 in which her niece had informed her that she wanted custody of Jonathan.

When Elizabeth arrived at the Hammond Avenue home, the fight over the children had already reached a boiling point. She parked her car in the driveway next to the bus and saw a large group of people yelling and fighting in the front yard. Elizabeth approached the group gathered around the front door. She testified that Marcus asked her to give him the car keys and she complied.

"Why'd he ask for the keys?" Gamoian asked. Elizabeth said she didn't know. She went back to the car to get her purse and then entered the house, placing her purse on an end table near the doorway. The yelling at the front door grew louder, and when Elizabeth heard her son Serafino threaten his cousin Marco, she returned to the front door. The anxiety she felt was almost too much to bear. She went into the kitchen to get a glass of water and then walked to the southeast bedroom. The door was closed.

"Did you hear any noises coming from inside that bedroom?"

"No, it was . . . it was quiet. I didn't hear . . . I didn't hear the babies or nothing. It was so quiet. I . . . I walked in the . . . I walked . . . I opened the door to the last bedroom."

Elizabeth said she stood in the doorway.

"Did you go inside the room?"

"No."

"Did you look inside the room?"

"Yes."

"What did you see when you looked inside the room?"

Elizabeth was breathing so hard she began to hyperventilate on the witness stand. She appeared to be having a panic attack and could barely speak.

"You need a few minutes, ma'am?" Judge Putnam asked.

There was no answer.

"Mrs. Wesson, you can step down there if you want and go outside and take a walk. As soon as you're ready, we'll start back up," Putnam advised.

About twenty minutes later Elizabeth returned to the witness stand and appeared to have calmed down.

Gamoian immediately picked up her questioning where she had left off.

"Now, when you looked inside the bedroom, what did you see?" Gamoian asked.

"I saw my daughter Lise," Elizabeth replied almost

inaudibly. The judge asked her to move closer to the microphone.

"And what was Lise doing?"

"My husband was holding her. There was a pile of blankets that high," Elizabeth said, motioning vaguely with her hand. "My husband was right next to the . . . right next to the blankets, and he was holding Sebhrenah . . . I mean he was holding Lise."

Elizabeth slurred her words and began rock slowly in her chair.

"Okay. And where in the room was Lise?" Gamoian asked.

"The coffins were standing up against the wall, and the blankets were next to the coffins," Elizabeth mumbled.

"And where was your daughter Lise when you saw her?"

"On top of the blankets."

"And how was her body positioned?"

Elizabeth began to tremble as she answered.

"I just . . . I just remember . . . I just see her eyes. I just see her eyes."

"How was Elizabeth positioned in relationship to the blankets?"

"I just see her eyes. I just see her eyes," Elizabeth repeated, in an almost catatonic state.

Gamoian persisted with the question, and at every turn Elizabeth repeated the same phrase:

Q. Well, was Lise sitting, standing, lying?
A. I just see her eyes. That's all I remember.
Q. Was Lise standing when you saw her eyes?
A. I just see her eyes. That's all I see.
Q. Was she sitting down when you saw her eyes?
A. I don't know. I just see her eyes.
Q. And you said that your husband was next to the blankets?
A. I think he was holding her.

Elizabeth explained that her husband was down on one knee cradling their daughter Lise. Elizabeth said he was crying.

Q. Where on her body was Mr. Wesson holding Lise?
A. Don't you understand? I just see her eyes. I don't see nothing else. I just . . . I just see her eyes.
Q. Again, what part of her body is he holding? Is she lying faceup or facedown?
A. Faceup.
Q. And what direction are her legs pointed?
A. They were toward me.
Q. And if Elizabeth is lying faceup, what side of her body is your husband kneeling with one knee up one knee down?
A. I don't know.
Q. You do not know?
A. No.
Q. And you say that your daughter Elizabeth looked at you?
A. I saw her eyes.

By this point the prosecutor was irritated and began to raise her voice.

Q. And what did you note about her eyes?
A. I just see her eyes.
Q. What did you note about her eyes? Were they looking at you?
A. I just . . . I just see her eyes.

"Was Lise looking at you when you saw her eyes, Mrs. Wesson?" the prosecutor repeated even louder.

"I just see her eyes," Elizabeth replied.

"I think we're going to take a break," Judge Putman interrupted. He turned to the jury. "Ladies and gentlemen, we'll have you come back in a few minutes."

The jury left the courtroom.

Putnam turned to Elizabeth. "Mrs. Wesson, is there something else you'd like to tell me as far as how you feel right now?"

"I just see her eyes," Elizabeth repeated.

"All right. We've heard that. Are you on any medication right now?" the judge asked.

"I just—" Elizabeth stopped and there was a long silence.

The judge told Elizabeth to step down from the witness stand and to take another walk. Putman told Elizabeth's court-appointed attorney, "Perhaps you can have somebody follow her and see if any medical attention is necessary. We'll take a break."

Putnam left the courtroom, and Elizabeth's lawyer and a bailiff approached her. She pressed her hand to her forehead. "I feel like I'm going to pass out, I'm feeling dizzy," she said.

Nearly everyone had left the courtroom. Marcus Wesson sat at the defense table playing an imaginary keyboard. He moved his fingers up and down the tabletop and swayed his body back and forth, oblivious to his wife's condition. When the judge entered the courtroom, Wesson stopped and put his hands in his lap.

Judge Putnam asked Mrs. Wesson's attorney, Douglass Foster, if Elizabeth was ready to resume her testimony. Neither the jury nor Elizabeth were in the courtroom.

"She's very emotional obviously, Your Honor. She said she's willing to give it a try," Foster said.

"I just want to say for the record I believe she is faking," the prosecutor said. "This is a continuing behavior with Mrs. Wesson. She was like this when police officers were questioning her, uncooperative, playing the victim. I'm not at all surprised as to how she's behaving on the stand."

Defense attorney Pete Jones spoke up. "I'd just like to say I've listened to her tapes and read her transcripts and

I don't think she's faking it. This was a horrendous tragedy. I think she's reliving it."

"Well I haven't heard the tapes or seen the transcript," Putnam said. The judge suggested that Gamoian question the witness in another area before returning to the subject of the murders.

The jury filed back in, and Elizabeth Wesson entered the courtroom and took her place on the witness stand. Gamoian questioned her about the family's financial troubles. Elizabeth periodically glanced in the direction of the defense table. In the middle of one of her answers, Gamoian interrupted her.

"Mrs. Wesson, you are always looking over at your husband. Is there a reason for that?"

Elizabeth gave a confused look. "I'm not looking at my husband. I'm looking at you," she said.

Again Gamoian returned to the day of the murders:

Q. You haven't thought over what you could have done to help Lise, to have helped Sebhrenah? You haven't thought that over in your mind since March the twelfth?

A. I think about that every day.

Q. What were you thinking when you were running? You've had time to look back at your actions. What were you thinking?

A. How could I protect them? I should have protected them.

Q. Then why did you run?

A. I just ran.

Q. Something frightened you, isn't that right?

A. I don't remember.

Q. Your husband frightened you?

A. I just ran.

Q. He wanted you to go in the bedroom and that scared you?

A. I just ran.

Q. Besides Mr. Wesson saying "Bee, come here," did you hear any other noise in the bedroom?

A. I didn't hear anything.

Q. And the blanket that Lise was on . . . did you see any of the other children on the blanket?

A. No.

Q. Did you see any of the other children underneath Lise?

A. No. I really don't remember that much that day.

While claiming not to remember exactly what she observed on the day of the killings, Elizabeth had already described the following scenario to police: Before entering the back bedroom, she moved a table aside that was blocking the doorway. (The table had likely been placed there by her daughter Kiani, who witnesses had seen barricading the bedroom door after Marcus went inside.) After entering the room, Elizabeth saw her husband bent down, holding their daughter Lise. Marcus beckoned his wife to him, and Elizabeth was overcome by terror. As she ran out of the house, she told detectives that she saw her daughter Sebhrenah in the living room, toward the front of the house. This was a huge point of contention for defense attorneys, who had pegged Sebhrenah as the murderer. The defense's case rested on the idea that Sebhrenah was inside the southeast bedroom and had perpetrated the crimes. On cross examination, the defense would get Elizabeth to admit that she might have confused her daughter Kiani for Sebhrenah. On that point, the defense's argument seemed to make sense. Sebhrenah had been found dead near the pile of bodies, while witnesses had seen Kiani come running out of the house just after her mother. In addition, Kiani told police that she had observed her mother enter the back bedroom. Several witnesses heard Elizabeth exclaim, "They're all gone!" as she exited the house, before passing out in the front yard. Clearly, she had seen something to indicate that the children were all dead, but Elizabeth claimed she didn't remember making that statement.

Q. Then why did you run out?
A. I don't know.
Q. Is that so that you wouldn't be killed?
A. I just ran.
Q. Because you didn't want to be killed.
A. I just ran.

At this point Marcus Wesson, who had been silent throughout the trial so far, interrupted.

"Objection, Your Honor," he announced. "The prosecutor is angry!"

The judge told Wesson to be quiet and to talk to his attorney if he had something to say.

"I mean no disrespect to the court," Wesson said.

"Talk to your attorney," Judge Putnam replied sternly.

The prosecutor didn't let the defendant's outburst faze her.

Q. Mrs. Wesson, what scared you on this day that you ran out of the house leaving your two daughters who were still alive?
A. I don't know.
Q. You don't know? Is it because you choose not to remember?
A. I only saw her and my husband. That's all I saw.
Q. Mrs. Wesson, is there a reason that you won't answer questions about March the twelfth of last year?
A. I'm answering your questions.

The prosecutor's voice took on an accusing tone.

Q. You lost nine children on March the twelfth. Don't you think what you saw, what you heard on that date, would be important in the investigation into the murder of nine of your children?

A. Do you want me to lie? I'm telling you I don't remember anymore! I don't remember what I said!

Q. Do you just remember what's convenient?

A. I remember that today is my daughter's birthday. She would have been twenty-seven.

"That's right! Sebhrenah would have been twenty-seven today!" Gamoian shot back. "And do you feel any obligation to make sure that Sebhrenah gets justice, Mrs. Wesson?"

"Isn't that what you're here for, to find justice?!" Elizabeth yelled. "You're supposed to find out, aren't you?! It seems that you wouldn't even need my testimony since you already made up your mind about everything!"

Elizabeth said she would have done anything to protect her children.

"Well, on March the twelfth what did you do to protect Lise?" Gamoian asked.

"I wasn't there," Elizabeth replied.

Again Gamoian raised her voice.

"You were there! You saw her eyes, isn't that right?"

Elizabeth began to sob.

"I should have stayed! I should have stayed inside there! I should have stayed! I should have stayed!"

"Why didn't you, Mrs. Wesson?"

Elizabeth continued to cry on the witness stand.

"We'll take another break," the judge announced.

Fifteen minutes later court resumed, but not for long. After just a few questions Elizabeth said she didn't feel well.

"Just rest a minute," the judge told her.

"My . . . I feel, um . . . I feel dizzy," she said, holding her forehead.

Again the judge adjourned court. The jury filed out of the courtroom.

"I can't breathe," Elizabeth said, leaning back in her chair. She appeared to be hyperventilating. Her attorney rushed to her side along with a bailiff. She told them she couldn't stand up.

An ambulance pulled up to the Fresno County courthouse and medics rushed to Department 53 to evaluate Mrs. Wesson. After a thorough evaluation they could find nothing wrong. She complained of shortness of breath and a headache, but her lungs were clear, she was alert, and her heart rate and blood pressure were all normal. The medic who performed the evaluation also reported to the judge that Elizabeth's blood sugar was perfectly normal and there was no medical reason he could see that would prevent her from testifying.

Again Elizabeth resumed her testimony, regaining what was left of her composure. The prosecutor asked her about when she first met Marcus. Elizabeth explained that when she was a girl, Marcus became intimate with her mother and they had a child named Adair. Gamoian pressed Elizabeth to tell the court about the first time she had sex with Marcus, and while Elizabeth admitted she was fourteen at the time, she refused to be more specific.

Marcus and Elizabeth were married when she was in the eighth grade. She'd been attending public school in San Jose, and Marcus told her that her mother approved of their union.

The prosecutor pressed Elizabeth to describe the act of her first sexual encounter with Marcus.

A. He penetrated me.
Q. How so?
A. Penetrated me.
Q. With what?
A. With his private parts.
Q. His penis?

A. Yes.
Q. And where on your body did he penetrate with his penis?
A. Down there.
Q. Your vagina?
A. Yes.

"You know what a vagina is, correct?" Gamoian asked sarcastically.

"Yes," Elizabeth replied.

Not long after their first sexual experience, Elizabeth became pregnant. She dropped out of the eighth grade and began to attend a school for pregnant teenage girls. The Wessons' first son Dorian was born in 1974. Elizabeth was fifteen years old.

Elizabeth denied that her husband would talk about sending the children "to the Lord" if the government tried to take them away. The prosecutor quoted the interview she had with police in which she told them that her husband would teach the family to "protect God's children at all costs."

"I mean, you lived with the man for thirty years," Gamoian said. "Was that his teaching, that the family protect God's children at all costs?"

"It wasn't like that," Elizabeth replied.

In spite of the fact that Marcus had impregnated his daughters and nieces, Elizabeth claimed she didn't realize Marcus had been unfaithful to her until after the murders.

"With all the newspapers and stuff, what everybody is saying, I guess I was just plain stupid," Elizabeth said.

"Do you still love him?" the prosecutor asked.

"Yes," Elizabeth replied. She explained that she had not had sex with her husband in eight years because her niece Ruby had told Marcus to leave her. Elizabeth said that she stayed in her marriage for the children's sake.

"I don't believe in divorce," she said.

"Well, do you believe in child molestation?" Gamoian quipped.

"No, I do not," Elizabeth answered, lowering her head.

Q. Well, how would you reconcile that if you found out your husband was molesting your girls?

A. You don't. You can't reconcile something like that.

Q. What do you do?

A. Just take care of your children and keep him away from your children.

Q. And did you do that with Mr. Wesson? Did you keep him away from your children?

A. I didn't know he was molesting them.

Q. Isn't it true that, in fact, you walked in on your husband and Sofina when she was orally copulating him?

A. No, I never did.

Q. Well, did you ask them who's the father of the babies they were having?

A. No, I never asked them.

Q. Why didn't you ask them?

A. 'Cause it wasn't my place.

Q. You're the mother, aren't you?

A. Yes.

Q. And mothers are concerned about the welfare of their children, aren't they?

A. They were happy. The girls were happy. They weren't depressed. They never gave any signs to me that they were unhappy.

Q. You weren't concerned, however, that your daughters are having premarital sex, right? That's against your religious beliefs?

A. I know what my beliefs are. It's just that things happen. My sister had children at seventeen, and I never asked her who the father was. I never—I just—I think it's mean and rude to ask something like that.

Q. Of your own daughters?

A. Of anybody.

Q. You think that's mean and rude?

A. If they want to tell me, they would have told me.

"Are you easily confused, Mrs. Wesson?" the prosecutor asked.

"I guess so. Since this has happened I have been confused," Elizabeth replied.

"You now have immunity. So why won't you answer these questions now?" Gamoian asked.

"It's not that I'm not cooperating, I just don't remember. I lost half my family that day. Then the day of the funeral they wanted me to come in and talk about it. I just couldn't do it. Could you?" Elizabeth asked.

"Set that aside for nine dead family members? Yes I could. Absolutely!" Gamoian retorted.

"Well I'm not you," Elizabeth said, lowering her head.

"You don't want to see justice done?" Gamoian said forcefully.

Elizabeth appeared to snap out of her catatonic state.

"You call this justice? Bringing me here and ridiculing my family? I don't like you!" she shouted.

"Why don't you like me?" the prosecutor retorted.

"Because you're insensitive. You're just a mean person. You just look mean."

"How about molesting little girls, is that mean?" the prosecutor shot back.

"No. That's gross," Elizabeth said, wincing.

"How about not protecting girls from someone molesting them?" the prosecutor asked.

"How could I protect them when they never told me anything?" Elizabeth replied.

Gamoian folded her arms. "So it's your testimony that none of your children ever told you that your husband was molesting them?"

"None of my children told me anything. The Marcus I know is a sensitive man. The man in the papers is not the man I know."

"Let me ask you this," the prosecutor said. "As you sit here today, do you believe that your husband fathered your daughter Kiani's child?"

"No!" Elizabeth retorted, shaking her head furiously.

"Why not?"

"Because I don't want to believe it! It's not true!" she shouted.

Again, Marcus Wesson interrupted. "Objection, Your Honor! I'm not getting properly represented!" he exclaimed. The defense attorneys attempted to quiet their client but it was of no use. The judge quickly excused the jury. As the jurors filed out, Marcus shouted, "I want the jury to hear! My counsel is not defending me properly. I'm not being properly represented!"

Judge Putnam had a scowl on his face. "Mr. Wesson, any objections you make don't mean anything to me. However, if you have some complaints about your attorneys I will hear those."

"Yes I do," Wesson responded.

"Do you want to address those privately or right here?" the judge asked.

"It's nothing serious. Right here. Basically I am not . . . I would like to admonish that I don't feel I should sit here and not say anything if I hear something disrespectful. The only reason I object is to get a point across. There are only two reasons I would object. One is disrespect of the court. This court is not being respected. There should be respect. The other is whenever there is improper inference I feel my counsel should stand up and make objections. Like there is all this talk about my daughters having babies and they were surrogate mothers!"

The judge let out a deep sigh. "Mr. Wesson, every time

you object, it is disrespectful to the court. It's not an easy process and your viewpoint of courtroom decorum may differ from mine. I may have to take you out of the court. You also need to know that any statements you make in court can be used against you."

Immediately Wesson apologized. "I did not know that speaking out was disrespectful. It won't happen again," he assured the judge. "My only problem is the continued disrespect of the court. I would like to see some kind of decorum in the court."

The jury filed back into the courtroom and Elizabeth resumed her testimony.

"Mrs. Wesson, why did you think your husband is in jail?"

"He did not kill my children. Sofia and Ruby set it off. Sofia went in there. She caused the fight. She shouldn't have been in that house! My children would have been alive!"

When the Wesson's 6-month-old son Donavan died from spinal meningitis, Elizabeth said she wasn't with him. She testified it was something she still regretted.

"Well, were you with Lise when she died?" the prosecutor asked.

"Why are you such a bitch?" Elizabeth snapped at Gamoian. "Why are you talking like that to me for? You are insensitive! Why are you talking like that toward me for? That's not a question! You are just an ugly person!"

Gamoian was unfazed. Elizabeth testified that she had become homeless since the murders and at times she would break into the home on Hammond Avenue and spend the night there.

"Because I lost everything on March 12. I lost half of my family. And you're asking me stupid idiotic questions about my life! I lost my family!"

The prosecutor asked Elizabeth why she never confronted her husband to find out if he was, in fact, fathering all the children being born in the family.

"Isn't that a burning question in your mind?"

Elizabeth paused and glanced down at the floor. "It still is," she said.

SIX

Twenty-year-old Serafino Wesson appeared nervous as he stepped into the courtroom. He was the youngest of Marcus Wesson's surviving sons. He had a husky build and, except for his lack of facial hair, bore a strong resemblance to his father. Like nearly all of his siblings, he spoke with a pronounced lisp; strangely, it was not a speech impediment either of his parents shared. On the witness stand Serafino would not exhibit the confrontational nature that was so apparent on the day of the murders. Instead, he was soft-spoken and polite. The prosecutor began by asking him to chronicle the events of March 12 as he remembered them.

Serafino testified that he and his brother Marcus Jr. were on their way to see the film *Passion of the Christ* with a friend, Michael Varin. Varin apparently had a crush on one of the Wesson girls, Kiani, and he wanted to stop by the Wesson home to see if she was there. When they arrived at the house, they saw squad cars everywhere and a group of family members gathered outside.

When Serafino discovered that his cousins Sofina and Ruby were there to retrieve their children, he became angry.

"They had no right to break up our family. I got angry like any normal person would," he testified.

"Didn't they have a right to get their children?" Gamoian asked.

"No. My dad made a deal with them that if the females ever left they could not take their children," he replied. "To me, they were being selfish. They were breaking the pact with my father and it wasn't fair."

Serafino continued his story, saying that he saw both of the oldest victims, his sisters Lise and Sebhrenah, in the house. Lise was crying and Sebhrenah stood in the doorway of the southeast bedroom.

"After Sebhrenah told me they were trying to force-fully remove the kids, I went to the front door because I wasn't going to let that happen," Serafino testified. He then stood in front of his father, who was still posi-tioned at the front door, telling the police they had no warrant, and he pushed an officer. Eventually Marcus left the front door and went into the back bedroom, but Serafino kept his post at the front door.

"I was afraid they were going to take my brothers so I was doing everything in my power to keep people out of the house."

Finally a police officer pulled out his gun and Serafino stepped aside. Marcus barricaded himself inside the bed-room, and after nearly an hour and a half he surrendered to police. After the elder Wesson was handcuffed, Sera-fino described looking into his father's eyes.

"In my mind I was like screaming at him, like, 'What happened? Tell me! Look at me! Tell me something.' But he just had this blank look on his face."

The prosecutor referred to a police interview in which Serafino described his father's expression as a "dead look."

"Do you recall that, in fact, your father was looking at you?" the prosecutor asked.

"No, he was like, you know . . . someone could just stare at you, but they're not looking at you. He was like just still."

"Was he calm?"

"Yes, he was calm."

"Like he always is, right?"

"This was a different calm," Serafino explained. "It was like . . . like he sees something. Like he seen something . . . like at the point where it has nothing to do. Nothing to do. But it was like a different calm."

"Well, can you explain how many different calms you've seen your father exhibit over the years?" the prosecutor asked.

"Well, like, you know, people that have been through a lot, you know. They know how to handle situations, and they have this certain calmness about them. And you know, they know how to deal with problems. Not like I did, being all aggressive. 'Cause that's no way to deal with it. And to me, my father always knew how to handle situations."

Again Gamoian quoted Serafino's interview with police in which he referred to his father's demeanor on the day of the murders, saying, "My dad was so calm. He was so calm it was creepy." Serafino testified that he didn't remember making that statement.

The prosecutor then asked him if he believed that his father had impregnated any of his sisters or cousins. Serafino said his sisters told him they had gone to the hospital and had sperm injected into them. At the time he believed the explanation.

"Do you think it's sick for a man to have sex with his own daughters?" the prosecutor asked. The question was followed by a long pause.

Serafino turned to the judge and asked, "Do I have to answer that?"

The judge nodded and advised Serafino to answer the question. Serafino looked down and after another long pause he said, "Yes."

The prosecutor asked Serafino if he knew the truth about his father's sexual relationships with the women in the family. Serafino said he didn't want to know the truth.

"Why not?" Gamoian asked.

Serafino replied, "Everybody hates him. All it will do is cause me to hate him. I'd rather not. I'm not going to go look for the truth. I'd like to keep him in my heart as he is today." Serafino added that he would always love his father. "There is such a thing as forgiveness. I'm not saying I know who did it, but I know he's the only one who knows what happened. So why hate him, since I don't know the truth of what happened?"

SEVEN

Twenty-seven-year-old Kiani Wesson was already crying when she took the witness stand. The young woman was dressed in black and held a tissue in her hand; she looked like a funeral attendee rather than a witness in a murder trial. Kiani had two children with her father—8-year-old Illabelle and 1-year-old Jeva—and both were among the murder victims. Kiani apologized to the court and attempted to compose herself.

"Did you go into the bedroom after the children were placed there?" the prosecutor asked.

"I went in there one time, when Rosie first put Jonathan in the room," Kiani replied. She then immediately recanted the statement, saying she had not entered the room.

"I was very dramatized [sic] that day. I was very upset. I just wanted to get out of there."

"Your children were murdered. Don't you realize that?" Gamoian said.

"Yes," Kiani replied.

"Do you think it was important to give truthful information to police?"

"Yes, of course."

Several witnesses observed Kiani barricading the southeast bedroom door with furniture after Marcus entered the room where the children were being kept. Kiani denied this from the witness stand.

"That was not me," Kiani said. "I did not pull no table."

She told the court that she heard a muffled "pop" sound not long after her father entered the room. After watching her mother Elizabeth run out of the house with a startled look on her face, Kiani explained what happened next.

"I was yelling at the crowd, 'It's all your fault! You're next!' "

Gamoian asked who specifically Kiani was addressing.

"Sofia and Ruby. I just meant that God's going to deal with them," Kiani testified.

The prosecutor suggested that Kiani knew what had happened in the room because the family had a murder-suicide pact.

"No, there was no plan in the family," Kiani said.

Gamoian referred to Kiani's interview with police in which she said there was such a plan.

"I don't remember saying that. At that point I knew that something tragic had happened. It was just the way he talked. It was just a figure of speech, I don't know. It was not our plan to do that."

"It was the plan if police or CPS came to take the children that you would kill the children and then yourselves. Are you denying that?" Gamoian asked.

"Yes, I'm denying that," Kiani replied.

"Are you denying making that statement to police?" the prosecutor asked.

"I don't remember what I said to police," Kiani said.

Gamoian changed the subject and asked Kiani if she and her father ever had sexual contact.

"Yeah," Kiani replied matter-of-factly.

"But you didn't think that was unusual?" Gamoian asked.

"No," Kiani answered.

"Was that okay with you?" Gamoian asked.

"Yeah, because I . . . I agreed with it, that's okay with

me." Kiani explained that her father began to touch her in a sexual way when she was nine and that they "married" when she was nineteen.

A. He would touch even down there, everywhere. Like you know he used to just like touch us down there.
Q. What do you mean? Your vagina area?
A. Yeah, uh-huh.
Q. And you felt okay with that?
A. Yeah, uh-huh. Yeah.

The prosecutor asked if Kiani had married her father in a legal or religious sense. Kiani said the marriage wasn't official. Gamoian challenged her, suggesting that having sex with her father would be considered sex outside of marriage, which Kiani already had said was wrong.

"But see there's a catch to that," Kiani explained. "I think the father and daughter are as one."

"Where did you learn that?" Gamoian said in a sarcastic tone.

"In the Bible," Kiani replied.

"Did you read that or did someone tell you that?" the prosecutor asked.

"I read it. I can't find it and I don't know where it's at . . . but I read it. I read it. It's some, it's a principle of it. It don't say exactly that, but um, it has it in the Bible."

The prosecutor asked if Kiani was ever forced to have sexual contact with the other girls.

"I do not want to talk about sexual contact with females," Kiani replied. "I can tell you this much. Nothing was ever forced upon anybody. We always had had choices. We had meetings. We talked about everything and we were the boss of what we wanted to do."

Gamoian asked if Marcus ever conducted a marriage ceremony between her and her cousin Ruby. Kiani de-

nied that it ever happened. The prosecutor then asked
how she justified having sex with her father, even as a
young girl.

"Well, Marcus said like that's the purpose of loving is
to learn."

"And it started as early as age nine for you?"

"It says in the Bible, too, 'Man leads to his daughters
bed,' " Kiani explained.

As Kiani recalled the explicit details of her sexual encounters with her father, Marcus sat quietly at the defense
table writing or drawing on a yellow pad of paper. He
stopped, lifted the paper, gazed at it, and then returned to
writing.

Kiani explained that between the ages of eight and
fourteen her father would just kiss her on the neck and
hold her.

"Did he put his tongue in your mouth?" the prosecutor
asked.

"No, but I put my tongue in his mouth," Kiani replied.

"How did you know how to do that? Who taught
you?"

"If you're a true woman you automatically know how
to do that," Kiani answered. Despite her assurances from
the witness stand that she felt there was nothing wrong
with having sex with her father, Kiani began to cry when
she recounted the first time they had intercourse.
Gamoian forced her to describe the act in detail as well
as the first time she orally copulated her father. Jurors
winced as the prosecutor asked Kiani to demonstrate
with her hands how she helped her father reach orgasm.
She cried as she made the motions with her hands. Many
of the jurors looked down in embarrassment.

Kiani seemed to go out of her way to insist that she did
not have intercourse with her father until she reached the
age of nineteen. The prosecutor was quick to point out
that Kiani was born in 1977 and gave birth to her first
child in 1995.

"Weren't you seventeen when you got pregnant?" Gamoian asked.

"No, nineteen," she replied.

"Can't you do math? You were eighteen when you gave birth," the prosecutor said.

Kiani just shook her head. "No, I was nineteen."

Kiani explained that she had plans to move out of the Wesson home and start a life of her own after having her second child. She said the women all agreed that if they decided to leave they would have to leave their children with Marcus.

"I didn't want to leave Jeva," she said. Again Kiani broke down and cried.

After a short break she composed herself.

"I love my father like a father," she said.

"Do you love your father like a boyfriend?"

"No. Like a father," Kiani insisted.

Gamoian asked Kiani to read aloud a letter she wrote to her father. Kiani took the paper from the prosecutor and read:

> *I love you very much, with all my heart.*
> *You are a very special person in my life.*
> *You are my one true love.*
> *I love you my Daddy, always know that.*
> *I am deeply in love with you.*
> *The words I say are not to impress*
> *I will never leave you.*
> *You mean too much to me to walk away.*
> *I will always be with you no matter what happens*
> *I love you too much*
> *My Sugar Daddy I love.*

"I was just expressing to him how I felt about him as a father," Kiani explained after reading it.

"Don't you agree it sounds more like you wrote it to a lover?" Gamoian asked.

"No," she replied.

"What does that mean when you call your father your 'Sugar Daddy'?"

"I still love him and everything but I'm still going my own way and getting married," she replied.

Not long after the murders Kiani responded publicly to media accounts of her family's unorthodox lifestyle. She wrote a handwritten letter that was faxed to the local newspaper and television stations. In it she claimed, "Nothing was forced upon us, everything was done by choice." She concluded the letter by saying:

> *I just want everyone to know that Marcus is not that horrible person that every one is portraying him to be, our history makes us what we are today and I thank my dad who raised us, because, I am proud of what I am today.*

"Are you happy with your life?" the prosecutor asked.

"Not right now. But yeah . . ." Kiani replied, unconvincingly.

"Jeva and Illabelle are gone. Are you happy about that?"

There was a long pause.

"No," Kiani replied. Again she began to cry.

EIGHT

"Everybody was screaming. And I just felt somebody slapping me in my face. I opened my eyes and I saw my sister Brandi above me telling me to wake up."

Ruby Ortiz woke and realized she wasn't having a nightmare. Then she heard five gunshots and jumped up. She looked over and saw several officers pointing their guns into the house.

Ruby testified that three days prior to the murders she had contacted a lawyer who advised her that Wesson had no legal claim to their daughter since his name did not appear on the child's birth certificate. Ruby had not even seen her uncle Marcus in four years when she showed up at the Hammond Avenue house on March 12. She had run away several times and always returned. The last time she left she knew she couldn't go back; Marcus was getting more violent, and she thought if she returned he would kill her.

After hearing the gunshots, Ruby ran to a police officer and begged him to go inside the house.

"I was afraid Marcus was going to kill the children." Ruby began to cry on the witness stand. When she saw Elizabeth and Serafino exit the house, Ruby knew something terrible had happened just by the expressions on their faces.

* * *

The prosecutor asked Ruby to recall the first time her uncle Marcus had molested her. Ruby said she was eight years old. She was crying on her bed and Marcus crawled under the covers with her. She said he began to caress her all over and then began to touch her between her legs. Ruby claimed that by the time she was ten years old Marcus was penetrating her vagina with his fingers.

"He would say that a father is supposed to give his daughter 'loving' or they would grow up to be whores because they would not know how to be faithful."

Ruby also explained that Marcus told her not to talk about their sexual contact with the other girls.

"And besides him touching you skin-to-skin on your vagina, inserting his fingers at these sessions, would he do anything else or would he have you do anything else to him?" the prosecutor asked.

"Yeah. He would, um, take his penis out of his pants and have me touch it. And he would tell me to like kiss his nipples and to suck them."

Several jurors winced as Ruby described how her uncle forced her to perform oral sex on him.

"I started to cough, but he held my head down and told me to swallow."

"Did he say anything about swallowing?"

"He said, 'A real woman will swallow. She'll take it.'"

Ruby said that when she was thirteen Wesson performed a private marriage ceremony in which they exchanged vows and she pledged her faithfulness to him.

"He just asked me if, um, I wanted to be his wife. That he believed in having more than one wife, and that he wanted me to be his wife. And I said yes. I loved him very much," Ruby explained. Immediately after the two "married," Ruby began to do her uncle's laundry and to cook for him. At fifteen, she began to have intercourse with Marcus; he explained it was time to consummate their marriage. Ruby testified that the first time they had sex it was painful and Marcus pulled out and ejaculated on the bed.

"Did he tell you why he didn't ejaculate inside of you?"

"He said that, um, I could not get pregnant."

Ruby claimed that Elizabeth Wesson walked in on their sexual encounters at least three times. The first incident occurred when Ruby was twelve and performing oral sex on her uncle. Ruby said that each time, Elizabeth told her to get out of the room.

Ruby became pregnant with her uncle's child while the family was living aboard the *Sudan*. Their daughter Aviv was born on June 15, 1996.

While working at the Radisson Hotel, Ruby fell in love with a coworker named Frank. She decided to run away from home and this time for good. She moved in with Frank and his parents, and after a couple of days called her aunt Elizabeth to let her know that she was safe.

"She started asking me, 'Well, why did you have to do this.' I go, 'Because, Aunt Lise, I do not love Marcus. I do not want to be married to him.' She goes, 'Well, what about Aviv?' I go, 'Well, if you want me to, I'll take Aviv.' She goes, 'You can't take her. You're supposed to stay here with her. You're married to Marcus, and you're not to suppose to leave.'"

Elizabeth told Ruby she should talk to Marcus, and Ruby refused.

"I already knew there was a chance he could convince me to stay again, and this time I wasn't going back," Ruby testified.

Several months later Ruby called to see how her daughter was doing. Elizabeth answered the phone and told her the children weren't there. Ruby claimed that Elizabeth told her not to call the house anymore. But Ruby persisted and continued to call. As time passed, Elizabeth was more understanding. She said that Aviv was fine but that Ruby should not see her, because it would just make it harder for the child. On the phone, Ruby began to cry.

"[Elizabeth] said that it's my own fault that I'm suffering because I wanted to leave and have a different life," Ruby testified. "And that it was my choice. That I could have stayed there and stayed in my daughter's life."

Later, Ruby and Elizabeth reconciled and Elizabeth apologized for how she had treated her. Elizabeth started stopping by Ruby's house periodically to ask for money or food. One day Elizabeth made a request that made Ruby suspicious.

"She came over, and she asked me if I had cake mix. And I was like, 'Cake mix?' I go, 'Oh, no. I don't have any. Why?' She goes, 'Because it's one of the kid's birthdays, and I want to, you know, have a cake for him or something. I wanted to make cupcakes.'"

It was February at the time, and Ruby knew that none of the children had been born during that month. Ruby confronted Elizabeth and asked her if the girls were having more babies.

"I go, 'So how many more babies are there?' And she got quiet. And I go, 'Aunt Lise, you might as well tell me.' She goes, 'Well, Rosa has another baby.' And she left it at that."

Just a month prior to the murders, Ruby found out that there were in fact three more babies: one born to her sister Rosa, another to her cousin Kiani, and a third to Sebhrenah. Ruby said when she discovered this, she became angry with her aunt.

"I told her, 'Marcus is not supposed to be having more babies with his kids.' And she's like, 'Well, *mija,* the girls, they want it.' She goes, 'What can I say. I can't say anything about it.' I go, 'Aunt Lise, that's what you should be telling them! That is enough! So what, he's going to start having kids with his grandkids?'"

NINE

She was the one he called the "good soldier." Rosa Solorio did not talk to other men like her sisters did. She was completely devoted to her uncle and she would have done anything to protect him. The 23-year-old niece of Marcus Wesson had two of his children—4-year-old Ethan and 18-month-old Sedona—and both had been killed on March 12. Following the murders, like a "good soldier," Rosa stood by the man she considered her father and her husband and she defended him publicly, granting interviews to several local TV stations.

On the witness stand Rosa appeared nervous and shy. She spoke softly with the familiar family lisp. The judge asked her to move closer to the microphone. She began to cry as she listed the names of the children who lived in the house at the time of the murders.

"Is it true that you were being evicted from the house the next day?" Gamoian asked.

"They were saying that we had to get out in about a week," Rosa replied. She testified that the family had plans to purchase another boat and to live off the California coast.

The prosecutor asked Rosa about the events of March 12. Rosa described the custody dispute she had with her sister Sofina over 7-year-old Jonathan. She said that after a violent struggle she was able to pry the boy away from her sister.

"Then I took Jonathan and Ethan into the back room," Rosa testified.

"What room?" Gamoian asked.

"The room where the incident happened."

Rosa said she pushed Sofina out of the room and the seven younger children were all inside.

"What were the kids doing at this point?" Gamoian asked.

"They were just playing. They didn't know what was going on."

Rosa explained that she felt as if Jonathan was her own son.

"I raised him," she said.

"Who was his biological mother?" Gamoian asked.

"Sofina," she replied.

"Who was his father?"

"I don't know," Rosa said, shaking her head.

Gamoian asked who fathered all the children in the home. Rosa said she didn't know.

"I can assume but I actually don't know," she testified.

Rosa broke down when describing the moment when Elizabeth Wesson ran out of the house on the day of the murders, looking pale and frightened.

"She started fainting and she's saying, 'They're all gone,'" Rosa said.

"Now, during the time that you were living in the Wesson family, was there anything discussed about vampires?" the prosecutor asked.

"Yes," Rosa replied.

"What was that?"

"Well, at the time we . . . we . . . um, we liked the vampire movies and we just like playing, um . . . we just like playing vampires sometimes."

Rosa explained that several of the children had vampire

names, including her daughter Sedona, whose middle name was Vadra; Sebhrenah's son Marshey was named after one of the vampires in Marcus Wesson's book. Rosa explained that she named her son Ethan Saint Laurent because it was important for him to have a biblical name. Rosa denied that Wesson himself had a vampire name or that he taught the family any vampire doctrine.

"And isn't it Mr. Wesson who was making the comparison between Christ and vampires, that they both live forever?" Gamoian asked.

"No," Rosa replied.

"No? That was just something that all of you in the family—"

"It was just common knowledge," Rosa replied.

Rosa explained that there weren't enough beds for the children so many of them slept on top of the coffins because it wasn't as cold as sleeping on the floor.

The prosecutor asked Rosa if she recalled telling police detectives that she was irritated with Sofina and Ruby.

"Yes," Rosa replied.

Gamoian quoted a statement Rosa made to police: " 'Because they were acting like they were actually the victims when they only lost one child and I lost two'?"

"Yes, I remember saying that," Rosa answered.

"You don't think they are victims?"

"I do. They are victims as to losing the children. But, um, other than that, no. And the only reason why I was saying that, because they were gone for so long and they left the kids to us. And all of a sudden they would want to come and take them."

Gamoian referred to a statement made by Lise and Sebhrenah on the day of the murders. Several witnesses heard them tell Sofina and Ruby, "Bow down to your master," while pointing at Marcus Wesson's feet. Rosa refused to implicate her uncle.

Q. And with regards to Lise or Sebhrenah saying that, "Bow down to your master," what sort of voice were they using?

A. Um, a loud angry voice.

Q. And who was that statement directed to?

A. It was directed toward themselves.

Q. Toward who? I'm not following you.

A. Well, um, they were talking to Sofia and telling them to bow down to them . . . to whoever was telling Sofia bow down to your master, they were referring to themselves.

Q. And so they were telling Sofina to bow down to them?

A. Yes.

Rosa admitted to calling her sister Sofina "the true Lucifer" on the day of the murders. "I was just calling her that because she went back on her word."

"While all of this was going on, did you turn to Mr. Wesson and ask 'Should we?'" the prosecutor asked.

"No." Rosa paused. "Actually, yes I said, 'Should we go out there and get the keys to the car?'"

Q. Who do you believe killed the nine people?

A. Ruby and Sofina.

Q. Is that what you still believe?

A. Yes.

Q. Why?

A. Because if they could have waited, it wouldn't have happened.

The prosecutor asked about the practice Wesson referred to as "loving." Rosa testified that when she turned eighteen, Marcus would touch her in a sexual way about once a month.

"Did you want him to?" Gamoian asked.

"Yes." Rosa seemed very uneasy discussing the subject.

"Why do you seem so uncomfortable talking about it if you didn't think anything was wrong with it?"

"Because I don't like talking about my private life," Rosa said. "He did it so we would be better women," she assured. Rosa testified that Wesson only rubbed her over her clothes until she was eighteen years old. Then at nineteen, she said, she orally copulated him for the first time.

"How did it happen?" Gamoian asked.

"It just happened," Rosa answered.

The prosecutor became more aggressive. "You just accidentally put your mouth on his penis?" Gamoian asked.

"Yes," Rosa replied.

"You knew how to orally copulate a man without any instruction?"

"Yeah."

"Did Mr. Wesson protect you from being molested?"

"He never had to, because I never was molested," Rosa replied.

Gamoian asked Rosa to describe in graphic detail how she orally copulated her uncle. As she did, many of the jurors seemed uncomfortable and squirmed in their seats. Some glanced down at the floor.

Rosa said she "married" Marcus when she was nineteen and that she knew he had also married several other women in the family. She testified that having multiple wives was "natural," that she had read about it in the Bible and in history books. She told the court that she still considered herself Wesson's wife and that she intended to be faithful to him forever.

She claimed that the mass suicide attempt when the family was living aboard the *Sudan* was just a joke:

A. We were not serious when we were writing that note.
Q. But you told police you were ready to die, did you not?

A. Yes.

Q. Then how was it a joke?

A. I just meant I had the Lord and I was ready to die at the time.

On the witness stand, Rosa blatantly contradicted several statements she made to police following the murders. In one instance she told police that Wesson had trained them how to kill the children and themselves in case anyone attempted to separate the family. On the stand she said no one had told her what to do.

"You just knew instinctively what to do?" Gamoian asked.

"Yes."

"Just like you knew how to orally copulate Mr. Wesson without being told?"

"Yes."

Gamoian asked how Rosa planned to carry out the murder-suicide plan.

"I would shoot in the temple and over the heart," she replied.

Rosa testified that she had been visiting her uncle in jail and that he claimed to be on a strict diet. Wesson claimed he had been eating nothing but vegetables and that he went four months without drinking water.

"Do you believe that?" the prosecutor asked.

"Yes," Rosa answered.

"Did you ask him how he was able to live?" Gamoian asked.

"No," Rosa said.

On cross examination, Rosa broke down and cried as Ralph Torres asked about one of the children at the center of the custody dispute, 7-year-old Jonathan.

"Did you want that little boy to die that day?" Torres asked.

"No," she replied, sobbing.

"Sebhrenah killed the others, then herself. Wouldn't she be responsible for what she did?" Torres asked.

A. Yes, but I feel had Ruby and Sofina not done it in the way they did, it wouldn't have happened.

Q. You know they didn't pull the trigger, right?

A. Yes.

Q. Would you have killed for Marcus Wesson?

A. No.

Q. Did he tell you to kill anyone that day?

A. No.

TEN

Among the evidence collected from the crime scene were items of questionable significance including a PlayStation, a PalmPilot, and a bottle of fake blood. Crime-scene investigators also took possession of twenty purses, a pair of nail clippers, and two gun catalogues. The more compelling evidence included: a green purse containing unused bullets, a gun scope, and a switchblade key chain that apparently belonged to Sebhrenah Wesson. Identification Bureau technicians also collected a black purse that contained Sebhrenah's ID and two pocketknives. The murder weapon, a .22 caliber Ruger pistol, had been tested for fingerprints and it had none; it had also been swabbed for blood and was found to have traces of Sebhrenah's DNA. Gunshot residue tests of both Marcus and Sebhrenah Wesson's hands came back negative.[38] The knife discovered in the pile of bodies fit perfectly into the sheath Marcus had in his pocket at the time of his arrest. While it was covered in blood, none of the victims had suffered stab wounds.

However compelling that evidence was, it did not compare in importance or consequence to the carnage found

---

[38] The gunshot residue tests on Sebhrenah Wesson were done after her body had reached the morgue; the defense argued the tests should have been done earlier at the murder scene. Tests were performed on Marcus Wesson's hands not long after his arrest.

in the southeast bedroom. Senior forensic pathologist Dr. Venu Gopal of the Fresno County Coroner's Office performed the autopsies on the nine victims. He testified in graphic detail about the wounds suffered by seven children and the two older victims, and had also determined their cause of death.

Dr. Gopal had a mustache and wore glasses and he spoke with a strong Indian accent. He began with the victim at the base of the pile of bodies, Sebhrenah Wesson. Gopal testified that judging by the ring of soot around the gunshot wound to her right eye, that was where the bullet first entered Sebhrenah's body. He noted that she also had a contusion to her upper eyelid. As he spoke, photos of the victims' bodies flashed on a white screen.

"Taking all that into account, consistent with the gun site imprint, the muzzle end of the gun was in contact with the skin when the bullet was discharged. I can say that the gun was in a position where the gun site should be at nine o'clock position to the body and it should be in contact with the skin."

The prosecutor put on latex gloves and retrieved a large padded envelope. She opened it, took out a gun and handed it to Dr. Gopal. He held up the murder weapon as he explained that the gun was pressed up hard against Sebhrenah's skin when the gun was fired. The only wound found on her was the bullet wound to her face; her cause of death was damage to the brain, and the manner of death was ruled a homicide.

Seventeen-year-old Elizabeth (Lise) Wesson suffered a gunshot wound to her upper eyelid. Dr. Gopal described it as an "intermediate gunshot wound," which indicated that the gun was fired anywhere from a distance of half an inch to two feet from Lise's face. The doctor explained that the bullet had traveled through her upper eyelid, the right eyeball, the socket, the right side of the neck, and came to rest at the back of her neck. There was no exit wound. Lise was one of two victims who had been shot more than once. Gopal said the second shot was fired into her lower right eye.

The prosecutor asked Dr. Gopal if he had ever seen a victim who had committed suicide with two gunshots to the face.

"In the face, yes, but in the same eye like this is highly unlikely if not impossible," Gopal answered.

The autopsy on 1-year-old Jeva showed that the child had been shot in the right eye. The gunshot site made an imprint at the ten o'clock position, Gopal explained; the bullet penetrated the right eye, the eye socket, the brain, and exited out the back of the head. As an autopsy photo showing a close-up of the baby's face appeared on the screen, many jurors appeared horrified. One juror sighed loudly. Another put her hand over her eyes.

The coroner continued: Eighteen-month-old Sedona also had a gunshot wound to the right eye, but the coroner characterized it as a "hard contact wound," meaning the baby was shot at very close range. The fired bullet collapsed the right eye, went through the eye socket, the brain, and then exited the back of the head.

The son of the oldest victim, Sebhrenah Wesson, was 18-month-old Marshey. Marshey was the only one who had been shot in his left eye. The coroner described the path of the bullet, saying it traveled through the left eye from front to back, slightly upward.

The autopsy of 4-year-old Ethan revealed a hard contact wound, meaning he was shot at close range. Gopal testified that the bullet traveled through his right eye, collapsed the right eyeball, and perforated the brain. Ethan also suffered a gunshot wound to the right side of his abdomen. Gopal said the second wound indicated the gun was fired from a distance of more than two feet.

"Because there was no bleeding in the abdomen or liver, it suggests it was postmortem or it happened in or around the death," Gopal stated. "The person's heart was not beating when this injury occurred."

Eight-year-old Illabelle was shot in the right eye. The bullet went through the right eyeball, the nasal bones, crossed over and perforated the muscles in the back of the neck. The bullet did not penetrate the brain and there was no exit wound.

Seven-year-old Aviv Wesson's autopsy revealed a gunshot wound to the right side of her face. The bullet penetrated the brain and did not exit the head.

Seven-year-old Jonathan Wesson had also been shot in the right eye. The bullet traveled to the back of his head, fracturing the skull.

"I am carefully wording this wound, because the gun muzzle was at an angle," Gopal said. "The gun was held at an angle, in my opinion."

As the coroner testified, Marcus Wesson wrote intently on a pad of paper and did not glance at the photos being projected onto the screen.

Under cross examination, defense attorney Ralph Torres questioned Dr. Gopal about the time of death of the victims and whether liver temperature tests were taken at the scene. Gopal said that liver temperatures were taken of five of the nine victims: Sebhrenah, Elizabeth, Jeva, Jonathan, and Sedona.

"What does this tell you about their time of death?" Torres asked.

Gopal explained there were many variables that made time of death difficult to determine.

"Is it possible that with these numbers, that Sebhrenah and Lise died at about the same time?" Torres asked.

"They are in the ball park figure," Gopal affirmed.

He concluded, "The two adults died probably later than the other seven children. That's the best we can do." The doctor explained further that he believed the children were killed one to two hours before the oldest victims, Elizabeth and Sebhrenah.

"Do you remember a conversation you had with me

when you said Sebhrenah's injuries were consistent with being self-inflicted?" Torres asked the doctor.

"I don't think I used the word 'consistent' but I can say yes, it can happen that way," Gopal answered.

ELEVEN

Included in the prosecution's long list of witnesses were Wesson's oldest sons, Dorian and Adrian Wesson, who both had been estranged from their family for several years. In addition to hearing them testify, the jury spent several hours listening to their interviews with police in which both young men made some frank admissions about their father. Dorian told a police detective, "In the beginning my father made sense. But in the last three years he's become insane." When asked if he believed that his mother knew about the sexual abuse going on in the house, Dorian replied, "Obviously she had to know about it. I mean that's one dumb person. My mother was like a shadow, she was always quiet, very submissive." Dorian told the jury that he felt "socially handicapped" by his upbringing.

Adrian told the court that as a boy he wanted to be like other children and was excited when his father asked him if he wanted to attend school. Adrian thought he would soon be in a classroom surrounded by other kids his age but soon discovered, to his great disappointment, that his father wanted him to attend martial-arts classes. Knowing it was his only chance to meet children outside of his family, Adrian began to study martial arts and eventually earned a black belt in aikido (some of the other Wesson boys did the same).

After the murders, Adrian told the police, "Just my father's whole outlook at life, the Bible. I thought he was pretty insane. He's not stupid. They always label him as being insane. You know, it's just kind of insane to do it. I would say he was insane . . . When I moved, when I left out of the house I was determined that I had to get out of the house."

Other prosecution witnesses included the 911 dispatcher who took the calls for help the day of the murders. Several family members accused Fresno police of a slow response to their calls for help. The jury heard recordings of five 911 calls made by two women from the Solorio family that day. Twenty-two minutes elapsed between the time of the first call to 911 and the arrival of police. By the time a third call was placed, the CHP dispatcher chuckled and told the police dispatcher the story being told by the callers was "embellished."

Reacting to the criticism of a dawdling response, the Fresno Police Department released the following timeline of events:

2:13 P.M. Police receive call about child custody dispute at the Wesson home.

2:23 P.M. First officer is dispatched.

2:35 P.M. Several officers respond to scene and decide they have no legal right to enter the residence.

2:50 P.M. Officers call the city attorney to ask if they have legal authority to enter the house; Marcus Wesson remains at the front door. The attorney tells police they have no cause to enter the house without the owner's permission.

3:03 P.M. Officers call Child Protective Services.

3:35 P.M. Wesson leaves his post at the front door and enters the house. Several women become hysterical outside, saying Wesson is armed with a handgun. Officers yell into the house for Wesson to respond. There is no answer.

3:47 P.M. Officers request SWAT team.

4:45 P.M. SWAT team arrives and surrounds the house.

4:47 P.M. Wesson emerges from the back bedroom covered in blood and is arrested.

By the time she was done making her case against Marcus Wesson, the prosecutor had called sixty-five witnesses to the stand and twelve weeks had passed. The judge ruled Gamoian would not be allowed to call her two expert witnesses to testify on the subject of mind control. With the help of psychological experts, the prosecutor had planned to argue that Wesson had effectively brainwashed his family to carry out a murder-suicide pact if the government ever tried to separate the family. After hearing what the two experts had to say in a closed session, Judge Putnam decided their testimony was contradictory and would just confuse the jury. The expert's analysis of Wesson's mental state was therefore not immediately made public.[39] Shortly after the murders, one of the prosecution experts offered an opinion about Wesson to a reporter at the *San Jose Mercury News,* who paraphrased J. Reid Meloy as follows: "But [Dr. Meloy] said Wesson's nomadic,

---

[39] The judge unsealed the transcripts in March 2005, after I made a motion to have them made public. The experts' findings are discussed in the last section of this book.

polygamous lifestyle had many hallmarks of a 'charismatic psychopath'—similar to cult leader David Koresh . . . who manipulates followers through a mixture of isolation, sexual indoctrination and his own paranoid preaching."[40]

Included in the prosecutor's list of experts was Park Dietz, a forensic psychiatrist who had testified in many high profile trials, including those of Jeffery Dahmer, "Son of Sam" killer David Berkowitz, and Yosemite murderer Cary Stayner. As jury selection was under way in Wesson's trial, Dietz became embroiled in a huge controversy involving his most recent testimony in the case against Houston mother Andrea Yates. Dietz concluded that Yates, who had drowned five of her children, was sane. He also testified that he had consulted the producers of the TV show *Law & Order,* and that an episode had aired that paralleled the Yates case. In the episode, Dietz testified, the woman was found not guilty of the murders by reason of insanity. There was only one problem: such an episode had never aired. The prosecutor had argued that perhaps Yates got the idea to kill her children from the show. The mistake ultimately caused a mistrial, and Dietz's name immediately disappeared from Lisa Gamoian's list of potential witnesses in the Wesson case.

The issue of insanity would not even come up during Wesson's three-month trial. Given Wesson's belief that he was a vampire and had written at length about his desire to start a new religion that mixed vampirism and Christianity, it appeared the defense had ample material with which to make an issue of their client's mental capacity, but the public defender would have to take a different tack. According to California law, the defense could not argue insanity as a defense without Wesson's

---

[40] Quote from the *San Jose Mercury News,* March 18, 2004.

cooperation, and there was no way Wesson would agree to such a strategy. Defense attorneys would have to focus on the lack of physical evidence linking Wesson to the killings, and they would have to convince the jury that Wesson had never instituted a murder-suicide pact. Several family members had already verified the existence of such a pact, but it was the defense's assertion that such a plan had not even been discussed for years. Wesson's attorneys would paint a picture of 25-year-old Sebhrenah as a religious zealot, fascinated with guns and knives and obsessed with the afterlife. The defense argued that Sebhrenah often said she wanted to die and couldn't wait to go to heaven.

The defense took about a week to make its case, calling only seven witnesses. The first witness was Allen Boudreau, a retired sheriff's official who performed an elaborate experiment at the Wesson home following the murders. He attempted to recreate the murder scene, positioning several people in and around the house as he fired a .22 caliber gun in the southeast bedroom. Many of those involved in the experiment reported hearing an inconsistent number of gunshots. The results of the experiment were supposed to explain why police officers had not heard gunshots, while several family members said they had. Boudreau also testified to what defense attorney Ralph Torres portrayed as a key piece of evidence: a postmortem photograph of Sebhrenah Wesson's hand that revealed a small black mark on her right pinky finger. Torres argued that the spot was produced by the murder weapon and proved that Sebhrenah had fired the gun, in spite of the fact gunshot residue tests done on her hands produced negative results.

Gary Cortner, a retired criminalist for the California Department of Justice, testified that the Fresno Police

Department had mishandled the evidence. Cortner said that the bodies were moved improperly, contaminating the crime scene. On cross examination the prosecutor asked, "Does it change the fact that nine people were killed with a .22 caliber pistol?"

"Certainly not," Cortner replied.

Dr. Robert Lawrence was a defense expert who studied the liver temperatures of the victims in an effort to determine their time of death, and he concluded that the seven younger children died between two and three o'clock in the afternoon. According to several witnesses, Marcus Wesson was still positioned at the front door of the house at that time. The autopsies also revealed that the younger children still had food in their stomachs and that Sebhrenah's and Lise's stomachs were empty. The defense argued that if the family all ate lunch together, this supported the idea that Sebhrenah and Lise died a significant time after the younger children since the oldest victims had time to digest their food. Dr. Lawrence also examined Sebhrenah Wesson's autopsy photos, concluding that the gunshot to her right eye was likely self-inflicted. All of this, the defense team reasoned, supplied more than a reasonable doubt that Wesson had committed the killings.

The question of whether to call Wesson himself to testify was one that perplexed his defense team. The prosecutor had not introduced Wesson's taped interviews with police as evidence, and the defense could not do so. If defense attorneys wanted their client's version of events to be considered by the jury, their only option was to call Wesson to the stand. Defense attorneys knew if they called their client to testify, the prosecutor would be allowed to cross examine him on all of the sex charges. That meant she could ask him to describe in graphic detail each of the alleged sexual acts, as she did with several of her own witnesses. It would cause the jurors to hate him more than they already did, the defense team reasoned, and it was a risk Wesson's attorneys weren't willing to take. The defense would rest its case, and the only person who knew what happened in the back bedroom at 761 West Hammond Avenue would not get a chance to tell his side of the story.

TWELVE

After three months of testimony it was finally time for the prosecutor to argue her case to the jury. Lisa Gamoian stood up, placed her arms on the back of her chair, took a deep breath and sighed.

"Did you ever think we'd get to this place?" she asked the jury. "I was beginning to wonder." Gamoian said she would provide jurors with a framework to interpret all the evidence they had seen and heard over the previous twelve weeks.

"That framework is the law," she said.

The prosecutor said that the evidence had shown that Wesson was guilty of nine counts of first degree murder. She explained there were several elements such a conviction required: The jury had to determine that the murders were unlawful killings with express malice, and they had to be willful, deliberate, and premeditated.

"Was it an accident? Obviously, it wasn't," Gamoian told the jury. The prosecutor argued that the killings were intentional, demonstrated by the fact that the gunshot wounds showed hard contact with the eyes of all of the victims. She said the killer had jammed the gun into their eye sockets and that the murders were most certainly premeditated.

"We have the gathering up of the victims into the southeast bedroom secluded away from anyone who could possibly rescue them or intervene in the killing process. And then we have our victims systematically lined up and just exterminated one right after another with the muzzle of that gun just jammed up to the eye. Obviously, there's careful thought and consideration. Our slayer is acting very coolly. Not irrationally. Not panicked. Very collected."

Gamoian said the motive in the case was clear: Wesson had taught the women in the family to carry out a murder-suicide pact if CPS ever tried to take the children.

"We've got the finding of the gun in the duffel bag, the loading of the gun, sliding back of the bolt mechanism to get it in firing position. Shooting of Jonathan and Aviv, Illabelle, Ethan, one right after another." Gamoian paused between each of the victims' names. "Marshey, Jeva, Sedona, Lise. Finally Sebhrenah. Very systematic. And what the crime scene tells us is that at one point our shooter, our slayer, had to reload, because we have an empty magazine on the floor under Illabelle's foot. Obviously, our slayer, our killer, dropped a magazine and loaded another to continue the shooting."

At least two bullets were misshapen, and the prosecutor postulated that meant the gun jammed at least twice, forcing the shooter to stop and reload.

"This is a very calm, cool, premeditated, collected slayer. Clearly, we have nine counts of premeditated murder."

The prosecutor explained that the jury could find Wesson guilty of first degree murder in one of three scenarios: that Wesson himself was the shooter, that he conspired in the killings, or that he aided and abetted the shooter.

As to the first theory—that Wesson was the shooter—the prosecutor argued that the .22 caliber gun belonged to the defendant; he was the only one in the family who ever fired it and he never taught anyone else to use it. Wesson was also the only one to emerge from the back bedroom alive and he had blood all over his clothes.

"At a minimum, based upon Mrs. Wesson's testimony—that Lise appeared to be crying while Mr. Wesson held her—he's in the bedroom when Lise is killed. And additionally Sebhrenah."

Under the second theory the jury would have to find that Wesson had the intent to commit, encourage, or facilitate the crime.

"We've got all three," the prosecutor said.

Gamoian called Wesson the inventor of the murder-suicide plan, referring back to Sofina's attempt to carry out the plan when the family was living aboard the *Sudan*. Gamoian pointed out that the boat contained all the tools needed to carry out the plan; after the murders, investigators found seven hundred rounds of live ammunition on board.

"Mr. Wesson told the older girls in the family, 'No, wait for my instruction, for my direction, before you do it.' That's what he told the girls. He'd fine-tuned the plan. He didn't revoke it. He didn't say, 'Don't do that.' He continued to promote that plan. To instigate it, to encourage it."

On March 12, the prosecutor argued, Wesson was simply facilitating that plan.

"Isn't that what he was doing at the front door keeping everyone out, blocking the doorway, not letting police officers inside, not letting Sofina take her child? All it would have taken was one word from Mr. Wesson. 'Let the kids go,' and that is it. But he didn't. Instead he said, 'Let's talk about it.' Bogus talk. Bogus talk. He was just buying time. He knew all the kids had been collected in the southeast bedroom. He full well knew what was going to occur in that southeast bedroom. He stands in the position of the shooter, even if you don't think he is the shooter."

The third and final theory of conspiracy required that

there had to be an agreement between two or more people to commit a crime, and there had to be an overt act done to carry out that plan. The prosecutor said there was clearly an agreement in this case between more than just two people.

"Mr. Wesson, Kiani, Gypsy, Rosie, Sofina, Ruby, Sebhrenah, they had all agreed to it. It was a regular discussion at the girl talks, right? Those Friday night girl talks. Mr. Wesson was always checking to see if the girls were obeying the rules, if they were talking to boys. One of the regular talks, likewise, was talk of the family not letting the kids be separated or the family be separated. And if that should happen, the government or CPS should come in, then the murder suicide pact would be instituted. Girls were directed to first kill the younger children, then themselves."

The prosecutor continued. "During their interviews with police the day after the murders, Gypsy, Kiani, and Rosie, Elizabeth, who do they blame? It's amazing. Who do they blame for the whole slaughter of a whole generation of this family? Not the designer of the murder suicide pact. Not the supposed slayer. No. They blame Ruby and Sofina because they were aware of the agreement, and they had agreed to it. In their minds, Ruby and Sofina are the ones who put this plan into action."

As for the sex charges, Gamoian pointed out that when some of the girls testified they were adamant that the sexual acts between themselves and the defendant were consensual.

"Any victim under the age of fourteen cannot consent by law," she pointed out. "Ruby testified that when she was eight years old, the loving . . . Mr. Wesson's rubbing, teaching her how to please a potential husband in the future, that began when she was eight! And the defendant was very instructive to an eleven-year-old, teaching her how to orally copulate him. 'Don't use your teeth. Just use your tongue and your lips.' These are Mr. Wesson's statements to an eleven-year-old! 'A real woman would swallow.' This is Mr. Wesson teaching 'loving' to the daughters in the family."

Gamoian argued that Wesson had a pattern of blaming the women in the family for just about everything that went wrong. "So is it any great surprise that he would try to lay off nine murders on Sebhrenah Wesson? No. But as I said, these are very exacting wounds. This wasn't someone who was wildly shooting in some sort of frenzy on this particular day, to systematically shoot children one right after another. Was Sebhrenah collected and calm enough to then mark her own child? Is that what she was doing? Marshey, her own son, was shot in a different eye. Isn't that more the defendant's style? So that he, again, can lay this off on Sebhrenah. Marking Marshey as somehow being different. Any way you slice it, any way, any theory you use, the defendant is responsible for nine counts of first degree murder that occurred on March the twelfth."

With a look of satisfaction on her face, Gamoian thanked the jurors for their attention and sat down. Throughout the prosecutor's closing arguments, Ralph Torres sat next to the defendant, leaning back with a look of skepticism. He leaned uncomfortably close to Wesson, his head nearly grazing Wesson's shoulder, leaving reporters in the gallery to speculate that Torres was trying to make his client seem less intimidating. Wesson would also periodically whisper something in Torres's ear and Torres would nod approvingly.

"It's been a hard long road," Torres began. "It sure has. My kids don't even remember me. And so thank God we're finally at the end."

Torres began by acknowledging the sex charges. "But this is first and foremost a murder case," he advised the jury. "In this case we have shown you through forensic science that Mr. Wesson did not kill his nine children. The prosecutor has admitted that much."

He argued there was no murder-suicide plan.

"Who called it a suicide pact? What witness called it that? The prosecutor makes it up. It sounds better. No witness that I heard called it a suicide pact and then related it to some sort of training."

Torres continued. "This family, of course, is dysfunctional to the tenth power. But that doesn't mean that we throw the rules of law of evidence out the window because we hate this situation. That these women as girls were hurt. And we don't like what happened. But ladies and gentlemen, this happens. People raise their kids dysfunctionally all the time."

The defense attorney said the prosecutor had misled the jury to believe that Wesson was inventing his own brand of religion. Torres argued that there were millions of Seventh Day Adventists around the world who believed in the Second Coming of Christ and the end of the world, and Wesson was no different.

"Please!" Torres insisted incredulously. "Is this the only family that believed that 9/11 may have been a sign of Armageddon?"

Torres argued that the Wesson family had problems just like every other family.

"What African-American father who's strong-willed would not discipline his kids?" he asked. Several jurors appeared doubtful. Torres glanced down and apologized. "Sorry, I lost my train of thought," he said, pausing. Torres encouraged the jury to consider the "larger picture."

"In the prosecution of this case, this man, we're looking at little tidbits. Is that justice? Is that fairness?"

Torres made reference to the audio recording made on the day of the murders at the front door of the house. He argued that Wesson remained calm and even asked for the involvement of the police. Torres said the evidence pointed to Sebhrenah Wesson as the shooter and perpetrator of the crimes.

"Sebhrenah was the quiet one. Why is it that the other girls didn't carry bullets in their purses? She shined her bullets. Who does that? None of the other girls did that."

Jonathan and Aviv, who were the two children at the center of the custody dispute, were the first to die, Torres argued.

"I will submit to you that Jonathan and Aviv died around 2:20 in the afternoon. That's way before the police arrive."

Wesson's attorney then played the audio recording made on the day of the murders by Louis Garcia. Large speakers sat on the defense table, pointing toward the jury box; the recording had been enhanced so the panelists could hear the alleged sound of gunfire.

"Everyone arrived at 2:10. The tape is turned on immediately, according to Louis Garcia." Torres played the tape, pointing out significant points along the way.

"Within two minutes and thirty seconds you hear screaming in the background. The ladies in the back are fighting. You can hear it."

About eight minutes into the recording, Torres argued, the first gunshots could be heard. "You hear them. Boom. Boom. Nobody seems to pay any attention." Marcus Wesson's voice could still be heard on the recording at the time of the first possible gunshots, Torres pointed out. As the tape played, jurors strained to hear the thumping noises.

More gunshots could be heard eleven minutes into the tape, Torres posited.

"So now, by that time I think Jonathan and Aviv were gone. Maybe Illabelle, too. Marcus Wesson is trying to talk to the family." Seventeen minutes into the recording Torres asked the jury to listen for two more gunshots.

"We have numerous shots mounting up. This is when the children died," he said.

At nineteen minutes, there was another "pop" or gun-shot. Police subsequently arrived and Torres pointed out two more places on the tape where gunshots could be heard; Marcus Wesson is still at the front door through-out it all.

"There it is. Boom," Torres said of the last alleged gunshot heard on the tape. Since Wesson was not in the room at the time of the killings, Torres argued that the prosecutor had not proved either an aiding and abetting or conspiracy theory beyond a reasonable doubt. The blood smears found on Wesson's clothes were consistent with touching the victims after they had been killed, Tor-res reasoned; Wesson had wiped the blood on his shirt or perhaps kneeled in Sebhrenah's blood.

"We know that Sebhrenah shot herself. It's overwhelm-ing. The evidence is overwhelming to show you that the children had passed before the adults. It's overwhelming when we show you that Sebhrenah shot herself and that there is no evidence that Marcus Wesson had knowledge of it, authorized it, or ordered it."

The prosecutor then made her rebuttal argument. She immediately addressed the playing of the recording, say-ing the defense's timeline was "fatally flawed" and that the sounds were not necessarily gunshots.

"I stopped counting. I mean, counsel identifies nine shots. I heard twenty-two of something at one point. And ultimately he identifies twelve. That's what Mr. Torres testified to today during his closing argument was twelve shots. Well, that's not even accurate, 'cause there were eleven shots that were fired."

Gamoian continued.

"I mean, Mr. Garcia is carrying this recorder in his pocket. His shirt pocket. I mean, I don't know, are his keys or cigarette lighter in the pocket that may be hitting up against that?"

One of the officers at the scene heard a baby's cry come

from the southeast bedroom; Gamoian said that disproved the defense's theory that the children were killed before police arrived. She said the whole demonstration didn't change the facts of the case.

"It doesn't change the long domination and control Mr. Wesson had over the girls. It doesn't change the agreement, this murder-suicide pact that he's been preaching for years and years that almost happened on the *Sudan*. It doesn't change any of that."

If Wesson himself hadn't pulled the trigger, the prosecutor argued, he spent those eighty minutes inside the southeast bedroom ordering the killings. As for how the blood got on his clothing, Gamoian said it was not because he was checking for signs of life.

"If anything this guy was checking to make sure they were dead," she said.

In addition, the prosecutor argued the defense's contention that Wesson was a practicing Seventh Day Adventist was erroneous.

"Where in the Seventh Day Adventist doctrine does it say anything about vampirism and comparing Jesus to vampires? How they both drank blood? How they both live eternally? Seventh Day Adventists don't believe that."

Wesson dictated the plan for his children to "go to the Lord" for years, Gamoian said. "It makes sense, doesn't it? The shot to the eye? He's very Old Testament oriented, according to his family. That's what he was doing here, isn't it? An eye . . . for an eye . . . for an eye . . . for an eye . . . for an eye . . . for an eye . . . for an eye . . . for an eye . . . for an eye!" The prosecutor repeated the phrase nine times for each of the victims, her voice growing louder and filled with more emotion each time.

"And you can bet Mr. Wesson was the last thing those kids saw before they were slaughtered, because he's Jesus! He's the Lord and that's where they were going!"

Gamoian paused and looked squarely at the jurors.

"Don't let Mr. Wesson evade responsibility! Don't let him hide behind the girls in the family! Don't let him rape Sebhrenah one last time by laying this off on her! Because that's what they want to do: rape her after her death. He's responsible! Hold him responsible!"

THIRTEEN

On June 17, 2005, whispers of a verdict spread quickly throughout the Fresno County courthouse. The jury of five men and seven women had reached a unanimous verdict on all twenty-three counts, and the decision came less than an hour into the jury's tenth day of deliberations. Family members were informed by phone that the jury had reached a decision. In a matter of minutes the hallway outside Department 53 had filled with reporters, curious attorneys, and members of the public. The Sheriff's Department set up a security check area in the hallway and searched bags and scanned with a metal detecting wand everyone who planned to attend the hearing.

Family members filed into the courtroom and sat in the back row. The group of family included many of the Wesson children and the defendant's wife, who appeared frail and broken. Elizabeth Wesson had already lost her composure and was sniffling. It was the only sound that could be heard in the otherwise silent courtroom. The judge took the bench and the jurors entered the room with stern looks. None made eye contact with Wesson as they took their seats in the jury box.

Court reporter Barbara Graves read the verdict forms. "We the jury in the matter of *People* v. *Marcus Delon*

Wesson, find the defendant guilty of the crime of murder in the first degree." It was a phrase she would repeat nine times. The jury had found that Wesson did not pull the trigger of the murder weapon, but it sided with the prosecutor's argument that Wesson either aided and abetted in the crimes or that he conspired in the murders. In addition, the jury found Wesson guilty of fourteen sex crimes, ranging from forced oral copulation and rape to continuous sexual abuse. Halfway through the reading of the verdicts, Wesson wiped tears from his eyes. The courtroom remained silent except for the sobs of Elizabeth Wesson and Rosa Solorio on the back row. The jury also found the special circumstance of multiple murders to be true, which meant the same jury would have to decide if Wesson deserved to die for the crimes.

Elizabeth Wesson collapsed as she made her way out of the courthouse. Her son Almae propped her up and told the photographers and reporters who swarmed around them, "Justice was not carried out." He helped his mother into a waiting car that sped off.

Before the penalty phase of the trial began, the court received a report of possible juror misconduct from local television station KMPH. On June 21, 2005, Judge Putnam held a private hearing in his chambers to discuss the issue. The report alleged that a juror had told her husband about the guilty verdicts before they were announced. According to KMPH's source, the spouse shared the information with his coworkers at a local Wal-Mart, and one of those coworkers had called the TV station just minutes before the verdicts were read to say that the verdict would be guilty on all counts. KMPH did not report the information as fact but also did not confirm the tip before airing the story. "We weren't able to verify the story," the station's news director, Roger Gadley, said unapologetically. Gadley could not attest to the reliability of the source, saying, "I can't imagine someone would make up something like this and stir up a big hornet's nest."

The judge called both Gadley and several KMPH employees into his chambers in an effort to get to the bottom of the accusations. Gadley refused to reveal the identity of the source, citing his protection under the Shield Law and calling it a "major issue for all journalists." Ultimately, the source of the story was revealed and called into court. Behind closed doors, the female Wal-Mart employee shared what she had heard. Judge Putnam also interviewed the juror in question and her spouse. After completing his investigation, Putnam decided that no juror misconduct had occurred and the penalty phase began.

The defense would call only two witnesses to testify. The defendant's 84-year-old mother, Carrie Wesson, had planned to make the trip from Seattle but suffered from osteoarthritis and cancelled the trip at the last minute. Instead, she wrote a letter to the court, pleading for her son's life. Wesson's sister, Cheryl Penton, took the witness stand, and when asked to identify her brother, she pointed at Wesson and said, "He's my brother." Wesson sat at the defense table with his eyes closed. Penton paused and said, "Open your eyes, Mark. I love you." She recalled her brother as a young boy, bringing home stray and injured animals and nursing them back to health. Penton also recalled an unstable childhood, saying that the family moved often and that their father was an out-of-work alcoholic who was mostly absent from his children's lives.

"You understand that your brother is facing the death penalty," attorney Pete Jones said. "If the jury spares his life would you stay in contact with him?"

A look of despair came over Penton's face. "Till I die," she replied quietly.

"Is it a relationship that is meaningful to you?" Jones asked.

"Yes," she said. There was a brief silence and then Penton began to sob.

The defense had hired at least two experts of their own to offer a mental evaluation of Wesson, and it was expected that their testimony would be offered as mitigating evidence during the penalty phase. If Wesson suffered from some sort of mental illness, perhaps the jury would opt for a sentence of life in prison rather than death. Jones would not say why he decided not to call either expert to testify.

The only other witness called in the penalty phase was Gregory Bledsoe, a childhood friend of Marcus Wesson. Bledsoe testified that when he was just a teenager, Marcus's father Ben Wesson propositioned him, offering him fifty dollars to let the elder Wesson perform oral sex on him.

Bledsoe stepped down from the witness stand, and it was time for the prosecutor to address the jury. Before she could utter her first word, Marcus Wesson interrupted the proceedings. "Your Honor?" he said.

"Yes, sir," the judge replied.

"Could I be heard now?" Wesson asked.

The judge shook his head. "Not right now, no," Putnam said.

"Your Honor?" Wesson repeated.

"You'll have to wait, Mr. Wesson. We'll continue the matter—"

Wesson would not quiet down. "My lawyers are fired," he proclaimed. "Could I be heard?"

"Not yet," Putnam advised.

"They're fired," Wesson repeated.

"Ms. Gamoian, go ahead," Putnam told the prosecutor.

"Thank you, Your Honor," she replied. Gamoian appeared completed unaffected by the defendant's outburst. She looked squarely at the twelve jurors.

"You know why I'm here," she began. "And you know what I'm about to ask you to do. When we first met, I asked you if you all had the courage to make a decision such as this, and you all confirmed that, in fact, you could make that decision. And so, I now stand before you and I fully realize the gravity and the enormity of what I'm about to ask you to do. Without any hesitation, no reservation, I'm asking you to return a verdict of death as to each count. All nine counts of the murders this man perpetrated on his own children."

Again Wesson interrupted the proceedings.

"Your Honor, my lawyers are fired!" he said. "Can I have a Marsden hearing?"[41]

Judge Putnam let out a long sigh. "Well, ladies and gentlemen, we're going to have to take a recess, then, and we'll have you back in as soon as we can."

The judge also asked everyone in the gallery to exit the courtroom.

After a closed hearing in which Wesson explained why he wanted to fire his attorneys, the judge denied Wesson's request and the prosecutor resumed her statement to the jury.

"Don't reward him with the gift of life," she urged. Wesson sat at the defense table shaking his head in protest.

"He not only controlled their minds, he controlled their bodies. He controlled their hopes and dreams. For Mr. Wesson the ultimate satisfaction came on March 12, because he controlled their deaths," Gamoian said. "He throws them out like trash. That's the respect he shows for his own children."

The prosecutor turned on a projector and the bloody

---

[41] A hearing to determine if a defendant can fire his or her counsel.

images of the dead children again flashed on the white screen.

"Will you ever get the image of Sedona out of your minds?" Gamoian asked the jury. "The one-year-old in a onesie shot through the eye? And the haunting image of Jeva, the youngest, with those little jeans she was wearing, shot in the eye! That's the kind of compassion that man showed! You can bet he was the last person they saw before they were shot. He solely sentenced each of his children to death. He didn't give them the consideration you're giving him. He was judge and jury."

Wesson shook his head vigorously as the prosecutor continued.

"He's the one who orchestrated these murders, these rapes, these molests. There is no lingering doubt. Life is a gift. Far more than he afforded a whole generation of children. Is this case extreme enough to warrant the death penalty? Is this horrific enough? Is it cruel enough? Is the taking of nine innocent lives, is that senseless enough? You decide. Thank you."

Pete Jones made one last plea to the jury to spare Wesson's life.

"There are no excuses for these crimes. These victims are gone forever. They should never be forgotten," Jones began. He told the jury that putting Wesson to death would be "the easy thing to do."

"By your verdicts you have branded him forever as a child molester and a rapist. And as he is led off in chains to his modern day dungeon, that brand will follow him wherever he goes."

Jones reminded the jury of Wesson's alcoholic father and his ultrareligious mother. "It does not take an expert to tell that Ben Wesson had a problem. A picture begins to emerge, a bridge between the boy that might have been and the man who sits here today. I'm not here to judge

Ben Wesson, but Marcus Wesson cannot be viewed in a vacuum."

Jones finished with the story of John Newton, who sailed a slave ship and who wrote the song "Amazing Grace," to illustrate the lesson of human frailty.

"You can't just look at photographs and hear a rant about evil and say 'That's it.' Giving Marcus Wesson death won't bring back any of the victims or undo anything he has done to the family on both sides of this courtroom. It's your decision not to impose the death penalty and I would ask you not to compromise that decision."

It took the jury fewer than nine hours to reach a verdict: death for each of the nine counts of first degree murder. A sentencing hearing was scheduled for the following month. After the verdict, defense attorney Ralph Torres told a group of reporters that they had given Wesson the "worst case scenario," and that Wesson was prepared for the jury's decision. Pete Jones expressed his deep disappointment, saying, "Obviously the results aren't what we hoped for or worked for, I'm going to be second guessing myself for a long time." Prosecutor Lisa Gamoian left court waving off reporters and made no public comment.

On July 27, 2005, the courtroom was packed one last time for Marcus Wesson's sentencing. Before pronouncing the sentence, the judge let anyone in the family address the court. Sofina knew at that moment what she wanted to say. She rose to her feet and walked to the lectern at the front of the gallery. She looked straight at her uncle, who was facing forward. He turned slightly and could see her out of the corner of his eye.

"I have something very simple to say," Sofina began. "I just wanted Marcus to know that you claim to be

Jesus Christ. You claim to be God. Look at you now. You're nothing. You're the lowest of low." Her voice did not waiver. "But I want you to know something. Since I have departed from you, your presence, I found my true God. And one thing I have learned is that he don't go against himself. And one of his commandments states, 'Thou shall not kill,' and you have done that. So I want you to know that nothing or anybody is going to prevent me from going to heaven to see my children and my sisters. I love them and they know it. And I just want you to know that you have been forgiven in my heart. Likewise, I have forgiven my sisters and my aunt Lise and my mother. So like I said before, nothing is going to prevent me from going to heaven. And I just hope, you know, through God's mercy that as you sit there in your cell that you think about what you have done to my family, my brothers, my sisters, my child Jonathan, little Aviv, Ethan, Illabelle, Sedona, Marshey, Jeva. These are children that belong not to you. They were for you to raise for the Lord. That was not for you to make that decision to take them away from this world. But they're gone now. Who knows why. They're in a better place. I believe that in my heart. So my life now is to continue to live that I may see them one day. That's basically all I have to say to you."

Sofina took her seat and her brother Marco Garcia stood up.

"You led God's children to the slaughter," he told his uncle. "So I know He will put much suffering and pain upon you, Marcus. There's nothing I want to enjoy more than to watch you slip into death. Nothing. Your soul will never rest."

The tension in the courtroom grew. The Wessons sat on the back row of the left side of the courtroom, the Solorios sat on the right. The first of the sons from the

Wesson side of the family, 30-year-old Dorian, spoke next. His head was shaved and he appeared to be wearing eye makeup.

"Marcus Wesson, which is my father," he said. "I just want to say to you that even though you are guilty of things and you may be wrong in the things you do, and I forgive you for what you have done, even though I consider it wrong. But I still love you as a father. And me, as your oldest son, will carry your name on. And I will always represent your teachings, but in a legal manner. And Marcus Wesson, my father, I will always love you within my heart and be a soldier of God. And though I may be arrogant and defiant, I will live an arrogant life, defying all things in life to the end, but in a legitimate way. Know I love you, and I may carry on your seed, and my children bear your fruits. For this is the beginning of God's true task. I may not make sense 'cause I'm full of emotions, but everything I heard previously was nothing but a grain of sand next to titanium steel. And I am your oldest son, and your spirit will live through me, but in a good way. I'll do things the right way. The way God wanted it to be. I'll be legitimate. But one thing, you will rest in me. So therefore, you are free through my soul. I just want to let you know that. And arrogance does run through me. And I'm young and cocky as hell. I'm done."

Dorian took his seat and his mother, Elizabeth Wesson, moved with uncertainty toward the lectern. She spoke in a whisper. "Marcus, what happened that day I do not blame you for it. I just want you to know that your children still love you. I love you. And I know that that day would have never happened if my nieces never came to my home. They had other legal ways to go about it. They should have went about it different. And the thing that they said that happened to them, they should have reported to the police a long time ago. They should not have wasted five years, two years, three years. Sofia knowing all this coming to my home regularly visiting me should have done something a long time ago. I don't blame you for anything. I blame Sofia, Ruby, and the rest of my family for this."

The Wessons' youngest son, Serafino, approached the lectern and spoke directly to his father. "I just want to tell you that the past, I let it go," he said. "I will never speak of it again. And I love you. And you know, I shall continue my life. Carry on my seed for you. And then, you know, people know who they are, you know. I can't judge nobody. But when God comes, he will do the judgment. And I'm just going to leave it in his hands. And I wouldn't . . . I will never shed another tear again because of this. I'm just going to live my life as I can, and I'll leave the rest in God's hand. And His judgment will come."

Rosa Solorio spoke briefly, telling her uncle, "God's prophets suffer the worst," and that she would always love him.

Kiani Wesson followed: "I am Marcus Wesson's oldest daughter, Kiani, and I'm proud to be his daughter. I just want to say that, um . . . that the people in the room . . . what happened to the children, we know that the one in that room did it. But I just want to say that I feel that the people to blame are people who came to our house that day. Even though we know somebody in that room, I feel they're at fault. But I still, um, love my sister Sofia, Ruby, and Brandi, very much. Because, you know, we had a good life together. Sofia and Ruby and Sebhrenah, Brandi, they were my best friends and sisters. That's all I had in my life. And I still love them. And I love them no less. It's just sad that it had to end up this way, and that it had to fall apart, our whole family that we enjoyed together all of our lives. We had a big family, and we enjoyed our times together. But I just want my father to know that I love him very much. And there's many people out there who are for him and love him very much. And I know that deep inside Sofia, Ruby, my sisters . . . that they would soon come to know . . . right now we're just all going through things. They would soon come to know that . . . that we're still all family, and God loves us all. And pretty soon judgment will be met, and we will all suffer for whatever we did wrong."

Wesson's 24-year-old son Almae then approached the lectern. "Your Honor, I'm Almae Wesson, the son of Marcus Wesson. And I just want to say that, Dad, I love you and, um . . . I love you a lot, Dad. And remember in the Bible when Jesus was walking, and they were spitting the rocks at him and all, you were in his situation right now. These guys here who you have . . . these guys here who are accusing you of these things . . . and just look at yourself as you're walking in Christ. And Jesus Christ is on your side. And . . . and Ruby and Sofia, Marco and all them, um, yes, they may go to heaven, but first they have to pay for what they have did and what they are doing." Almae began to weep and leaned on the lectern to prop himself up. "And we all love you, Dad. And again, no matter what anybody says, God is on your side. And I am proud to be your son and proud you're my father. And if I don't see you before you go . . . and I love you, Dad. That's it." Marcus Wesson motioned to his son with his hand, almost as if to dismiss him. Almae immediately stopped crying. He bowed and backed away from the lectern.

After hearing so many of the Wesson children blame her for the murders, Ruby couldn't sit still any longer. "My name is Ruby Ortiz. I just want to tell Marcus that I know it's sad today. I see our family split apart. And his children think that their siblings hate them when I could never hate my sisters or my brothers. I love them, and I'll always love them. And I do not blame them for anything. For anything. I have no hate in my heart for them. And regardless of how much Marcus puts us against each other, God will never let that happen. Because someday I know the family will come back together again, and he will not, Marcus will not prevail in this matter. He's the only person I blame for my child being dead and for all the children that died. They were all innocent, and they did not deserve whatever sin . . . they did not deserve the sin that was put upon them. They did not deserve that. And I know . . . well, I don't know what he talks to his children about, but I hope he does not tell his children that it's my fault or my sister Sofia's fault. 'Cause the only thing I ever went there for was because I loved my child. And I never rested a day without her. There was never a day that I did not have pain in my heart for my daughter Aviv. And anyone being a mother would know that feeling of losing a child. And even if I didn't see her for as long as I did, my pain is still there, and it will always be there forever. And he's who I blame for that. And I believe, like Serafino said, only God can judge. That is true. God will judge. Judgment will come upon you for whatever sins you have committed."

The judge asked if anyone else wanted to speak, and there was silence. Putnam then addressed Wesson, citing his "mind-numbing history of exploitation." The judge said Wesson controlled his family, from the way they lived to how some of them died.

"Therefore, Marcus Delon Wesson, it is the judgment and sentence of the court that you shall suffer the death penalty. Said penalty to be inflicted within the wall of the state prison of San Quentin, California, in the manner prescribed by law and at a time to be fixed by this court in the warrant of execution."

Days later Wesson was transported to Marin County, about thirty miles south of Marshall, where the *Sudan* was stilled moored. There, he entered Death Row at San Quentin State Prison, overlooking the very bay he had once dreamed would be the starting point of his voyage around the world.

PART SEVEN:

LETTERS FROM DEATH ROW

On September 9, 2005, Marcus Wesson began to correspond with me from his prison cell at San Quentin's Death Row. After his arrest, Wesson had been interviewed by five detectives for ten hours over two days, but none of it was ever introduced as evidence during the trial. Since the defense never called him to testify, I had written him several letters in an effort to hear his side of the story. Toward the end of the trial, Wesson interrupted the proceedings to request a hearing to fire his attorneys. He made a statement to the court that ostensibly contained his version of events, and he had already told police what happened on the day of the murders; but the judge sealed any and all documents that provided insight into Wesson's point of view.

Primarily I wanted to know what happened inside the southeast bedroom for those eighty minutes on March 12, 2004, when Wesson was barricaded inside, refusing to come out. I explained to Wesson that I had covered his trial from beginning to end and that I was writing a book about the case. I told him I wanted to include his version of events, pointing out that he was the only one left who could explain what had happened. I also had many questions about how his spiritual writings related to his life. Among other startling revelations, he admitted to me in the letters that he considered himself to be the "Master" of a new brand of religion and that his power and position was shared by only one other: Jesus Christ.

On September 9, 2005, Wesson wrote the following letter to me from San Quentin prison. He began by quoting a line from the letter I had written him:

> Hello Monte:
>
> ". . . since you are the only one left who can tell the world what happened":
>
> It is of the foregoing words that I do languish: The world should know what really happened but I was not allowed the chance to tell of such. I only hope that you can understand of mine intentions to preserve of its revelation until I establish of it to the Supreme Court, then I will divulge of its entirety to you only. Maybe sooner than you think.

Wesson went on to discuss his book at length, explaining that the name of the entire work was "In the Night of the Light for the Dark," even though several derivations of that title had emerged. At times Wesson also referred to the volumes as "The Book of Vampyr." I posed a number of questions about the manuscript, hoping Wesson couldn't resist the chance to explain the "religion" he claimed to have created. I began by asking him how he situated himself in the telling of the narrative:

Q. I notice at times you are speaking from the perspective of "the Master," or the Head Vampire, and at other times the narrative seems to parallel your own life and the lives of your family members. To what extent is the book autobiographical?

A. The extent of the book's autobiographical compose is as you have noticed: At times I speak from the per-

spective of "the Master" and at other times the narrative does parallel mine own life and the lives of certain
of my family members.

Q. In the preface of the book you invite the reader to
"come and study on this bold journey to the dark and
the unknown and the divine: vampire the true essence of man. Yes, this book has the answers to all
living the dead and undead the beginning and the
end." Do you intend this book to reach a mass audience?

A. I intend for this book to reach of those interested in
truth of the unknown to most of man. The size of the
audience is immaterial to me at this time.

Q. Are you attempting to start your own unique brand of
spirituality or religion?

A. It is well established within mine understandings of
this Biblical parallel; of the essence of Christ's blood—
the partaking thereof—the resulting eternal life: to the
need for life giving of the so-called vampire's blood
toward of those in of said vampires following; such as
his Fledgelings, as in Christ's deciples. Biblical accounts of the importance of blood is striking in simi-
larity to the so called vampires need for blood for life
maintenance: Read Leviticus. This aforementioned
spirituality is unique only to myself and one other.
Yes!

Q. From a spiritual perspective do you consider yourself
a vampire?

A. Yes; I do consider myself as of such said; from a
spiritual perspective, yet; only as the Master.

Wesson often referred to vampires as a lost species or
race. I asked him if he was attempting to rebuild that race
within his own family. His initial response to the question was incoherent and nearly incomprehensible. Yet
when I asked specifically about the depiction of his children as "fledglings," Wesson responded:

A. I named my children *after* the characters to reestablish what once was of old. The characters were before mine children were; my children are simply a perpetuate thereof.

Q. Did you name these characters after your children in an attempt to invent a piece of fiction or were you mythologizing your own experience with a much grander goal?

A. My experiences, yes. Mythologizing, no. To-ward a grander goal: Nothing is of such grandeur as the truth.

Q. You apparently refer to the murder-suicide attempt that you thwarted aboard the boat. When you say, "They are confident in the gun," are you referring to that plan?

A. "They are confident in the gun": There was never a plan of such in of mine own parameters; of such discussion was held by of those outside of my constituents. The term "they are confident in the gun" is totally irrelevant as to relate to my family: said term is of those whom *depend* on a gun. I do not believe in guns as a power as some "entities" do believe: The term "gun" as I use it, is not limited to a 22 pistol, or of any explosive, nuclear reaction or light intensity laser, or particle beam. All of man is subject to these projectiles, but there are powers that render a man totally none affected by such weaponry. Note the biblical "burning furnace." I was referring to the weakness of man to think that; of a gun is the ultimate power. War is evidence of man's dependency on this power to attain power.

Q. You speak of your book in Biblical terms. Do you believe this book is divinely inspired?

A. The book was not divinely *inspired*, it was divinely written; *the book has 800 more pages that will be added to it: "The lost seed of righteousness."* It will be finished in less than two years. Once the 800 pages

are inter-fitted throughout the three existing books—
then it could be understood: Right now; the book is
not complete, therefore difficult to understand.

I finished my barrage of questions by pointing out
that I covered the trial and frequently observed him
playing an imaginary piano while seated at the defense
table. I asked him if he was composing songs. He responded:

*I have written 28 songs since in jail. I only play pi-
ano by ear.* ☺ *Country Western, Sailing—one Rock
song.*

Sincerely,
Marcus Wesson

After receiving the letter, I only had more questions.
Over the next several weeks I wrote Wesson several more
times, seeking clarification. Most importantly, he still had
not told me what had happened in the bedroom, and I was
determined to hear his side of the story. Nearly two
months went by and I had not received a response. As-
suming Wesson had been advised not to discuss the case
with me, I contacted his former attorney, David Mugridge,
who had represented Wesson for only a matter of days
before figuring out that Wesson was in no position to pay
for his own defense. Perhaps Wesson had told Mugridge
his story. I discovered that he had, but as I expected, Mugridge told me he couldn't violate attorney-client privi-
lege.
"What if Wesson said it was okay?" I asked Mugridge.
He said he would seriously consider cooperating if Wesson released him to give me the information. In my next
letter to Wesson I asked him if he would allow Mugridge
to tell me his story. Mugridge also wrote to Wesson, saying that I had contacted him with questions about the

case. I received this response from Wesson written on December 4, 2005:

Dear Monte:

I am in receipt of your letter today—as indicated by the above date. Within the inverted triangle of your letter's presentation: I did write to David Mugridge in response to his letter written to me dated; October 10-2005: I wrote November 12. Said letter requested permission to "completely" answer questions about my case in order to help write a book. I did give to David Mugridge permission to talk to "Monte": Monte Francis only: David Mugridge was given permission to and is still given permission to present his point of view on a variety of subjects surrounding my case. Said letter was mailed to: [Wesson lists Mugridge's address and phone number]. Said letter was mailed as legal mail. I; during my interview with David Mugridge, along with his associate; Gary Harvey; I told David details of my experience in the "south east bedroom": It would be of a definite benefit for you to get this story from a legal perspective and from another person besides of my own witness to myself. Mr. Mugridge can offer that perspective, legally. I have been told numerous times not to discuss my case with anyone but, of that is not the reason that I have not written: Whereas; I have forgotten any pertinent data; I am quite sure that Mr. Mugridge can present a more favorable story. Thus, protecting of myself from any misstatements of my previous testimony to the police.

Wesson wrote that he wanted to "maintain a virtual silence" on the murders because he worried that he might present a slightly different sequence of events than he had laid out for the police. Strangely, he added

that he should not comment on the subject of his book—
that it was "evidence in a criminal trial," and comment-
ing on it now might endanger his hope of a "decent
appeal." (He had, of course, already divulged a great
deal of information about the book to me.) He concluded
the letter:

> *I Marcus Wesson, hereby this letter, dated Decem-*
> *ber 4-05; do give my permission to Monte Francis*
> *to talk with David Mugridge about my interview*
> *with him concerning my case. No other permission*
> *is granted or implied.*

> *My life at San Quentin is perfect: I am acquiring all*
> *that I had planned to acquire mentally and spiritu-*
> *ally as well as physically.*

> *I do not plan to finish my fourth book in prison. I will*
> *give you a preview someday. Promise!*

> *Well; Monte Francis. Please forgive my lack of re-*
> *sponse to your letters. I do not intend to be so im-*
> *polite. I receive your letters on the average of 21*
> *days after mailing, along with a few other little*
> *problems on my behalf. Take care—maybe Mr.*
> *Mugridge will have something noteworthy. Until*
> *then—Merry Christmas.*

> *Feel free to write!*

> *Marcus Wesson*

After receiving the letter, I phoned David Mugridge
and set up a time for us to talk. On December 16, 2005,
I met with Mugridge in his Fresno office. Just as the interview was about to get under way, his phone rang. It
was Elizabeth Wesson on the line and she had received

word that Mugridge and I were meeting. She told Mugridge she didn't want him to talk to me, explaining that more publicity would only make matters worse for her family. She went on to say that she would attempt to reach Marcus and that she was sure she could get him to reconsider allowing Mugridge to speak on his behalf. To my dismay, the interview was over. Although Wesson had given clear and explicit permission for Mugridge to talk exclusively to me, as a courtesy he agreed to give Elizabeth time to contact Marcus in an attempt to change his mind. I thought it implausible that Elizabeth could sway her husband, considering their relationship, but I told Mugridge I understood the position he was in, and although disappointed, I left his office empty-handed.

Earlier that day, I attended a hearing in Judge Putnam's courtroom where a number of routine matters were discussed, including my request to have some of the testimony from the trial unsealed. I wanted to read the testimony of the two prosecution experts who had testified in a closed session, to gain some kind of perspective on Wesson's mental condition. I knew the experts had not interviewed Wesson in person and had based their opinions on his interviews with police and his writings. Perhaps the experts inadvertently revealed pertinent information about what had happened in the room where the murders occurred, I thought. Putnam had supplied both prosecutor Lisa Gamoian and defense attorney Pete Jones with copies of my letter to the court. When asked if either attorney objected to the unsealing of the transcripts, Gamoian just shook her head. Jones issued an impassioned argument against letting me see the transcripts, calling the testimony of Dr. Mohandie and Dr. Meloy "incompetent" and "prejudicial." Jones also raised the concern that Wesson was not present in court and at the time did not have appellate counsel to represent his interests in the matter.

The judge turned to Jones. "I assume you're ready to issue some points and authorities on this," Putnam said.

"Sure," Jones replied, shrugging his shoulders.

Putnam gave Jones a month to provide a basis for keeping the records sealed. The judge also suggested that I seek legal help to make a more formal written motion to the court.

Two weeks later I phoned Mugridge. He had given Elizabeth until the Monday after Christmas to contact her husband and had not heard from her. He placed me on hold for several minutes while he called Elizabeth. When he came back on the line, he said she wasn't home and that he had left a message. Since she had not attempted to contact him four days past his deadline, Mugridge began to tell me about his dealings with Wesson.

He explained that he had been contacted by a colleague, attorney Gary Harvey, just shortly after Wesson's arrest. Harvey handled civil cases and had assisted Wesson during the family's real estate dispute with Frank Muna. When Wesson was given a chance to contact a lawyer from jail, he immediately called Harvey. Recently, Harvey had taken an interest in criminal law, but he knew he didn't have the experience or expertise to handle a case in which the district attorney was likely to seek the death penalty. But he knew who could take on a case of that magnitude, and he immediately called his friend, David Mugridge.

Mugridge was intrigued by the request but didn't want to take on the case unless Wesson himself wanted his counsel. On March 16, 2004, Mugridge agreed to go to the Fresno County Jail with Harvey. When they arrived, Mugridge waited in the jail annex while Harvey went in to see Wesson.

"I told Gary, 'Go in and talk to him and let him know that I'm outside but that I don't want to come in until he has been advised that I am here and he asks me to come in. Otherwise I'm just not going to do it,' " Mugridge said.

After talking to Wesson, Harvey returned to the annex and told Mugridge that Wesson wanted to meet with him to discuss retaining his services. Mugridge went inside and met with Wesson for the first time. During their first meeting, Wesson and Mugridge did not discuss the murders; rather, Mugridge simply wanted to determine if Wesson had the resources to retain a private attorney. He warned Wesson that hiring counsel in a case like his could cost a least a quarter of a million dollars.

"I told him that very rarely can people afford to retain private counsel, because normally, people don't have the money to do that," Mugridge recalled telling Wesson. "I advised Mr. Wesson that unless he could afford to hire private counsel, it would be foolish for him to try to engage somebody to represent him without submission to assets. Anyone who would take the case would be doing so simply for publicity and could end up doing him some significant harm."

Wesson told Mugridge that he had some assets and property but couldn't estimate their worth. The next day, Mugridge appeared in court with Wesson and informed Judge Brant Bramer that he was in discussions with Wesson to determine if he had the means to retain an attorney. An investigation of Wesson's assets revealed that the family did not have the money required to mount an adequate defense.

At this point in the story, Mugridge told me he had another call and put me on hold. I had a sinking feeling that it was Elizabeth on the other line. Several minutes later Mugridge was back on the line to confirm my fear: Elizabeth Wesson had just called, and he said he couldn't discuss the case any further.

"She's told me some things I can't tell you, but has

asked me not to say anything," Mugridge explained. "I just don't want this to come back and haunt me."

"But we both have letters that state explicitly that Wesson wants you to talk to me," I countered.

But Mugridge had made up his mind; he wasn't going to say any more. However, before we hung up, he agreed to reconsider finishing the interview if either of us received another letter from Marcus. The letter would have to reaffirm Wesson's position in spite of Elizabeth's concerns.

I immediately wrote to Wesson and explained the situation, and waited for his response. Included in my letter was one last invitation to him to tell me his story. I wrote, "Maybe we can just keep it simple to avoid any confusion. Perhaps you can answer me this: Did you pull the trigger, and if not, who did?"

On February 2, 2006, I was back in court. I had filed a formal motion to have the expert testimony unsealed, arguing that the judge would have to find an "overriding interest" to keep the testimony secret. After reviewing my argument and the counterargument from the defense, Judge Putnam agreed with me, and ordered the transcripts unsealed.

Upon reviewing the transcripts, I discovered that the experts had spoken at length about Wesson's manipulation of his family and had offered opinions that Wesson had brainwashed or used "coercive persuasion" on most if not all of his family members. Neither expert had personally interviewed Wesson but had based their assessments on Wesson's interviews with police, his spiritual writings, and daily transcripts from the trial.

Forensic psychologist J. Reid Meloy testified that Wesson used his control and dominance in the family to initiate a murder-suicide pact. Meloy also offered a view that Wesson alone had the dominance to move the pact forward or to stop it. Explicitly, Meloy posited that

Wesson had to be in the room when all the victims were killed:

Q. And with regards to the level of dominance and control that Mr. Wesson did have in the family on March twelfth, would one of the adult females—would that have been something that she would have initiated on her own independent of Mr. Wesson, the murder-suicide pact?

A. In my opinion, absolutely not. I think it was shooting in the eyes.

Q. And with respect to predatory violence, that is more consistent with someone who is calm?

A. Correct.

Q. Rather than someone who is yelling, posturing, that sort of thing?

A. Absolutely.

On cross examination, attorney Pete Jones asked:

Q. And were you asked to render an opinion concerning whether Mr. Wesson actually fired the gun?

A. Not specifically, no.

Q. Would it be—would it not be logical to infer from your testimony that based on your analysis of the information you were provided, that only Marcus Wesson could have been the one to fire the gun on March twelfth?

A. Correct. That he was directing.

Q. That he was directing?

A. Yes. He was either firing the gun or he was directing the killings.

Q. It seems to come through loud and clear to me that you've formulated an opinion that Mr. Wesson was a psychopath. Is that just me, or is that a fair inference?

A. For this hearing that is a fair inference.

While he considered Marcus Wesson a psychopath, Meloy testified that he could find no indication that Wesson suffered from a psychotic illness. Under cross examination, Meloy admitted that he had not included any mass murders committed by women in his study. The defense was prepared to cite studies showing that women were just as likely to commit mass murder when the killings involved children.

Psychologist Kris Mohandie, Ph.D., was less specific when talking about his findings with regard to Wesson's case, although he agreed with Meloy that Wesson had to be the one to order the killings:

Q. Given what you know about this case, in your opinion would any of the girls in the family have made an independent decision to kill the children and then herself?

A. No.

Q. Why?

A. They didn't even make small decisions. I mean, using the term "small decisions." Smaller decisions like, are we going to work? Are we not going to work? Are we going to have children? Are we not going to have children? All those decisions. Pretty much every major decision in the family was controlled by Mr. Wesson.

Q. And do you have an opinion as to whether or not Mr. Wesson would have to initiate, give the green light if you will, for the murder suicide pact? Have to tell them to do it?

A. It would be my opinion that he would have to give his approval and/or direction to do so, yes.

Despite that opinion, Mohandie testified that Wesson's level of control in the family was so overwhelming that it could have been enough to compel Sebhrenah to kill the others and then herself. While not stated explicitly, the implication was that Wesson might not have had to be in the room at the time of the murders.

After hearing the two experts testify, Judge Putnam decided the doctors had contradicted each other and had used different methodologies. He ruled that the testimony would just confuse the jury and didn't allow either doctor to take the witness stand. It might have been a blessing in disguise for the prosecutor. The liver temperature tests on the victims indicated a likelihood that the younger victims were already dead by the time Wesson entered the bedroom, contradicting Meloy's assertion that Wesson had to be in the room at the time of the killings, or was the one who pulled the trigger. It would have been a major sticking point for the defense and seemed to work against the main thrust of the prosecutor's argument: that Wesson conspired to commit murder and was responsible either way. As it turned out, the prosecutor wouldn't need her experts to convince the jury that Wesson was guilty.

By mid-March, I still had not received a response to the last letter I'd sent Wesson. I simply wanted someone to confirm what I had already been told "off the record" by more than one source: that Wesson claimed he did not pull the trigger and that he had watched as Sebhrenah shot Lise and then herself. According to Wesson's story, the seven younger children were already dead when he entered the room. With some coaxing, attorney Pete Jones confirmed that Wesson's statement about the murders was consistent with what the defense had argued at trial. "This was not a contrived defense," Jones assured me.

As my publishing deadline approached, I couldn't sleep. For months I had thought about the case, but I still hadn't settled on a clear reason why Wesson would order or carry out, the murders. I took out Wesson's thousand-page book and began to randomly flip through its pages. I came to a passage in the third section with the subtitle, "The Family." I read the following words:

```
The purpose is to gather multiply
duplicate in micro cosim the exact-
ness of the hierarchy in his spiri-
tual world of his master for only by
the order of all things in this
light is there light . . . The work-
ings of a family is a physical mani-
festation of the spiritual hierarchy
of his master . . .
```

I remembered that Wesson had told me in one of his letters that he had named his children *after* the characters in his book. It left me with the impression that Wesson revered the characters in his spiritual world as superior; they had preceded his children in their existence. Perhaps, I thought, Wesson was simply trying to recreate his spiritual characters in the physical world by impregnating his daughters and nieces. As sick as it was, it would truly make him the "Master" he professed to be. I thought: How can someone be a "Master vampire" if he has no one to control or dominate? In his book, Wesson had referred to his children as vampires or as his "fledglings," and in the second section of his book, Wesson had called death a "sacrifice to save the human soul." In his spiritual world, somehow killing the children made sense. In the real world, it was unfathomable. I read on:

```
For the same line to last for centu-
ries in all integrity one needs to
re-induce the same blood character-
istics once in a while from a royal
being of perfect blood . . .
```

Wesson had begun to believe his own ramblings. In his mind, the children he fathered with his daughters and nieces were helping him to realize his position as the "Master." They had literally brought the musings of his book to life.

While I struggled to make sense of Wesson's demented logic, nothing helped me fully absorb the gravity of what had happened and what Wesson's children had endured. There was no way to truly empathize or to fathom the years of control, the isolation, or the physical and sexual abuse. I remembered what one of the jurors had said not long after deciding that Wesson should suffer the death penalty.

"Those kids never had a chance," she said, shaking her head.

The case had long since faded from the public eye. Years from now, I wondered, who would remember the Wesson children: how they had lived, or the horrible way they died?

EPILOGUE

After the trial was over, aside from a sit-down interview with Wesson himself, it was the interview everyone wanted. Most of the members of the Wesson family had already talked to television and newspaper reporters, mostly to accuse Sofina Solorio and Ruby Ortiz of causing the murders by sparking the family dispute of March 12. But neither Solorio nor Ortiz themselves had granted one-on-one interviews with anyone. How did the women at the center of the family dispute feel about the man they once considered an uncle and a husband, and who had been convicted for killing their children? No one knew.

While on the witness stand, the 911 dispatcher had revealed Sofina's cell phone number, and many of the reporters in court that day (myself included) had written it down. I wasn't sure it was still a working number, so I was surprised when Sofina answered the phone. She sounded pleasant, and politely explained that while the trial was going on she didn't want to make any kind of public comment. When it was all over, she said, she might have something to say. During the last six weeks of the trial I kept in close contact with Sofina. She lived out of town and frequently read my daily accounts on the Internet of what had occurred in court. After Wesson's sentencing, I phoned her and asked if she would be willing to offer her reflections on the case for a televi-

sion news story. Sofina agreed to talk. She gave me di-
rections to the house where she was staying, so I went
there and briefly interviewed her on camera. She was as
pleasant in person as she seemed over the phone, and yet
under that pleasant exterior, she was headstrong and
confident. Perhaps it was the reason she had escaped
Wesson's control, I thought, and so many of the others
had not. During that first interview, I asked her to react
to the statements of so many of her family members who
had accused her of causing the killings.

"I just want to say that it's not our fault," Sofina told
me. "We didn't pull the trigger. We all have a choice in
life. They all made their choice."

She said her son Jonathan was a resilient child and that
he didn't deserve to die. She recalled the last time she saw
him alive and the moment he was torn from her arms.

"He was in my hands that day. He was in my grasp,"
she said. "We had this eye contact. He knew what was
going to happen. It was like he was telling me, 'It's okay,
Mom.' It was like he already knew. It's that eye contact
that keeps me going."

Her feelings about her uncle Marcus Wesson were un-
derstandably complicated. I asked her how she felt about
the death penalty.

"I still don't believe in it, but he got it and that's because that's what he deserves," she said without hesitation. She then began to weep when I asked her how she
would feel on the day of her uncle's execution.

"He did what he did but he was important to me," Sofina said through tears. "And for him to just be gone . . . it's
going to hurt . . . because he was important to me. When
that day comes, it will be like somebody died. Somebody
that I knew and that I once loved."

After the interview was over, I thanked Sofina and
rushed back to the television station to meet my deadline,
which was less than a half hour away. I apologized for
being so abrupt and told Sofina I would call her in the

coming weeks, so we could talk more at length about the case.

About two months following Wesson's sentencing, I arranged to meet with Sofina in San Jose. I made the forty-five-minute drive from my home in San Francisco and met with her at her aunt's house. When I arrived, she greeted me with a big smile. We talked for the next several hours. I took notes at the kitchen table while she talked and made homemade salsa. Her three-year-old daughter Alyssen[42] sat in the front room watching cartoons.

One of the things I hadn't figured out was how Sofina was able to survive her experience in the Wesson family. How was she able to find the courage to overthrow Wesson as the creator of this insulated world she had lived in and then move on with her life after the death of her son? She had a good job with Santa Clara County, taking care of children who were mentally retarded, or who had special needs. She was professionally successful and was well-liked by her employer and coworkers. Why was she able to function successfully in the real world and so many other Wesson family members were not? Sofina shrugged her shoulders when I asked her the question. She reminded me that Wesson didn't come into her life until she was eleven years old and that she had always felt that her personal faith in Jesus Christ was what grounded her. I remembered from the trial that Sofina was the only one who ever challenged Wesson when it came to his manipulation of the scriptures.

"I've always been honest," she said, chopping a tomato on a wooden cutting board. "When I wanted to get out of the situation, he stabbed me. He felt that he had to do that in order for me to stay there. But no. That was just the

---

[42] Alyssen is the daughter of Sofina Solorio and Milton Richardson, a man Sofina worked with at the Radisson Hotel.

beginning of, 'You know what, you're full of crap. I don't have to be in this situation anymore.'"

"It sounds like that was a turning point for you," I suggested.

"No, that was not the turning point," she replied. "The turning point was when he separated me from the rest of the family." Sofina reminded me that Marcus forbade her sisters and cousins to talk to her during the last two years of her time in the Wesson home. She was also not allowed to be around her son, and Marcus would not allow the boy to call her "Mom."

"When Jonathan was ten months old, Marcus took him away," Sofina said. "He couldn't talk to me until he was five years old. They used to spank him to keep him away from me."

After the family moved to the house on Hammond Avenue, Marcus slowly began to lift those restrictions and would allow Sofina to visit Jonathan. By that time, she had started a new life in San Jose, but she drove to Fresno every chance she got because she cherished every minute she could spend with her son. She felt she had to make up for lost time. Sofina returned to Fresno several times a month and would bring food and money to the family. She secretly gave Jonathan treats and small gifts and told him not to tell anyone. The gifts included a matchbox car, a small plastic baby spoon, and her old name tag from the hotel where she used to work. She wanted him to have something to remember her by since she only saw him once every few weeks.

"Jonathan was my child. I would have done anything for him. And I did do anything for him," she said. Sofina said the Wesson children always looked forward to her visits and would ask her to buy them things.

"Mom, when you come next time can you buy me some shoes?" Jonathan asked Sofina during one of her visits. She assured her son that she would, and a few weeks later took him to the shoe store. He tried on a pair of brown and black shoes.

"They fit you?" she asked as Jonathan looked at his feet in a mirror.

"Yeah, but can you get me some black ones?" he asked.

"But Jonathan, those have black in them," Sofina replied.

"No, I want *all* black," the boy insisted.

Sofina acquiesced to her son's request and bought him an all black pair.

"Even though it was innocent, he wanted black," Sofina told me, now sitting at the kitchen table. "And that was a sign already. It was another sign for me. Black shoes, black pants, and a black jacket."

Sofina got up and retrieved a family photograph that showed her cousin Sebhrenah Wesson wearing white makeup and bright red lipstick. She explained that some of the children were already trying to look like vampires.

"By having the other kids and naming them after vampires, and [Marcus's] book and all that . . . that's crazy," Sofina said. "And that's the reason I was like, 'No, you can't have Jonathan. Jonathan's not going to be living this life. You didn't give that life to me.' Yeah, now that I'm older I'm going to live a godly life. But what's the choice Jonathan had? Vampirism? I didn't want him to be like sixteen years old and wearing black and spikes and stuff like that. Or even worse . . . being a Christian on the outside but having all these hateful feelings on the inside. I knew that's where it was heading. That's why I was like, 'I need to get Jonathan now.'"

Sofina paused. She seemed to be deep in thought. "I don't know. Sometimes I don't know if I regret going there that day. Because I was allowed to talk to and see Jonathan at that point. It wasn't supposed to happen that way. I wasn't going to bring all the family there. I was going to go there myself. And with Marcus it was going to be 'Yes,' or 'No.' Marcus broke some promises, and because he did . . . if he was a man of his word he would have let me have Jonathan."

Even though jurors had found Wesson guilty of nine counts of first degree murder, they had decided that there wasn't evidence to show that Wesson himself had pulled the trigger. I asked Sofina if she believed that her uncle had shot and fired the gun that killed her son and the rest of the children.

"To me, it was done and he was in the room," she replied. "Whether he pulled the trigger or not, it doesn't matter. He was there. He could have prevented it from happening. He planned this for years, before the kids were even born. And it happened."

She continued, "Marcus was not the person I thought he was. That's what saddens me the most. He's a selfish, manipulating person . . . he is this ugly being. He wasn't the person he led us to believe he was. He was something different. Like a demon."

I wanted to know if Sofina had sought any kind of help to deal with the loss of her son. I asked her if she had ever talked to a counselor or therapist about it. She told me that she hadn't, but that there was one thing she still wondered about. She explained that not long after the murders, the Coroner's Office contacted her to say they had found some items in the pocket of her son's overalls. She arranged to pick them up and made the three-hour drive from her home to Fresno. The items were given to her in a plastic bag, and they included a plastic baby spoon, three pieces of yarn, a pin from the Radisson Hotel that read "Sofina," and a matchbox car. She wondered what it meant that her son had kept her secret gifts to him in his pocket. I paused, then asked her what she thought it meant. Tears welled up in her eyes. "I felt that it had a lot to do with me," she said. "Even though I wasn't there all the time, he was connected to me. And that was the only

way he could be close to me . . . the things he had." She
bowed her head and a long silence followed.

The voice of her daughter Alyssen came from the other
room. The little girl was upset and wanted help changing
the TV channels. "Excuse me," Sofina said, getting up
from the table. She walked into the living room where
her daughter sat on the floor in front of the television.
The three-year-old had long curly hair and her arms were
in the air, asking for her mother's embrace. Instinctually,
Sofina picked up her daughter and made the unspoken
promise mothers are known to make. *I will never let you
go. Everything's going to be all right.* Life had already
taught Sofina it was a promise mothers meant but could
not always keep.

ACKNOWLEDGMENTS

I am deeply indebted to many people for their help with this book. First, I am grateful to Sofina Solorio for choosing to speak the secrets of her past. My friend, Matt Kreamer, helped me enormously with editorial suggestions, and Jeremy Cesarec's advice and encouragement was also helpful. Craig Wiley and the folks at Waterside Productions had the faith in me to take on this project, and for that I am appreciative. For their contributions and support, I am thankful to Peter Hubbard, Caroline Van Ness, Matthew Francis, Stacey Toyoaki, Jill Baxter, Pete Jones, David Mugridge, Sherry Spears, the staff at the Fresno County Courthouse, and my friends and colleagues at KSEE. Finally, I deeply appreciate my family's unwavering support, and my mother, who was the first to value the writer in me.

Shocking true accounts of murder Texas-style from

KATHRYN CASEY

SHATTERED
THE TRUE STORY OF A MOTHER'S LOVE, A HUSBAND'S BETRAYAL, AND A COLD-BLOODED TEXAS MURDER
978-0-06-158202-8

EVIL BESIDE HER
THE TRUE STORY OF A TEXAS WOMAN'S MARRIAGE TO A DANGEROUS PSYCHOPATH
978-0-06-158201-1

A DESCENT INTO HELL
THE TRUE STORY OF AN ALTAR BOY, A CHEERLEADER, AND A TWISTED TEXAS MURDER
978-0-06-123087-5

DIE, MY LOVE
A TRUE STORY OF REVENGE, MURDER, AND TWO TEXAS SISTERS
978-0-06-084620-6

SHE WANTED IT ALL
A TRUE STORY OF SEX, MURDER, AND A TEXAS MILLIONAIRE
978-0-06-056764-4

A WARRANT TO KILL
A TRUE STORY OF OBSESSION, LIES AND A KILLER COP
978-0-380-78041-9